P9-CRP-553

THE BIG DROP

JAMES RICKARDS

BESTSELLING AUTHOR OF *THE DEATH OF MONEY* AND *CURRENCY WARS*

FOREWORD BY PETER COYNE

For Ann

ISBN: 978-1-6212915-3-4

19 18 17 16 15 1 2 3 4 5 6 7

Published by Laissez Faire Books, 808 St. Paul Street, Baltimore, Maryland
www.lfb.org

Cover and Layout Design: Mena Fusco

CONTENTS

Foreword

Seven years after the 2008 crisis, "The Big Drop: How to Grow Your Wealth During the Coming Collapse" could strike you as a trite title for a worn out topic. Countless books have been published forecasting financial calamity.

What rescues this tome are the experiences, connections and scientific know-how of the writer.

Many have watched their net worth evaporate before their eyes. Fewer have recovered only to experience it again. Still fewer have had the stamina to learn *why* it happened and regain everything they had lost despite the odds.

But only a few of those people, if any, have also had the desire and wherewithal to help thousands of others avoid the same fate.

Jim Rickards is one of those men.

Jim's personal history plus his countless and ongoing professional encounters in intelligence work, non-profit endeavors, finance and academia are responsible for the book you hold in your hands — and for our monthly financial newsletter, *Jim Rickards' Strategic Intelligence*.

The fact that you're reading this foreword means one thing, you've joined our ranks. You couldn't ask for a better guide for your investments.

"I want to help everyday Americans" Jim told me candidly

after partnering with us at Agora Financial to launch his advisory. "There are people in positions of real power who see what I see, but won't be honest with people about it. They're perfectly prepared for other people to lose all their money."

"The next collapse — the big drop — is coming. You can see it coming because of the dynamics."

Not everyone will be prepared. But those who are will be happy they were in the aftermath. This book is a means to that end.

On February 6, 2015, we wrote about the slowly unfolding "de-dollarization" in the *Daily Reckoning*. "The dollar would die with a whimper" we suggested, "not with a bang." Soon after, I received the following note from a reader:

> *My mother tells the story of her first day working as a bank teller. It was when my father was in Vietnam — circa 1968.*
>
> *Her manager, a guy who was otherwise reasonable, took her aside and told her the following: 'You probably won't be working here long because the dollar is going to become worthless. It will be good for nothing more than kindling for the stove.'*
>
> *She was also told that the money she was contributing to Social Security was a waste since the program was a pyramid scheme and would collapse in a few years.*
>
> *Nearly fifty years later, here we are. The dollars in my wallet are still accepted for goods and services and my mother is still receiving the social security she paid into.*
>
> *The sky has always been about to fall… but never seems to get around to it.*
>
> *People lap this stuff up and there's always, always, always someone there to make a buck on it.*

At first glance, such cynicism might seem worthy of credence.

Since 1971, learned men in the minority, newsletter editors, fringe pundits, goldbugs and gadflies have predicted the end of the dollar standard. Despite them all, here we are.

But as Jim points out in Chapter 11, "The Beginning of the End for the Dollar", the reader's argument is specious at best — and downright dangerous at worst.

What the reader who wrote that note may not realize, or chooses not to recall, is that the dollar actually *did* lose over half its purchasing power in five short years from 1977 to 1981. Inflation in those five years was over 50 percent. If you had a job, maybe you got a raise or the value of your house went up. But, if you were relying on savings, insurance or a fixed income, half your value was lost forever. Maybe that bank manager knew something after all.

In fact, the international monetary system *has* collapsed three times in the past 100 years. First, in 1914 after World War I, then in 1939 after the gold exchange standard and finally, in 1971 when President Nixon ended the convertibility of dollars into gold.

The monetary system seems to collapse "about every thirty or forty years and it's been about forty years since the last one" writes Jim.

"That doesn't mean the system is going to collapse tomorrow morning like clockwork. It does suggest, however, that the useful life of the international monetary system, if you will, is about thirty or forty years. We're at the end of that period so we shouldn't be surprised if it collapses again."

The Big Drop: How to Grow Your Wealth During the Coming Collapse shows you how to protect and build your wealth ahead of and during the coming monetary collapse. Perhaps even more interesting, it may play a part — however small — in helping to sidestep disaster altogether.

No doubt, you've heard of a self-fulfilling prophecy.

Say you're hired as a truck driver from New York to

Baltimore — but you believe you are going to be the worst courier of all time. As a consequence, you're distracted and take 95 North to Maine. By thinking you'd be the worst truck driver, you became it. Your prophecy became true because of itself.

But have you heard about the opposite phenomenon? The self-*negating* prophecy?

Jim tipped us off to the concept. He, in turn, learned it from its originator, Robert K. Merton, a respected sociology professor at Columbia University who passed away in 2003.

"A self-negating prophecy is when you make a prediction" Rickards related. "You can help it not come true. By alerting people to the risk, they can behave in ways that make it not come true, which is what you want."

"By sounding a warning — that the 'Big Drop' is right under our nose — based on troubling trends that are in play today, it helps people do things that collectively will help move us in the right direction."

Therefore, as you read, you should repeat the words of the *Financial Times* review of Jim's forecast in your head: "Let's hope he's wrong." But also remember to prepare as if he's right.

Jim admits, the outlook is grim. But he also makes it clear there are unique and lucrative opportunities for the sagacious.

Everything you need to get started is right here, in your hands. Read on...

Peter Coyne
Managing Editor Rickards' Strategic Intelligence
Managing Editor The Daily Reckoning

Introduction: In the Year 2024...

The following describes a fictional dystopia in the spirit of Brave New World or 1984. It is not a firm forecast or prediction in the usual analytic sense. Instead, it's intended to provide warning, and encourage readers to be alert to dangerous trends in society, some of which are already in place...

As I awoke this morning, Sunday, Oct. 13, 2024, from restless dreams, I found the insect-sized sensor implanted in my arm was already awake. We call it a "bug." U.S. citizens have been required to have them since 2022 to access government health care.

The bug knew from its biometric monitoring of my brain wave frequencies and rapid eye movement that I would awake momentarily. It was already at work launching systems, including the coffee maker. I could smell the coffee brewing in the kitchen. The information screens on the inside of my panopticon goggles were already flashing before my eyes.

Images of world leaders were on the screen. They were issuing proclamations about the fine health of their economies and the advent of world peace. Citizens, they explained, needed to work in accordance with the New World Order Growth Plan to maximize wealth for all. I knew this was propaganda, but I couldn't ignore it. Removing your panopticon goggles is viewed with suspicion by the neighborhood watch committees. Your "bug" controls all the channels.

I'm mostly interested in economics and finance, as I have been for decades. I've told the central authorities that I'm an economic historian, so they've given me access to archives and information denied to most citizens in the name of national economic security.

My work now is only historical, because markets were abolished after the Panic of 2018. That was not the original intent of the authorities. They meant to close markets "temporarily" to stop the panic, but once the markets were shut, there was no way to reopen them without the panic starting again.

Today, trust in markets is completely gone. All investors want is their money back. Authorities started printing money after the Panic of 2008, but that solution stopped working by 2018. Probably because so much had been printed in 2017 under QE7. When the panic hit, money was viewed as worthless. So markets were simply closed.

Between 2018–20, the Group of 20 major powers, the G-20, abolished all currencies except for the dollar, the euro and the ruasia. The dollar became the local currency in North and South America. Europe, Africa and Australia used the euro. The ruasia was the only new currency — a combination of the old Russian ruble, Chinese yuan and Japanese yen — and was adopted as the local currency in Asia.

There is also new world money called special drawing rights, or SDRs for short. They're used only for settlements between countries, however. Everyday citizens use the dollar, euro or ruasia for daily transactions. The SDR is also used to set energy prices and as a benchmark for the value of the three local currencies. The World Central Bank, formerly the IMF, administers the SDR system under the direction of the G-20. As a result of the fixed exchange rates, there's no currency trading.

All of the gold in the world was confiscated in 2020 and

placed in a nuclear bomb-proof vault dug into the Swiss Alps. The mountain vault had been vacated by the Swiss army and made available to the World Central Bank for this purpose. All G-20 nations contributed their national gold to the vault. All private gold was forcibly confiscated and added to the Swiss vault as well. All gold mining had been nationalized and suspended on environmental grounds.

The purpose of the Swiss vault was not to have gold backing for currencies, but rather to remove gold from the financial system entirely so it could never be used as money again. Thus, gold trading ceased because its production, use and possession were banned. By these means, the G-20 and the World Central Bank control the only forms of money.

Some lucky ones had purchased gold in 2014 and sold it when it reached $40,000 per ounce in 2019. By then, inflation was out of control and the power elites knew that all confidence in paper currencies had been lost. The only way to re-establish control of money was to confiscate gold. But those who sold near the top were able to purchase land or art, which the authorities did not confiscate.

Those who never owned gold in the first place saw their savings, retirement incomes, pensions and insurance policies turn to dust once the hyperinflation began. Now it seems so obvious. The only way to preserve wealth through the Panic of 2018 was to have gold, land and fine art. But investors not only needed to have the foresight to buy it… they also had to be nimble enough to sell the gold before the confiscation in 2020, and then buy more land and art and hang onto it. For that reason, many lost everything.

Land and personal property were not confiscated, because much of it was needed for living arrangements and agriculture. Personal property was too difficult to confiscate and of little use to the state. Fine art was lumped in with cheap art and mundane personal property and ignored.

Stock and bond trading were halted when the markets closed. During the panic selling after the crash of 2018, stocks were wiped out. Too, the value of all bonds were wiped out in the hyperinflation of 2019. Governments closed stock and bond markets, nationalized all corporations and declared a moratorium on all debts. World leaders initially explained it as an effort to "buy time" to come up with a plan to unfreeze the markets, but over time, they realized that trust and confidence had been permanently destroyed, and there was no point in trying.

Wiped-out savers broke out in money riots soon after but were quickly suppressed by militarized police who used drones, night vision technology, body armor and electronic surveillance.

Highway tollbooth digital scanners were used to spot and interdict those who tried to flee by car. By 2017, the U.S. government required sensors on all cars. It was all too easy for officials to turn off the engines of those who were government targets, spot their locations and arrest them on the side of the road.

In compensation for citizens' wealth destroyed by inflation and confiscation, governments distributed digital Social Units called Social Shares and Social Donations. These were based on a person's previous wealth. Americans below a certain level of wealth got Social Shares that entitled them to a guaranteed income.

Those above a certain level of wealth got Social Donation units that required them to give their wealth to the state. Over time, the result was a redistribution of wealth so that everyone had about the same net worth and the same standard of living. The French economist Thomas Piketty was the principal consultant to the G-20 and World Central Bank on this project.

To facilitate the gradual freezing of markets, confiscation of wealth and creation of Social Units, world governments coordinated the elimination of cash in 2016. The "cashless society" was sold to citizens as a convenience. No more dirty, grubby coins and bills to carry around!

Instead, you could pay with smart cards and mobile phones and could transfer funds online. Only when the elimination of cash was complete did citizens realize that digital money meant total control by government. This made it easy to adopt former Treasury Secretary Larry Summers' idea of negative interest rates. Governments simply deducted amounts from its citizens' bank accounts every month. Without cash, there was no way to prevent the digital deductions.

The government could also monitor all of your transactions and digitally freeze your account if you disagreed with their tax or monetary policy. In fact, a new category of hate crime for "thoughts against monetary policy" was enacted by executive order. The penalty was digital elimination of the wealth of those guilty of dissent.

The entire process unfolded in small stages so that investors and citizens barely noticed before it was too late. Gold had been the best way to preserve wealth from 2014–18, but in the end, it was confiscated because the power elites knew it could not be allowed. First, they eliminated cash in 2016. Then they eliminated diverse currencies and stocks in 2018. Finally came the hyperinflation of 2019, which wiped out most wealth, followed by gold confiscation and the digital socialism of 2020.

By last year, 2023, free markets, private property and entrepreneurship were things of the past. All that remains of wealth is land, fine art and some (illegal) gold. The only other valuable assets are individual talents, provided you can deploy them outside the system of state-approved jobs.

Shock Doctrine: How We Get From 2015 to 2024

One of the most influential books among global power elites in the past 10 years is *Shock Doctrine: The Rise of Disaster Capitalism*, by Naomi Klein, published in 2007. The shock doctrine is an essential concept for understanding how power elites such as central bankers, finance ministers and the ultra-rich work behind the scenes to advance their agendas. It's also how today's world could quickly turn into the dystopian 2024 I describe above. This is not conspiracy mongering or science fiction; this is fact.

Shock doctrine is simple. Political leaders use crises to ramrod policies into place no one would accept in normal times.

The shock doctrine begins with the fact that power elites have agendas that take decades or even centuries to implement. These agendas include things like world money, global taxation, control of physical gold, population control and other plans intended to increase the power and wealth of the few at your expense. Political elites are not fools. They understand that their agenda is highly unpopular. They also understand that democracy empowers everyday citizens and makes their unpopular plans hard to implement. This is where the shock doctrine comes in useful.

A shock can take many forms. It can be a financial panic, terror attack, natural disaster, assassination or other extreme event of a kind that seems to come out of the blue but is actually somewhat regular and predictable. When the shock occurs, people become fearful and look to their leaders for comfort. People begin to value order above liberty. It is at these critical moments that the elites stand ready with a "plan" that will restore order but also secretly advance their agenda.

In effect, inevitable shocks are used as a cover to implement plans that you would not accept in ordinary times. Order is restored at the expense of liberty. When the shock wears off, the new order remains but liberty is lost forever. This is the shock doctrine at work. After each episode, the elites retreat and wait for the next shock, which is always just a matter of time.

A good example is the USA Patriot Act, passed by the U.S. Congress in 2001. This was the legislative response to the Sept. 11 terrorist attacks. There were a lot of good items in the Patriot Act that aided the global war on terror and helped to eliminate Osama bin Laden. But there is also much that has been abused in the years since.

You and I have lost our privacy and have our private communications, emails, phone calls and other records collected. If you've traveled abroad lately, you may have seen the new kiosks at Customs that take a digital retinal scan of each returning traveler. This is something that used to be handled with a paper passport. That retinal scan goes into a digital data bank, perhaps to be used to pursue political enemies, as happened in the recent IRS scandal. Privacy and liberty are mostly gone as the result of policy responses to various shocks such as Sept. 11. There are many other examples.

For investors, the important question is how will the shock doctrine be used next? What is the unfinished business of the power elites? What is the next part of the hidden agenda to be revealed? And what shock will be used as cover to advance that agenda?

These questions have definite answers that we will explore in this book. Regardless of those agendas and coming shocks, there are things investors can do today to avoid being manipulated by the power elites.

There are investments such as gold, land and fine art that are not digital and cannot be wiped out by computers. There are wealth preservation strategies that are not subject to current tax. There are portfolio diversification strategies that are robust to many types of shocks even if each particular shock cannot be predicted exactly.

These strategies should be implemented now before the next shock arrives and options become limited or unavailable. The power elites will continue to play the shock doctrine game. But you do not have to be the victim. The key is to know how the shock doctrine works and prepare now before the next shock strikes.

CHAPTER 1

The Financial Warning You Were Never Supposed to Hear

You may be surprised to learn what I'm about to tell you. But the globe's most connected financial insiders recently signaled that the markets are on the brink of catastrophe. Many of these global elites are already taking steps to prepare for the worst. Fortunately, it's not too late for you to take concrete steps to protect your own wealth ahead of time.

There's an old saying in the stock market that when prices are about to collapse "nobody rings a bell." In other words, it's up to you to be alert to important turning points in markets. No analyst or adviser is going to tell you exactly when the bull market is over. In fact, they probably don't know themselves; the experts will be taken just as much by surprise as everyday investors.

Yet sometimes, the global power elites do ring a bell. But they ring it for the wealthiest and most powerful individuals only. Everyday investors like you are not intended to hear it. One of these insider warnings was sounded recently…

On June 29, 2014, the Bank for International Settlements (BIS) issued its annual report, which said markets had become "euphoric." That report went on to say that "Time and again…seemingly strong balance sheets have turned out to mask unsuspected vulnerabilities."

The BIS, based in Switzerland, is a private meetinghouse for the most powerful central bankers in the world. It exists under a unique legal structure that is not accountable to any government.

During World War II, the BIS, under the direction of an American CEO, fenced Nazi gold to help the Germans fight the Allies.

The BIS is also the leading institution for central bank gold manipulation today. No institution in the world keeps more central bank secrets than the BIS. When they warn about market bubbles, you should take heed. But they weren't the only ones...

Three months later, on Sept. 20, 2014, the G-20 finance ministers met in Australia. The G-20 is a group of 20 economies including rich countries such as the U.S. and emerging markets such as Brazil, China and India.

Since the crisis of 2008, the G-20 has been the most important forum for directing global economic policy. The final report of their September meeting said, "We are mindful of the potential for a buildup of excessive rifsk in financial markets, particularly in an environment of low interest rates and low asset price volatility."

A few days after the G-20 meeting, a private think tank based in Switzerland called the International Center for Monetary and Banking Studies, ICMB, with strong links to major banks and government regulators, issued its so-called "Geneva Report" on the world economy, which it has done since 1999.

The latest Geneva Report said, "Contrary to widely held beliefs, six years on from the beginning of the financial crisis... the global economy is not yet on a deleveraging path. Indeed, the ratio of global total debt... over GDP...has kept increasing... and breaking new highs." The report then goes on to warn about the "poisonous" impact of that debt today.

On Oct. 11, 2014, shortly after the Geneva Report release, the International Monetary Fund (IMF) issued its own warnings. The head of the IMF's most powerful policy committee said capital markets are "vulnerable to 'financial Ebolas' that are bound to happen..."

The IMF's final press release said, "Downside risks arise from...increased risk-taking amidst low volatility in financial markets and heightened geopolitical tensions."

Finally, while attending the same IMF meeting in Washington, the vice chairman of the Federal Reserve, Stan Fischer, warned that world growth may be weaker than expected, which could delay the Fed's next move toward raising interest rates.

The message is impossible to ignore. The world's most powerful financial institutions and think tanks, the BIS, G-20, ICMB, IMF and the Fed are all warning about excessive leverage, asset bubbles, slow growth and systemic risk. They are doing this publicly, and seemingly in a coordinated fashion, since all of these warnings were issued within 100 days from late June to early October 2014.

As if on cue, the Dow Jones index peaked on Sept. 19, 2014, and then began a 700-point nose dive that continued through Oct. 10, 2014, at the start of the IMF meeting. The market temporarily bounced back, but the volatility and nervousness has continued through today.

Are The Global Financial Elites Trying To Tell You Something?

All of the reports and press releases noted above are written in highly technical language and were read only by a relatively small number of expert analysts. Some of these reports may have been picked up and mentioned briefly in the press, but they didn't make the front pages.

For you, such pronouncements are just more financial noise in a flood of information that washes over you every day on TV, radio, the Web, in newspapers and in other publications. The power elite were not signaling you — they were signaling each other.

Have you noticed that government officials, billionaires and major CEOs rarely seem to suffer when the financial system collapses, as it does from time to time?

It's not a coincidence that it's everyday investors and middle-class savers who see their 401(k) accounts and stock portfolios take a beating during collapses. This is because the elites have inside information. They see the catastrophe coming and warn each other to get out of the way in advance.

Not every billionaire is a full-time financial expert. Some made their money in telecommunications, social media, Hollywood or other endeavors. But they do share tips and inside information at private conclaves in Davos, Sun Valley, Aspen, Jackson Hole and other hangouts of the rich and famous.

They see trouble coming and scramble out of the broad stock market and into hard assets, art, cash, land and other safe havens. When the collapse comes, they emerge from their financial bunkers to snap up valuable companies that small investors have been panicked into selling at bargain-basement prices. As soon as elite institutions like the BIS and IMF start sounding the alarm, the smart money knows where to hide.

These elite warnings serve another purpose in addition to giving fellow elites a heads-up. They insulate politicians and officials from blame after the crash. When the collapse comes, you can be sure the BIS, G-20, IMF and the rest will point to the statements I just told you about and say, in effect, "See, we told you it was coming. Don't blame us if you didn't take action."

The warning has been sounded. The time for defensive action is now. Fortunately, it's not too late to take some of the same defensive measures as the power elites.

Welcome to the New Depression

The United States is living through an economic depression that began in 2007. It's part of a larger global depression, the first since the 1930s. This New Depression will continue indefinitely unless policy changes are made in the years ahead.

The present path and future course of this depression have profound implications for you as an investor. If you don't grasp this once-in-a-lifetime dynamic you are at risk of seeing all of your wealth wiped out.

Calling the current economic malaise a depression comes as surprise to most investors I speak to. They have been told that the economy is in a recovery that started 2009.

Mainstream economists and TV talking heads never refer to a depression.

Economists don't like the word depression because it does not have an exact mathematical definition. For economists, anything that cannot be quantified does not exist. This view is one of the many failings of modern economics.

But no one under the age of 90 has ever experienced a depression until now. Most investors like you have no working knowledge of what a depression is or how it affects asset values. And economists and policymakers are engaged in a conspiracy of silence on the subject. It's no wonder investors are confused.

The starting place for understanding depression is to get the definition right. You may think of depression as a continuous decline in GDP. The standard definition of a recession is two or more consecutive quarters of declining GDP and rising unemployment. Since a depression is understood to be something worse then a recession, investors think it must mean an extra-long period of decline. But that is not the definition of depression.

The best definition ever offered came from John Maynard Keynes in his 1936 classic, *The General Theory of Employment, Interest and Money*. Keynes said a depression is, "a chronic condition of sub-normal activity for a considerable period without any marked tendency towards recovery or towards complete collapse."

Keynes did not refer to declining GDP; he talked about

"sub-normal" activity. In other words, it's entirely possible to have growth in a depression. The problem is that the growth is below trend. It is weak growth that does not do the job of providing enough jobs or staying ahead of the national debt. That is exactly what the U.S. is experiencing today.

The long-term growth trend for U.S. GDP is about 3%. Higher growth is possible for short periods of time. It could be caused by new technology that improves worker productivity. Or, it could be due to new entrants into the workforce. From 1994 to 2000, the heart of the Clinton boom, growth in the U.S. economy averaged over 4% per year.

For a three-year stretch from 1983 to 1985 during the heart of the Reagan boom, growth in the U.S. economy averaged over 5.5% per year. These two periods were unusually strong, but they show what the U.S. economy can do with the right policies. By contrast, growth in the U.S. from 2007 through 2013 averaged 1% per year. Growth in the first half of 2014 was worse, averaging just 0.95%.

That is the meaning of depression. It is not negative growth, but it is below-trend growth. The past seven-years of 1% growth when the historical growth is 3% is a depression exactly as Keynes defined it.

Pundits point to 4% GDP growth in the second quarter of 2014 as proof that the economy is expanding robustly. Talk of depression seems confusing at best and disconcerting at worst. But second-quarter growth was driven by inventory accumulation, which adds nothing to GDP in the long-run. When inventories are converted to final sales, U.S. growth was only 0.65% in the first half of 2014. That is not a pace that will sustain an economic recovery.

Other observers point to declining unemployment and rising stock prices as evidence that we are not in a depression. They miss the fact that unemployment can fall and stocks can go up during a depression. The Great Depression lasted from

1929 to 1940. It consisted of two technical recessions from 1929–1932 and again from 1937–1938.

The periods 1933–1936 and 1939–1940 were technically economic expansions. Unemployment fell and stock prices rose. But the depression continued because the U.S. did not return to its potential growth rate until 1941. Stock and real estate prices did not fully recover their 1929 highs until 1954, a quarter century after the depression started.

The point is that GDP growth; rising stock prices and falling unemployment can all occur during depressions, as they do today. What makes it a depression is ongoing below trend growth that never gets back to its potential. That is exactly what the U.S. economy is experiencing. The New Depression is here.

Investors are also confused about depression dynamics because they are continually told the U.S. is in a "recovery." Year after year forecasters at the Federal Reserve, the International Monetary Fund and on Wall Street crank out forecasts of robust growth. And year after year they are disappointed. The recovery never seems to get traction. First there are some signs of growth, then the economy quickly slips back into low-growth or no-growth mode.

The reason is simple. Typically, a recovery is driven by the Federal Reserve expanding credit and rising wages. When inflation gets too high or labor markets get too tight, the Fed raises rates. That results in tightening credit and increasing unemployment.

This normal expansion-contraction dynamic has happened repeatedly since World War II. It's usually engineered by the Federal Reserve in order to avoid inflation during expansions and alleviate unemployment during contractions.

The result is a predictable wave of expansion and contraction driven by monetary conditions. Investors and the Fed have been expecting another strong expansion since 2009, but it's barely materialized.

Growth today isn't strong because the problem in the economy is not monetary, it is structural. That's the real difference between a recession and a depression. Recessions are cyclical and monetary in nature. Depressions are persistent and structural in nature. Structural problems cannot be solved with cyclical solutions. This is why the Fed has not ended the depression. The Fed has no power to make structural changes.

What do I mean by structural changes? Shifts in fiscal and regulatory policies. The list is long but would include things like lower taxes, repeal of Obamacare, approval of the Keystone Pipeline, expanded oil and gas production, fewer government regulations and an improved business climate in areas such as labor laws, litigation reform and the environment.

Power to make structural changes lies with the Congress and the White House. Those two branches of government are barely on speaking terms. Until structural changes are made by law, the depression will continue and the Fed is powerless to change that.

The difference between 3% growth and 1% growth may seem small in a single year but it's enormous over time. From the same starting place, an economy that grows 3% per year for 35 years will be twice as rich as one that grows 1% per year. After 70 years, about an average lifetime, the 3% economy will be four times as rich as the 1% economy.

These differences not only affect your wealth but also the ability of the economy to service its debts. The 3% economy can manage annual deficits of 2% of GDP. The 1% economy will eventually go broke with the same deficits. The difference between 3% growth and 1% growth is lost wealth that can never be recovered. It is the difference between the United States' success and failure as a nation.

Depressions pose other grave dangers to your wealth. In a depression, there is always the danger than disinflation — or falling inflation — tips into outright deflation. Deflation increases the real value of debt and forces many companies and ultimately the banks themselves into bankruptcy.

On the other hand, the Fed may try so hard to fight the deflation that they end up causing inflation that destroys the real value of your savings, insurance, annuities, retirement checks and any other form of fixed income. So far, the Fed has managed to walk a fine line between deflation and inflation, but the situation is highly unstable and is likely to tip one way or the other quickly and soon.

The depression in the U.S. will continue indefinitely until structural changes are made. The 25-year depression in Japan that began in 1990 is a perfect example of this. The U.S. is now like Japan, and the rest of the world is heading in the same direction. Investors like you are in constant danger; both deflation and inflation are real threats.

The good news is that structural changes do not happen overnight. They require action by the White House and Congress and such action is the product of debate and compromise that we can see coming.

If no action is on the horizon, the depression will continue and you can seek shelter from inflation *and* deflation.

A balanced portfolio of cash, gold, land, fine art, government bonds, alternative investments and stocks in the energy, transportation, agriculture and natural resource sectors should do the job. If, however, action is on the horizon, investors can prepare for the expected boom by positioning in technology, venture capital, financials and other pro-growth cyclical sectors.

You cannot know which outcome will prevail. But with the right understanding of these depression dynamics and watching your monthly *Strategic Intelligence* issues and updates closely you can know the signs of change and see what's coming. In fact, as a *Strategic Intelligence* reader you'll be among the first to know.

Everything that Made 2008 a Nightmare Is Worse Today

In 2008 all we heard about was too big to fail. Today, however, the banks that were too big to fail in 2008 are bigger. The five largest banks have a higher percentage of the total assets in the banking system. They have much larger derivatives books and a higher concentration of assets that would seem to be moving in the wrong direction.

We all know the San Andreas Fault in California can cause massive earthquakes. We don't know how big. They can be quite big, as we saw in San Francisco in 1906. But nobody thinks it's a good idea to go out and make the San Andreas Fault bigger. We're not sending the Army Corp. of Engineers out there to make the fault line bigger. In financial services, however, that's what we're doing. We're making the fault line bigger by allowing a greater concentration of assets.

Why is that? Well, there are two reasons.

Number one, policymakers don't use correct models. They don't understand that they're creating more risk with their policies. They probably think that they're making the system a little bit safer. In fact, they're creating more risk. They're a little bit blind in that sense.

The other reason is, if you want to slaughter a group of pigs, it's good to get all those pigs into one pen, so to speak. By forcing all the banking assets into a small number of banks it makes it easier for the government to steal people's money in three ways. Number one, obviously, is inflation. If you've got all this money in the bank, even with one-quarter of one percent or half of one percent — the Fed says they want 2 percent — it's enough to steal your money in small increments.

Beyond that, if there's another financial meltdown they'll be able to lock down the system and freeze bank deposits more easily. If there were more banks it would be harder to corral all of them. It would be easier for people to move from bank to bank.

Conversely, if there are a few mega-banks, you only need a couple phone calls to lock down the whole system. You could reprogram the ATMs to tell people they could only have $300 a day. Even if you try taking $2,000 out of an ATM today, you can't do it.

All the government has to do is dial the withdrawal limit to $300 for gas and groceries. They figure that's all people need and won't let you get the rest of your money. They won't steal it in so many words, but they won't let you have it. That's easier to do if there is a very small number of banks.

So people need to be alert to these kinds of programs that are in place. Regulators, government and large banks work together to steal people's money either indirectly through inflation or directly through asset freezes.

Recently, the FCC passed a rule that locks down money market funds. A lot of people think their money market fund is as good as cash. They think they can call their broker and have cash in the bank the next day.

Well, this new rule says the FCC can freeze money market funds or impose an exit fee so you get 95 cents on the dollar instead of 100 cents. There probably was a little flier in fine print inside your statement not too long ago about it. Most people probably opened the statement and threw the flier in the trash.

These are not things I'm making up. They're not scare stories about things that might happen in the future. They've already happened. The concentration of bank assets has happened. The freeze ability of money market funds has happened. These things are already in place. They're just waiting to be used in the next panic.

The Dollar Is Dying With a Whimper, Not a Bang

The same force that made the dollar the world's reserve currency is working to dethrone it.

July 22, 1944, marked the official conclusion of the Bretton Woods Conference in New Hampshire. There, 730 delegates from 44 nations met at the Mount Washington Hotel in the final days of the Second World War to devise a new international monetary system.

The delegates there were acutely aware that the failures of the international monetary system after the First World War had contributed to the outbreak of the Second World War. They were determined to create a more stable system that would avoid beggar-thy-neighbor currency wars, trade wars and other dysfunctions that could lead to shooting wars.

It was at Bretton Woods that the dollar was officially designated the world's leading reserve currency — a position that it still holds today. Under the Bretton Woods system, all major currencies were pegged to the dollar at a fixed exchange rate. The dollar itself was pegged to gold at the rate of $35.00 per ounce. Indirectly, the other currencies had a fixed gold value because of their peg to the dollar.

Other currencies could devalue against the dollar, and therefore against gold, if they received permission from the International Monetary Fund (IMF). However, the dollar could not devalue, at least in theory. It was the keystone of the entire system — intended to be permanently anchored to gold.

From 1950–1970 the Bretton Woods system worked fairly well. Trading partners of the U.S. who earned dollars could cash those dollars in to the U.S. Treasury and be paid in gold at the fixed rate.

In 1950, the U.S. had about 20,000 tons of gold. By 1970, that amount had been reduced to about 9,000 tons. The 11,000-ton decline went to U.S. trading partners, primarily Germany, France and Italy, who earned dollars and cashed them in for gold.

The U.K. pound sterling had previously held the dominant reserve currency role starting in 1816, following the end of the

Napoleonic Wars and the official adoption of the gold standard by the U.K. Many observers assume the 1944 Bretton Woods conference was the moment the U.S. dollar replaced sterling as the world's leading reserve currency. In fact, that replacement of sterling by the dollar as the world's leading reserve currency was a process that took 30 years, from 1914 to 1944.

The real turning point was the period July–November 1914, when a financial panic caused by the start of the First World War led to the closures of the London and New York stock exchanges and a mad scramble around the world to obtain gold to meet financial obligations. At first, the United States was acutely short of gold. The New York Stock Exchange was closed so that Europeans could not sell U.S. stocks and convert the dollar sales proceeds into gold.

But within a few months, massive U.S. exports of cotton and other agricultural produce to the U.K. produced huge trade surpluses. Gold began to flow the other way, from Europe back to the U.S. Wall Street banks began to underwrite massive war loans for the U.K. and France. By the end of the First World War, the U.S. had emerged as a major creditor nation and a major gold power. The dollar's percentage of total global reserves began to soar.

Scholar Barry Eichengreen has documented how the dollar and sterling seesawed over the 20 years following the First World War, with one taking the lead from the other as the leading reserve currency and in turn giving back the lead. In fact, the period from 1919–1939 was really one in which the world had two major reserve currencies — dollars and sterling — operating side by side.

Finally, in 1939, England suspended gold shipments in order to fight the Second World War and the role of sterling as a reliable store of value was greatly diminished apart from the U.K.'s special trading zone of Australia, Canada and other Commonwealth nations. The 1944 Bretton Woods conference was merely recognition of a process of dollar reserve dominance that had started in 1914.

Today, The Dollar Is Slipping

The significance of the process by which the dollar replaced sterling over a 30-year period has huge implications for you today. Slippage in the dollar's role as the leading global reserve currency is not necessarily something that would happen overnight, but is more likely to be a slow, steady process.

Signs of this are already visible. In 2000, dollar assets were about 70% of global reserves. Today, the comparable figure is about 62%. If this trend continues, one could easily see the dollar fall below 50% in the not-too-distant future.

It is equally obvious that a major creditor nation is emerging to challenge the U.S. today just as the U.S. emerged to challenge the U.K. in 1914. That power is China. The U.S. had massive gold inflows from 1914–1944. China has massive gold inflows today.

Officially, China reports that it has 1,054 metric tonnes of gold in its reserves. However, these figures were last updated in 2009, and China has acquired thousands of metric tonnes since without reporting these acquisitions to the IMF or World Gold Council.

Based on available data on imports and the output of Chinese mines, it is possible to estimate that actual Chinese government and private gold holdings exceed 8,500 metric tonnes, as shown in the chart below.

Assuming half of this is government owned, with the other half in private hands, then the actual Chinese government gold position exceeds 4,250 metric tonnes, an increase of over 300%. Of course, these figures are only estimates, because China operates through secret channels and does not officially report its gold holdings except at rare intervals.

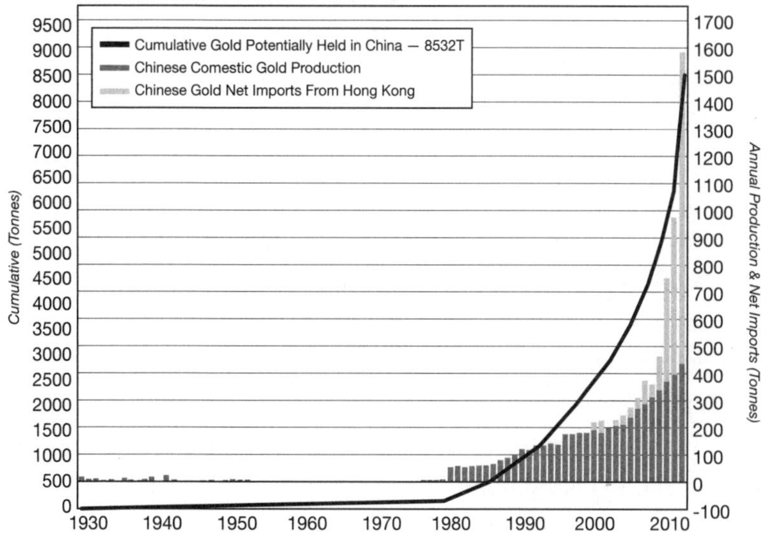

China's gold acquisition is not the result of a formal gold standard, but is happening by stealth acquisitions on the market. They're using intelligence and military assets, covert operations and market manipulation. But the result is the same. Gold is flowing to China today, just as gold flowed to the U.S. before Bretton Woods.

The Anti-Dollar Alliance

China is not alone in its efforts to achieve creditor status and to acquire gold. Russia has doubled its gold reserves in the past five years and has little external debt. Iran has also imported massive amounts of gold, mostly through Turkey and Dubai, although no one knows the exact amount, because Iranian gold imports are a state secret.

Other countries, including BRICS members Brazil, India and South Africa, have joined Russia and China to build institutions that could replace the balance of payments lending of the International Monetary Fund (IMF) and the development lending of the World Bank. All of these countries are clear about their desire to break free of U.S. dollar dominance.

Sterling faced a single rival in 1914, the U.S. dollar. Today, the dollar faces a host of rivals — China, Russia, India, Brazil, South Africa, Iran and many others. In addition, there is the world super-money, the special drawing right (SDR), which I expect will also be used to diminish the role of the dollar. The U.S. is playing into the hands of these rivals by running trade deficits, budget deficits and a huge external debt. What are the implications for your portfolio? Once again, history is highly instructive.

During the glory years of sterling as a global reserve currency, the exchange value of sterling was remarkably stable. In 2006, the U.K. House of Commons produced a 255-year price index for sterling that covered the period 1750–2005.

Inflation Exploded After the Sterling Lost Its Lead Reserve Role

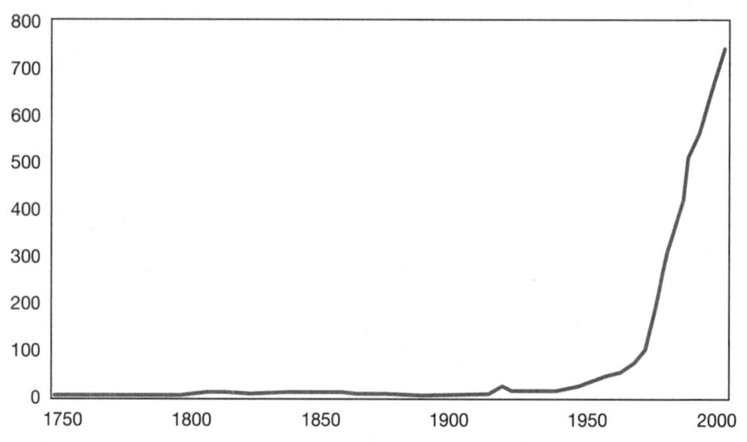

Source: Inflation: The Value of the Pound, 1750–2005, Research Paper 06/09, Feb. 13, 2006, U.K. House of Commons

The index had a value of 5.1 in 1751. There were fluctuations due to the Napoleonic Wars and the First World War, but even as late as 1934, the index was at only 15.8, meaning that prices had only tripled in 185 years.

But once the sterling lost its lead reserve currency role to the dollar, inflation exploded. The index hit 757.3 by 2005. In other words, during the 255 years of the index, prices increased by 200% in the first 185 years while the sterling was the lead reserve currency, but went up 5,000% in the 70 years that followed.

Price stability seems to be the norm for money with reserve currency status, but once that status is lost, inflation is dominant.

The decline of the dollar as a reserve currency started in 2000 with the advent of the euro and accelerated in 2010 with the beginning of a new currency war. That decline is now being amplified by China's emergence as a major creditor and gold power. Not to mention the actions of a new anti-dollar alliance consisting of the BRICS, Iran and others. If history is a guide, inflation in U.S. dollar prices will come next.

In his 1925 poem *The Hollow Men*, T. S. Eliot writes: "This is the way the world ends/ Not with a bang but a whimper." Those waiting for a sudden, spontaneous collapse of the dollar may be missing out on the dollar's less dramatic, but equally important slow, steady decline. The dollar collapse has already begun. The time to acquire insurance is now.

On the Knife-Edge of Runaway Inflation and Destructive Deflation

Today's investment climate is the most challenging one you have ever faced. At least since the late 1970s, perhaps since the 1930s. This is because inflation and deflation are both possibilities in the near term. Most investors can prepare for one or the other, but preparing for both at the same time is far more difficult. The reason for this challenging environment is not difficult to discern.

Analysts and talking heads have been wondering for five years why the recovery is not stronger. They keep predicting that stronger growth is right around the corner. Their forecasts have failed year after year and their confusion grows. Perhaps even you, who have seen scores of normal business and credit cycles come and go for decades, are confused.

If this "cycle" seems strange to you there's a good reason. The current economic slump is not cyclical; it's structural. This is a new depression that will last indefinitely until structural changes are made to the economy. Examples of structural changes are reduction or elimination of capital gains taxes, corporate income taxes and the most onerous forms of regulation.

Building the Keystone Pipeline, reforming entitlement spending and repealing Obamacare are other examples. These are other structural policies have nothing to do with money printing by the Fed. This is why money printing has not fixed the economy. Since structural changes are not on the horizon, expect the depression to continue.

What's the first thing that comes to your mind when you think of a depression? If you're like most investors I've spoken to, you might recall grainy, black-and-white photos from the 1930s of unemployed workers in soup lines. Or declining prices. Yet if you look around today, you'll see no soup lines, read that unemployment is only 6.2% and observe that prices are generally stable. How can there be a depression? Well, let's take each one by one.

The soup lines are here. They're in your local supermarket. Government issues food stamps in debit card form to those in need, who just pay at the checkout line.

Despite popular beliefs, unemployment is at 1930s levels too. If the Bureau of Labor Statistics measured the rate using the Depression-era method, it would be much higher than 6.2%. Also, millions today are claiming disability benefits when unemployment benefits run out — that's just another form of unemployment when the disabilities are not real or not serious, as is often the case.

What about prices? Here the story is different from the 1930s. Prices declined sharply from 1929–1933, about 25%, but they have been relatively stable from 2009–2014, rising only about 10% over the five-year period.

The Federal Reserve's money printing is responsible. The Fed had an overly tight monetary policy in the early 1930s but has employed unprecedented monetary ease since 2009. Ben Bernanke, who was in charge at the time, was reacting to what he viewed as the erroneous Fed policy of the 1930s. In a 2002 speech on the occasion of Milton Friedman's 90th birthday, Bernanke said to Friedman, "Regarding the Great Depression. You're right, we did it. We're very sorry. But thanks to you, we won't do it again."

But this did not mean that Bernanke had single-handedly discovered the cure for depression. Fighting deflation by itself does not solve the structural problems of the economy that lead to depressed growth. Instead, Bernanke, and now Yellen, have created an unstable dynamic tension. *Depressions are naturally deflationary.*

In a depression, debtors sell assets to raise cash and pay their debts. That pushes down asset prices. Falling asset prices, in turn, put other investors in distress, causing further asset sales. So it goes on in a downward price spiral.

Printing money is naturally inflationary. With more money chasing a given quantity of goods and services, the prices of those goods and services tend to rise.

The relative price stability you're experiencing now is an artifact of deflation and inflation *acting at the same time*. Far from price stability, what you're seeing is an extremely unstable situation. Think of the forces of deflation and inflation as two teams battling in a tug of war.

Eventually, one side wins, but the battle can go on for a long time before one team wears out the other side. If central banks stop causing inflation, deflation will quickly overwhelm the economy. If central banks don't give up and keep printing money to stop deflation, they will eventually get more inflation than they expect.

Both outcomes are very dangerous for you as an investor. The economy is poised on the knife edge of destructive deflation *and* runaway inflation. Prices could quickly and unexpectedly fall one way or the other.

This doesn't mean you should throw up your hands and say "I don't know." Plenty of analysts will tell you why you should fear inflation. And prominent policymakers such as Christine Lagarde of the IMF and Mario Draghi of the ECB have warned of deflation. Yet analysis has to be more than a matter of guesswork or stating a bias. The correct analysis is that *both* deflation and inflation are possible. Anyone who warns just of inflation or deflation is missing half the puzzle.

If you knew deflation was coming, you'd have an easy time constructing a profitable portfolio. You would have some cash and invest primarily in bonds. The value of cash goes up during deflation as prices decline, and bonds rally as interest rates decline. You might want to own some raw land in that case also.

During a deflationary period, the nominal value of the land might go down, but the costs to develop the land go down faster. The key would be to develop it cheaply in time for the next up cycle.

If, on the other hand, you knew inflation was coming, it would also be easy to construct a robust portfolio. All you would need to do is buy commodities like gold and oil, and stocks of companies with hard assets in sectors such as transportation, energy, natural resources and agriculture. You could also purchase fine art, which has excellent wealth preservation properties in an inflationary environment.

What should you do when the outcome is on the knife edge and could tip either way toward deflation or inflation?

The answer is prepare for both, watch carefully and stay nimble. Your initial portfolio should have gold, fine art, raw land, cash, bonds, select stocks and some alternatives in strategies like global macro hedge funds and venture capital.

Not all of those strategies will pay off, but some will do well enough to outperform others and preserve wealth.

Once the trend toward inflation or deflation becomes clearer, I'll alert you to sell assets positioned for the opposite outcome. That way, you can redeploy that month to prepare for the dominant outcome. For example, if inflation begins to spin out of control, I may tell you to convert cash and bonds into gold and land. If deflation gets the upper hand, I will advise you to liquidate some of your stocks in favor of more cash and bonds, and so on.

In future *Strategic Intelligence* issues, I'll maintain close watch on the tug of war between inflation and deflation for you. I'll give you early warnings about which way to pivot. For now, however, the outcome is uncertain and you need to place some bets on both inflation and deflation happening. But be ready to cut losses on losers and double down on winners when the time comes.

CHAPTER 2

Five Crisis Scenarios

Enemy Hedge Fund Scenario

A country like China or Russia could conduct a financial attack on the United States using the trillions of dollars of reserves they have in their sovereign wealth funds.

China is a good example. They have $4 trillion dollars in reserves. By reserves, I just mean their savings account. If you make $50,000 a year and you spend $40,000 on rent or car or whatever and you've got $10,000 left over, you can put it in the bank or you can use it to buy stocks and bonds. That $10,000 is your savings, or your portfolio, if you will.

Individual countries are no different. Countries earn money by having a trade surplus or getting direct foreign investment and they have to decide how to invest it. That's what's called their reserve position.

A lot of it goes into liquid assets, but the sovereign wealth funds are set up to invest in less liquid instruments, normal stocks and bonds too. They could, however, also be used to fund a hedge fund with layers of Cayman Island trusts, Maltese banks, cyber center intermediaries and, perhaps some corrupt lawyers or bankers, though, you could also have unwitting, unknowing lawyers and bankers who think they're working for a legitimate hedge fund and don't know who's really behind it. That's what's called layering — it's the use of trust and other vehicles to disguise the true ownership.

This fund could come into the market and can buy and sell on a continual basis, not really trying to make money. That's because its purpose would not be to make money like a normal hedge fund. Instead, it would actually have a malevolent geopolitical financial warfare intent.

It could build up its credit lines, build up its credibility, get facilities with major banks and then one day, just flood the market with sell orders in a particular stock. They could sell the big stocks too like Apple, Google and the like.

They could use options to amplify their attack — and they wouldn't do it on a sunny day. They would most likely pick a day when the market was already down, maybe three or four percent already. That would be a big day down say, down, by as much as six-hundred points. By piling on, this enemy hedge fund could create a panic and then disappear the next day, taking its money and going back to Beijing or wherever it came from.

A hedge fund entity could be set it up, funded, and left to be operated normally for years or even longer until one day, it attacks U.S. financial markets. That's one scenario that could play out and the United States certainly needs to be alert to that.

Inflation Takes Hold

The important thing to understand about inflation is that the Fed wants it. That's very hard for people to understand because most people remember the late 1970s or early 1980, when we had out of control inflation.

From 1977 to 1981, cumulative inflation over that five-year period was *fifty percent*. That means, if you were a saver, had annuity, an insurance policy, a retirement income or any kind of fixed income at all, you lost half of your purchasing power in five years.

People go back to the creation of the Fed in 1913 and they explain that the dollar has lost ninety-five percent of its purchasing power since 1913 — one hundred years. That's true, but the late seventies was a case where it lost fifty percent of its purchasing power, not in 100 years, but in five years. That could happen again.

The Fed spent 30 years getting the inflation genie back in the bottle. It started with Paul Volcker and continued through the 1980s, 1990s and the early 2000s. They succeeded, eventually getting inflation under control.

Now, however, the Fed is trying to open the bottle and let the genie out once again. They have their reasons. First, the United States can't pay its debt so inflation is a way to reduce the value of that debt. They still owe the same amount of money — around $17 trillion — but in real terms, it's worth a lot less.

We can't pay $17 trillion, but maybe we could pay $8 trillion so, they can reduce their bill by cutting the value of the dollar in half.

The Fed also wants to get the economy going again. To do so, they're using what's called financial repression. You force the banks to buy bonds and use other regulatory means to keep interest rates low. Meanwhile, you try to stoke inflation. Whenever inflation is higher than interest rates, you have what's called a negative real rate.

That's like free money. In fact, it's better than free money. The bank actually pays you to be a borrower because you get to pay the bank back in cheaper dollars.

The Fed is trying to engineer a situation like that to get people borrowing, lending and spending again. They think that will get the economic machine going. But what they don't understand or what they misapprehend is that once they do that, they'll have to change expectations.

Right now, inflation expectations are extremely low. Investors fear the opposite of inflation right now — deflation. It's very hard to change those expectations, but once you do, they can go out of control.

The Fed thinks they can dial inflation up to three percent or four percent and then dial it back down to two. They're going to find out that, instead, it goes from two to three to four to nine and all of a sudden, you're back to the very destructive borderline hyperinflation that we saw in the late 1970s.

They are playing with fire.

Deflation Takes Hold

No one knows what deflation looks and feels like today. We worried for decades about inflation, and today, the Fed's trying to get more inflation. Deflation, however, is a real danger.

The reason it's a danger is that we are not in a normal cyclical recovery. We're in a new depression. This is a global depression that began in 2007 and will run on indefinitely. The Fed's trying to treat the depression with monetary remedies, but it won't work. The reason it won't work is that depressions are structural.

Monetary solutions and liquidity solutions are cyclical. They help you out of the business cycle. If credit becomes too tight, the Fed loosens. If things get a little hot, the Fed tightens.

That's the normal kind of sine wave business expansion and contraction we've seen since World War II. But today is different. It's more like the Great Depression.

Depressions are structural. You cannot get out of them without structural changes in fiscal policy or regulatory policy.

In a depression, people want to deleverage. They sell assets and get cash to pay off debts to reduce their balance sheet.

What happens when they sell assets? It lowers the price.

That puts the next investor in distress. He now has to sell assets to deleverage his balance sheet and the process feeds on itself. That is very, very difficult for the Fed to control.

It actually creates a state of mind where cash is more valuable. In a deflation, cash actually goes up in real terms. In fact, cash can be one of your best assets in a deflationary environment.

The natural state of the world today is deflationary because we're in a depression. The government, however, can't tolerate deflation. They have to cause inflation. That's why the Fed's money printing is going on.

The best way to understand this is to picture two tectonic plates, like the San Andreas Fault. There's the Pacific plate and the North American plate. They're pressing on each other.

One plate is inflation and the other is deflation. The opposite forces of money printing and depression dynamics are the forces pushing them together.

They're pressing and pressing. Like a fault line, not much happens at first. At some point, however, it's going to break.

It could break either way. It could break into inflation, which we talked about, but it could also break into deflation.

The assets that will perform very well in a deflationary environment are things like cash and believe it or not, gold.

Over the long-term, I think inflation is more likely because the government wants it. That said, deflation is the state of the world today and you cannot rule it out.

Geopolitical Crisis

The fourth scenario I'd like to highlight is a geopolitical shock. People yawn and say, "Gee, haven't we had enough of those lately?"

It could, however, be something like an assassination or a more momentous event than what we've seen so far. Or, one of today's current geopolitical struggles could spin out of control.

When Russia invades Crimea, that's something that could trigger a crisis. When the Islamic State declares a caliphate, that's another. When Libya completely falls apart, and they stop pumping oil, that's another.

I frequently make the point that any snowflake can cause

an avalanche, which is true. But not every snowflake does.

A lot of snowflakes fall harmlessly, except that they make the ultimate avalanche worse because they're building up the snow pack. Then, when one of them hits the wrong way, and starts an avalanche, it cascades out of control.

Sometimes people have this idea that all geopolitical events are little things. They mistakenly believe they should be waiting for a massive event that will trigger the next crisis with a bang. That's actually not good science.

The way to think about the trigger for the next crisis is that it might not look that different from the little things. All that is necessary to trigger the crisis is for an event to react with the system the wrong way. If an event happens on a bad day or when markets were leaning a certain way, — that could be the straw that breaks the camel's back.

The straw that breaks the camel's back is not different than all the other straw. It's just that it was at the tipping point, and one piece of straw broke the camel. Likewise, onc snowflake starts an avalanche... and one small event can trigger a crisis.

The one thing that causes the big drop might not be that different than the events we've seen already. Except that the system is getting more and more unstable, and it might not take that much to make it collapse.

Market Collapse

The fifth scenario is a market collapse. This is something that would happen very suddenly and unexpectedly. The forces of inflation and deflation that I wrote about take a while to play out, but this collapse could happen very suddenly and catch investors completely unaware. We've come within hours or days of total global financial gridlock and total market collapse in the last 16 years.

Everyone knows about the 2008 crisis. People have a

sense of that. But few people know it also happened in 1998 as a result of the Russia default and the collapse of hedge fund Long Term Capital Management (LTCM).

I was involved in LTCM. I actually negotiated that bailout. I was in the room. I saw the $4 billion moved into our bank accounts to prop up the balance sheet. The money came from Wall Street.

There was a lot of give and take that almost didn't happen and we were literally hours away from markets collapsing. We muddled through that, but officials learned all the wrong lessons.

Instead of banning derivatives, backing away from overleverage and putting a lid on banks, public policy did the opposite. Congress repealed Glass Steagall, which allowed banks to act like hedge funds, they repealed Schwab's regulation, which meant that you could trade derivatives on anything.

They repealed or increased broker-dealer leverage from 15 :1 to 30:1. The Securities and Exchange Commission (SEC) did that in 2006. The Basel III capital requirements also allowed greater bank leverage. Basically, the officials looked at LTCM's failure and said, "The games on. You can do whatever you want, with as much leverage as you want and with as much opaqueness as you want."

Is it any surprise that in 2008 we had another collapse?

Then, Bear Stearns went down, then Fanny Mae, then Freddie Mac, followed by Lehman Brothers and AIG. One by one the dominos fell.

We were days away from total collapse. Morgan Stanley would have been next; Goldman Sachs would've been right behind it, then Citibank, Bank of America and then J.P. Morgan. All the dominos were falling.

What the government did, was drop a steel curtain between two of the dominos. They stopped the process after Lehman Brothers and AIG. That's why Morgan Stanley didn't fall — but they were days away from collapse.

The point is, how much more stress can the system take?

The system almost collapsed in 1998 and it almost collapsed in 2008. It's three strikes, and you're out.

The next collapse — the big drop — is coming.

You can see it coming because of the dynamics. The difference is, next time, the crisis will be bigger than the Fed.

The Fed was able to bailout LTCM, Morgan Stanley and Goldman Sachs. But when the Big Drop comes, it's going to be too much for the Fed to handle. They've used up all their dry powder; they've taken their balance sheet to $4 trillion.

What are they going to do, take their balance sheet to $8 trillion?

How can they take their balance sheet that high to re-liquefy against the next collapse without destroying confidence in the dollar?

The answer's simple: They can't.

That's why, after the Big Drop, the system won't get another chance.

"It Can't Happen Here"

People tell me all of the time that these sorts of scenarios can't happen here.

I have to remind them that it *has* happened here. I point out that the international monetary system has collapsed three times in the past hundred years — in 1914, 1939 and 1971.

The global financial system has come very close to complete collapse twice in the past 16 years in 1998 and again in 2008.

The stock market also dropped 22 percent in a single day October 19, 1987. That would be the equivalent in today's terms of the Dow Jones dropping *four thousand points.*

Not forty, not four hundred, but *four thousand* points. The Mexican Peso Crisis in 1994, the dotcom bubble, the NASDAQ collapse provide more examples — sending the stock market from five thousand points to two thousand points in a very short period of time.

Yet, these things keep happening.

It's true we get bailouts and money printing from the Fed, but we're at the point where the risk is bigger than ever. We've had our warnings, we've had our lessons, we haven't learned them, and we're making the same mistakes. When the Big Drop comes, it's going to be bigger than the Fed.

CHAPTER 3

The Threat of Inflation

Money Illusion

A money illusion sounds like something a prestidigitator performs by pulling $100 bills from a hat shown to be empty moments before. In fact, money illusion is a longstanding concept in economics that has enormous significance for you if you're a saver, investor or entrepreneur.

Money illusion is a trick, but it is not one performed on stage. It is a ruse performed by central banks that can distort the economy and destroy your wealth.

The money illusion is a tendency of individuals to confuse real and nominal prices. It boils down to the fact that people ignore inflation when deciding if they are better off. Examples are everywhere.

Assume you are a building engineer working for a property management company making $100,000 per year. You get a 2% raise, so now you are making $102,000 per year. Most people would say they are better off after the raise. But if inflation is 3%, the $102,000 salary is worth only $98,940 in purchasing power relative to where you started.

You got a $2,000 raise in nominal terms but you suffered a $1,060 pay cut in real terms. Most people would say you're better off because of the raise, but you're actually worse off because you've lost purchasing power. The difference between your perception and reality is money illusion.

The impact of money illusion is not limited to wages and prices. It can apply to any cash flow including dividends and interest. It can apply to the asset prices of stocks and bonds. Any nominal increase has to be adjusted for inflation in order to see past the money illusion.

The concept of money illusion as a subject of economic study and policy is not new. Irving Fisher, one of the most famous economists of the 20th century, wrote a book called *The Money Illusion* in 1928. The idea of money illusion can be traced back to Richard Cantillon's *Essay on Economic Theory* of 1730, although Cantillon did not use that exact phrase.

Economists argue that money illusion does not exist. Instead, they say, you make decisions based upon "rational expectations." That means once you perceive inflation or expect it in future, you will discount the value of your money and invest or spend it according to its expected intrinsic value.

Like much of modern economics, this view works better in the classroom than in the real world. Experiments by behaviorists show that people think a 2% cut in wages with no change in the price level is "unfair." Meanwhile, they think a 2% raise with 4% inflation is "fair."

In fact, the two outcomes are economically identical in terms of purchasing power. The fact, however, that people prefer a raise over a pay cut while ignoring inflation is the essence of money illusion.

The importance of money illusion goes far beyond academics and social science experiments. Central bankers use money illusion to transfer wealth from you — a saver and investor — to debtors. They do this when the economy isn't growing because there's too much debt. Central bankers try to use inflation to reduce the real value of the debt to give debtors some relief in the hope that they might spend more and help the economy get moving again.

Of course, this form of relief comes at the expense of savers and investors like you who see the value of your assets decline. Again a simple example makes the point.

Assume a debtor bought a $250,000 home in 2007 with a $50,000 down payment and a $200,000 mortgage with a low teaser rate. Today, the home is worth $190,000, a 24% decline in value, but the mortgage is still $200,000 because the teaser rate did not provide for amortization.

This homeowner is "underwater" — the value of his home is worth less than the mortgage he's paying — and he's slashed his spending in response. In this scenario, assume there is another individual, a saver, with no mortgage and $100,000 in the bank who receives no interest under the Fed's zero interest rate policy.

Suppose a politician came along who proposed that the government confiscate $15,000 from the saver to be handed to the debtor to pay down his mortgage. Now the saver has only $85,000 in the bank, but the debtor has a $190,000 house with a $185,000 mortgage, bringing the debtor's home above water and a giving him a brighter outlook.

The saver is worse off and the debtor is better off, each because of the $15,000 transfer payment. Americans would consider this kind of confiscation to be grossly unfair, and the politician would be run out of town on a rail.

Now assume the same scenario, except this time, the Federal Reserve engineers 3% inflation for five years, for a total of 15% inflation. The saver still has $100,000 in the bank, but it is worth only $85,000 in purchasing power due to inflation.

The borrower would still owe $200,000 on the mortgage, but the debt burden would be only $170,000 in real terms after inflation. Better yet, the house value might rise by $28,000 if it keeps pace with inflation, making the house worth $218,000 and giving the debtor positive home equity again.

The two cases are economically the same. In the first case, the wealth transfer is achieved by confiscation, and in the second case, the wealth transfer is achieved by inflation. The saver is worse off and the debtor is better off in both cases. But confiscation is politically unacceptable, while inflation of 3% per year is barely noticed. In effect, inflation is a hidden tax used to transfer wealth from savers to debtors without causing the political headaches of a real tax increase.

Why do central banks such as the Fed pursue money illusion policies? The answer involves another academic theory that doesn't work in the real world. The Fed believes that underwater debtors are from a lower income tier than savers and investors. This means the debtors have what's called higher marginal propensity to consume, or MPC.

The MPC measures how much you spend out of each dollar of wealth you gain. If you gained $1,000 and decided to spend $50, your MPC would be 5%. If you spent nothing after getting an additional $1,000, your MPC would be 0%.

Academic theory says that poorer debtors have a higher MPC than wealthier savers. This means that if inflation transfers wealth from savers to debtors, total spending will go up because the debtors will spend more of the money than the savers would have. This is said to benefit debtors and savers, because debtors gain from the increased wealth, while savers gain from more overall spending in the form of jobs, business revenues and stock prices. This makes inflation a win-win.

This theory sounds neat and tidy, but it has serious flaws. By lumping all savers together, the theory fails to distinguish between truly wealthy savers and middle-class savers. It may be true that if you're a very wealthy saver, you have a low MPC. If you are spending a certain amount on vacations and fine wine and the Fed steals some of your savings through inflation, you will probably spend just as much on vacations and fine wine.

But if you're part of the middle class who is struggling with an unemployed spouse, children's tuition, elderly parents' health care and higher property taxes, your savings and investments are a lifeline you cannot afford to lose. If your savings are eroded by inflation, the pain is real and your spending may be cut. There is no free lunch.

Insidious Cantillon Effects

Cantillon in the 1730s suggested an even more insidious flaw in the central bank's reasoning. He said that inflation does not move uniformly through an economy. It moves with lags, something Milton Friedman also said in the 1970s. Inflation, according to Cantillon, moves in concentric circles from a small core of people to an ever widening group of affected individuals.

Think of the way ripples spread out when you drop a pebble in a pond. Cantillon said that the rich and powerful are in the inner circle and see the inflation first. This gives them time to prepare. The middle class are in the outer circles and see the inflation last. They are the victims of lost purchasing power.

This Cantillon Effect may explain why wealthy investors such as Warren Buffett are buying hard assets like railroads, oil and natural gas that will retain value when inflation hits. Official measures of inflation are low today but those in the inner circle already see it coming first, just as Cantillon suggested.

If you're in the wider circles, however, you may stay in conventional stock and bond portfolios too long and will see the value of your assets diluted by inflation. You may not realize it until it's too late, either. The money illusion deceives everyday investors.

Money illusion has four stages. In stage one, the groundwork for inflation is laid by central banks but is not yet apparent to most investors. This is the "feel good" stage where people are counting their nominal gains but don't see through the illusion.

Stage two is when inflation becomes more obvious. Investors still value their nominal gains and assume inflation is temporary and the central banks "have it under control."

Stage three is when inflation begins to run away and central banks lose control. Now the illusion wears off. Savings and other fixed-income cash flows such as insurance, annuities and retirement checks rapidly lose value. If you own hard assets prior to stage three, you'll be spared. But if you don't, it will be too late because the prices of hard assets will gap up *before* the money illusion wears off.

Finally, stage four can take one of two paths. The first path is hyperinflation, such as Weimar Germany or Zimbabwe. In that case, all paper money and cash flows are destroyed and a new currency arises from the ashes of the old. The alternative is shock therapy of the kind Paul Volcker imposed in 1980. In that case, interest rates are hiked as high as 20% to kill inflation… but nearly kill the economy in the process.

Right now, we are in late stage one, getting closer to stage two. Inflation is here in small doses and people barely notice. Savings are being slowly confiscated by inflation, but investors are still comforted by asset bubbles in stocks and real estate. Be nimble and begin to buy some inflation insurance in the form of hard assets before the Stage Three super-spike puts the price of those assets out of reach.

Hyperinflation It Can (Still) Happen Here

Six years and $4 trillion of Federal Reserve money printing after the 2008 crash, you may think to yourself, *if hyperinflation were ever going to happen in the U.S., it would've already.*

In fact, when I write "hyperinflation," you might only think of two images. One, a reckless third-world country like Zimbabwe or Argentina printing money to cover government expenses and worker salaries to the point where trillions of local "dollars" or pesos are needed to buy a loaf of bread.

The second image is of the same phenomenon in an

advanced country such as Germany, but long ago. Perhaps you think of grainy, black-and-white photos from the 1920s.

The last thing you probably think of is a hyperinflation in a 21st-century developed economy such as the United States. We tell ourselves that hyperinflation might happen in faraway or long-ago places, but it can't happen here.

Yet it can happen here. In fact, the United States flirted with hyperinflation in the late 1970s, and before that in the late 1910s. Other episodes arose after the Civil War and the American Revolution. Hyperinflation acts like a deadly virus with no cure. It may be contained for long periods of time, but once it breaks out into a general population, there may be no stopping it without enormous losses.

To explain why, it's essential to know what hyperinflation is, how it begins and how it feeds on itself. In a complex system such as the U.S. economy, small initial blunders can have catastrophic consequences once feedback loops and behavioral changes take over.

There is no universally agreed-upon definition of hyperinflation. But one widely used benchmark says hyperinflation exists when prices increase 50% or more in a single month. So if gasoline is $3.00 per gallon in January, $4.50 per gallon in February and $6.75 per gallon in March, and if prices of food and other essentials are going up at the same pace, that would be considered hyperinflationary.

It also tends to accelerate once it begins, so the monthly 50% increase soon becomes 100%, then 1,000%, etc., until the real value of the currency is utterly destroyed. Beyond that point, the currency ceases to function as currency and becomes litter good only for wallpaper or starting fires.

Many investors assume that money printing by governments to cover deficits is the root cause of hyperinflation. Money printing does contribute to hyperinflation, but it is not a complete explanation. The other essential ingredient is velocity or the turnover of money. If central banks print money and that money is left in banks and not used by consumers, then actual inflation can be low.

This is the situation in the U.S. today. The Federal Reserve has expanded the base money supply by over $3 trillion since 2008. But very little actual inflation has resulted. This is because the velocity of money has been dropping at the same time. Banks are not lending much, and consumers are not spending much of the new money; it's just sitting in the banks.

Money printing first turns into inflation, and then hyperinflation, when consumers and businesses lose confidence in price stability and see more inflation on the horizon. At that point, money is dumped in exchange for current consumption or hard assets, and velocity increases.

As inflation spikes up, expectations of more inflation grow, and the process accelerates and feeds on itself. In extreme cases, consumers will spend their entire paycheck on groceries, gasoline and gold the minute they receive it. They know holding their money in the bank will result in their hard-earned pay being wiped out. The important point is that hyperinflation is not just a monetary phenomenon — it is first and foremost a psychological or behavioral phenomenon.

As you'll see below, hyperinflation does not affect everyone in a society equally. There are distinct sets of winners and losers. The winners are those with gold, foreign currency, land and other hard assets including factories, natural resources and transportation equipment. The losers are those with fixed income claims such as savings, pensions, insurance policies and annuities. Debtors win in hyperinflation because they pay off debt with debased currency. Creditors lose because their claims are devalued.

Hyperinflation doesn't emerge instantaneously. It begins slowly with normal inflation and then accelerates violently at an increasing rate until it becomes hyperinflation. This is critical for investors to understand because *much of the damage to your wealth actually occurs at the inflationary stage, not the hyper-inflationary stage.* The hyperinflation of Weimar Germany is a good case in point.

In January 1919, the exchange rate of German reichsmarks to U.S. dollars was 8.2 to 1. By January 1922, three years later, the exchange rate was 207.82 to 1. The reichsmark had lost 96% of its value in three years. By the standard definition, this is not hyperinflation, because it took place over 36 months and was never 50% in any single month.

By the end of 1922, hyperinflation had struck Germany with the reichsmark going from 3,180 to the dollar in October to 7,183 to the dollar in November. In that case, the reichs-mark did lose half its value in a single month, thus meeting the definition of hyperinflation.

One year later, in November 1923, the exchange rate was 4.2 *trillion* reichsmarks to one dollar. History tends to focus on 1923 when the currency was debased 58 billion percent. But that extreme hyperinflation of 1923 was just a matter of destroying the remaining 4% of people's wealth at an acceler-ating rate. The real damage was done from 1919–1922, *before* the hyperinflation, when the first 96% was lost.

If you think this can't happen here or now, think again. Something like this started in the late 1970s. The U.S. dol-lar suffered 50% inflation in the five years from 1977–1981. We were at the takeoff stage to hyperinflation, exactly where Germany was in 1920 on a relative basis. Most wealth in savings and fixed income claims had been lost already. Hyperinflation in America was prevented then by the combined actions of Paul Volcker and Ronald Reagan, but it was a close call.

Today the Federal Reserve assumes if inflation moves up to 3% or more in the U.S., they can gently dial it back to their preferred 2% target. But moving inflation to 3% requires a huge change in the behavior and expectations of everyday

Americans. That change is not easy to cause, but once it happens, it is not easy to reverse, either.

If inflation does hit 3%, it is more likely to go to 6% or higher, rather than back down to 2% because the process will feed on itself and be difficult to stop. Sadly, there are no Volckers or Reagans on the horizon today. There are only weak political leaders and misguided central bankers.

Inflation will accelerate as it did in the U.S. in 1980 and in Germany in 1920. Whether hyperinflation comes next remains to be seen, but it can happen more easily than most people expect. By then, the damage is already done. Your savings and pensions will mostly be gone.

The assets you need now to preserve wealth in the future are simple and timeless. Gold, silver, land and select tangibles in the right amounts will serve you well. Mutual funds designed specifically to protect against inflation should also be considered.

One such mutual fund is the West Shore Real Return Income Fund (NWSFX:US). Its assets include units of physical gold, fine art and other tangible assets intended to preserve wealth in inflationary conditions.

Full Disclosure: I'm global strategist for the West Shore Group, which manages the fund. Still, I believe NWSFX is a good representation of the assets that are necessary to protect your wealth.

Excess Reserves Held At Banks

The reason the Fed is paying interest on excess reserves today is to give banks the money to pay higher insurance premiums to the FDIC. Remember, the Dodd-Frank bill raised the insurance premiums on the banks that they have to pay for their deposit insurance. That would have hurt bank earnings. So the Fed said, "Fine, we'll just pay you on the excess reserves, take the money and pay your premiums."

This is just another game — another shadow play providing a backdoor way of financing the FDIC premiums with printed money so the banks don't actually have to bear the cost. That's the reason they're doing it.

Beyond that, the notion that, if they stop paying the interest that, all of a sudden, the banks will say, "Well, we've got to make some money. We'll go out and lend all this money," I don't agree with that at all. In fact, it's not right.

The dynamic is different than these theorists suppose. The real problem is that, to have inflation, you need two things: Money supply and velocity.

Velocity is simply the turnover of money. If I go out tonight and I buy a drink at the bar, then I tip the bartender, and the bartender takes a taxicab home, and the taxicab driver puts some gas in his car, that money has a velocity of three. You've got the bartender, the taxicab, and the gas station. But, if I stay home and watch TV or buy gold and leave it in a vault, that money has a velocity of zero.

The nominal GDP, the nominal gross value of all the goods and services in the US economy, is simply the money supply times velocity. You need both to cause inflation.

You need money supply times velocity to be greater than potential GDP. Then, the excess shows up in the form of inflation. Today the Fed has taken the money supply to the moon yet velocity is collapsing. That's the problem.

More or less money printing or payment of interest on excess reserves won't cause inflation. What would cause inflation is the change in velocity, which is behavioral. It's the change in the psychology. That's what you have to look for. It's what the Fed actually calls "inflationary expectations."

And so I like to say, if you want inflation, it's like a ham-and-cheese sandwich. You need both the ham and the cheese. Money printing is the ham and velocity is the cheese.

The thing to watch for is a change in inflationary expectations or a change in behavior. That can happen very quickly, and that's why inflation is so dangerous. It might not show up at all, and then, suddenly, it will come very quickly because it's very difficult to change the behavior. But, once you do, it's very difficult to change it back again. That's why inflation runs out of control.

Four Trillion Dollars and Counting

Over the past five years the Federal Reserve has ballooned its balance sheet above four trillion dollars. People say, "Well, that's got to cause inflation." But it doesn't automatically mean inflation.

What it means is that you *could* have inflation. The potential is there. Certainly, if the Fed hadn't printed that much money, the potential for inflation would be much lower.

But the money by itself is not enough. You need money plus the change of behavior. You need something that's going to catalyze people's behavior. Think of the money supply as a big pile of dry wood or maybe a big drum of gasoline. The behavior is the match — it's the thing you throw in that lights the fire — or, in this case, the hyperinflation.

We should absolutely be concerned about the money. The problem is that because there has been no inflation thus far, the Fed is going to keep printing.

We haven't seen that much inflation yet. That's a fact. Paul Krugman sees that and says, "See. I told you. You can print all the money you want and you don't get inflation. So go print some more."

My answer is: That's not quite correct. You can print all the money you want and we haven't had inflation. But that's only because the behavior hasn't changed. Again, once the behavior does change, two things happen. First, the inflation can come very quickly, much more quickly than people expect.

Second, once you change behavior it's very hard to change it back again.

Right now, the Fed says, "We want two percent inflation." Some of the FOMC members will tell you privately that they wouldn't mind seeing three percent inflation. To get it, they're going to keep printing and printing and printing until they get the three percent inflation.

But there are two problems. Most obvious is, they're printing all of that money. They might actually destroy confidence in the dollar before they get to three percent inflation.

This is where the British, Russia, China and other foreign countries buying gold all play out. These are governments backing away from the dollar because they don't like what they see.

The second problem is, the Fed might get to three percent inflation, but then cruise past it to nine percent inflation. Again, once you turn that battleship around you can't turn it back very easily.

The Fed thinks they're playing with a thermostat. It's like if your house is too cold you dial it up. If your house is too warm, you dial it down. The Fed wants to dial it up. They want a little more inflation and they think if things get a little too hot they can dial it down again.

What they're going discover, probably the hard way, is that it's not a linear. It's not a reversible process. When they get it to three percent inflation, which is not easy, it might go right to nine.

That's when investors will lose a lot of money.

Helicopter Money and Peer-to-Peer Lending

Printing money by itself does not cause inflation. It's a necessary condition, but it's not a sufficient condition. You do need the money to cause that kind of inflation, but you need something else. You need this change in behavior or velocity.

A lot of people say, "Well, all that money sloshing around is going to lead to a lot of lending." That's not how it works.

Banks don't need reserves to lend. They'll make the loan and then go get the reserves. The fact that the Federal Reserve is throwing reserves at the banks does not mean that people want to borrow and it does not mean banks want to lend.

In fact, people don't want to borrow and the banks don't want to lend. This is why we're seeing that some of the hottest companies around are Lending Tree and Social Finance. These are peer-to-peer lenders.

People use Internet platforms to dis-intermediate the banks. They take the banks out of the equation and say, "Hey, there are people over here with money and people over there who want to borrow money. We'll match the two online." Essentially, it's like an Uber for money lending.

You wouldn't have the opportunity for peer-to-peer lending if the banks were doing their job. Right now, they're not doing their job. The short answer why is that reserves are never constrained on lending. The banks can lend all they want. Then they'll go get the reserves if they need them. That's why all of the reserves are piling up right now.

This could lead to what's called "helicopter money." Helicopter money is the way the *government* takes the banks out of the equation. The banks aren't doing their jobs — they've been given all this money by the Fed, but they're not lending it. Candidly, people don't want to borrow, at least not on the terms the banks are offering.

The private sector solution to that problem is peer-to-peer lending. But there's also a government solution, which is helicopter money. The image people think of is the Fed printing a lot of money and then dumping the bills out of sacks from a helicopter in the skies above. Then, people are supposed to run around, scoop that money up and go spend it.

That's a nice image, but the way it actually works is that the government cut taxes, starting with the payroll tax. Half the people in American don't pay income tax. A lot of people are surprised to hear that, but it's true. Conversely, almost everybody who's working pays the payroll tax. By cutting the payroll tax, the government is able to put money right in people's pockets because it affects everyone.

That tax cut increases the federal deficit. The Fed, however, says to the Treasury, "Hey, guys. Don't worry about it. We've got your back. Go borrow the money to fill the hole in the deficit and we'll print the money."

That's the kind of money printing where you don't rely on the banks to make loans. You put the money right in people's pockets with a tax cut. You deficit finance the tax cut and you print money to pay the deficit. That's helicopter money.

While we're seeing peer-to-peer lending and social media today, we might see helicopter money in 2016.

Remember, it's an election year and politicians love tax cuts. This game is not over because at the end of the day, the government has to get inflation. They're not getting it. They've been trying to get inflation for five years and haven't succeeded.

At present, deflation is a greater danger. What I try to explain to investors is, you shouldn't think of one or the other. Don't think we're definitely going to have inflation or we're definitely going to have deflation. Think of it as a tug of war where two forces are pulling against each other and, at any point, one side is winning.

At writing, deflation is winning. But sooner than later, inflation might start to win. And what I try to do in *Strategic Intelligence* is help you understand that dynamic, keep you informed and give you portfolio suggestions so you can win either way.

How High Could Inflation Get?

In the last fifty years, inflation in the U.S. went as high as thirteen percent. But let's say it didn't get that high. Instead, let's say it got to nine percent.

Nine percent inflation will cut the value of the dollar in half in about eight years. Eight years is not a long time. If you've got three children and they're heading off to college, by the time the first one goes and the last one finishes, that's probably eight or nine years.

What does that do to your retirement income, insurance policies, your annuities and your savings?

It cuts them in half. It potentially cuts your retirement in half. That's something to be concerned about.

Now, inflation might not stop at nine percent. Or, it could go to ten or twelve percent. As I mentioned, we saw thirteen percent inflation in 1980 so it's not impossible. That's in the lifetime of many Americans. They probably remember that.

Of course, hyperinflation in a modern industrialized nation is something much more extreme. Everyone talks about Zimbabwe in recent years or nationalist China in 1949.

But Germany was not Zimbabwe. Germany was the third largest economy in the world in 1929, a major industrial power and exporter yet they had a hyperinflation. It was the result of bad policy and psychology taking over. Hyperinflation usually starts out with bad policy but once people realize what's going on, they'll do the rest. Then, they dump the money as fast as they can.

You know what happened during Weimer hyperinflation? People were getting paid *twice a day.* Not once a month or twice a month or once a week.

They would actually break for lunch and the wives would come down to meet the husbands at the factory gate. The husbands would get paid in stacks of notes, which had been brought over by the bank or in a car or a wheelbarrow.

Then, they would run right out and they would buy a ham, a bottle of wine, a stick of butter or whatever they needed for that day. Then, they'd do the same thing again at the end of the day when they'd get another pay pack.

Of course, by 5:00 p.m. the price had probably doubled since lunchtime. The point, however, is if you got the ham you don't care if the price doubles, quadruples or goes up a billion times. Think about ham as a hard asset. I think of a bar of gold the same way.

Once you dump the dollars or whatever currency and get the hard asset, you're protected. You don't really care. You might care, but the money going to zero as it hyperinflates doesn't hurt you anymore because you've got the hard asset. In the case of a family trying to get through the day, that ham might have been dinner. Then they go out later that night and perhaps buy a loaf of bread for the next morning. That's how bad it was.

The point is people treat money like it's radioactive during a hyperinflation. You get some money in a paycheck but you don't want it. You want to dump it as fast as you can. And when you give it to the guy who sells me the ham, he dumps it immediately too. He pays the wholesale. In a hyperinflation, money's like a hot potato. You want to get rid of it.

The velocity pushes infinity, which means the currency approaches zero. That's the psychology behind it. So it's not all about money printing. It's about changing the psychology. Now, you need the money. You can run out of money. That's happened from time to time, but it's the combination of the two. It's the printing money by the central bank and the change in psychology by the people that can cause hyperinflation.

Today, we have the money printing — more than four trillion dollars. The psychology hasn't changed, but my point is that psychology and confidence are fragile things.

They can change quickly. And when they do it's very hard to change them back. You need to be prepared for that.

We don't have much inflation today. That's a fact. And there's no sense arguing we do. The data says otherwise. But we could have it suddenly and that's the reason to have some hard assets. Don't go all in or fifty percent, but have a slice of your portfolio in hard assets. That's your insurance policy.

Getting the Timing Right

There are a lot of analysts who, since 2008, have been are saying, "The next crisis is right around the corner. We're going to have hyperinflation. Buy gold. Do this. Get ready now."

Many people have bought into that narrative and have been disappointed. They say, "Well, wait a second. We don't really see much inflation. In fact, deflation appears to be more of a danger in recent times. Oil's down... gold's down... commodities are down. At some point, that narrative loses its credibility.

Here's what I say to confused investors. Inflation, much higher inflation is a danger. But so is deflation.

So, again, my advice for investors is be prepared for both. The investor who's doing this is Warren Buffet.

Warren Buffett's not only buying hard assets but he also has fifty-five billion dollars in cash. The hard assets are his inflation insurance. The cash is his deflation insurance.

It's a lesson not to put all of your bets on one side of the table. My advice is having some inflation protection. Have some hard assets, whether it's gold, energy stocks, silver, land, fine art. But don't go all in — make that a slice. If the hyperinflation comes or even extreme inflation comes faster than we expect, that's going to preserve your net worth.

On the other side, however, have some deflation protection. That could include bonds, fixed income and cash.

When I recommend cash to investors, a lot of them reply, "Well, I hate cash. It has no yield. It just sits there. It's not sexy or interesting."

They don't understand what cash does. The first thing cash does is it takes the volatility out of the rest of your portfolio. If stocks, gold and commodities have been volatile, having cash reduces the impact. It's a little bit technical, but that's what it does. It helps you sleep a little bit better at night.

Cash is also great deflation hedge. Remember, during deflation the value of cash goes up. It doesn't deliver high yield, but in real terms, it's becoming more valuable every day.

The third thing cash offers you is optionality or the ability to pivot. You might not be in cash forever, but you should consider having some now.

That way, you're ready for anything. If deflation takes off you're glad you have bonds.

If inflation takes off you're glad you got the gold and other hard assets.

And, if there's confusion, you're glad you have the cash because it reduces your volatility and lets you pick up bargains.

If the market crashes and you have equities in one part of your portfolio, you might lose on that. But then, you have cash and can go buy bargains. That's the way the smartest investors do it. They're ready for anything.

Hugo Stinnes: The Inflation King

Hugo Stinnes is practically unknown today, but this was not always the case. In the early 1920s, he was the wealthiest man in Germany, at a time when the country was the world's third-largest economy.

He was a prominent industrialist and investor with diverse holdings in Germany and abroad. Chancellors and Cabinet ministers of the newly formed Weimar Republic routinely sought his advice on economic and political problems.

In many ways, Stinnes played a role in Germany similar to the role Warren Buffett plays in the U.S. today. He was an ultra-wealthy investor whose opinion was eagerly sought on important political matters, who exercised powerful behind-the-scenes influence and who seemed to make all the right moves when it came to playing markets.

If you're a student of economic history, you know that from 1922–1923 Germany suffered the worst hyperinflation experienced by a major industrial economy in modern times. As I explained, the exchange rate between the German paper currency, the reichsmark, and the dollar went from 208 to 1 in early 1921 to 4.2 *trillion* to 1 in late 1923. At that point, the reichsmark became worthless and was swept down sewers as litter.

Yet Stinnes was not wiped out during this hyperinflation. Why was that?

Stinnes was born in 1870 into a prosperous German family that had interests in coal mining. He worked in mines to obtain a practical working knowledge of the industry and took courses in Berlin at the Academy of Mining. Later, he inherited his family's business and expanded it by buying his own mines.

Then he diversified into shipping, buying cargo lines. His own vessels were used to transport his coal within Germany along the Rhine River and from his mines abroad. His vessels also carried lumber and grains. His diversification included ownership of a leading newspaper, which he used to exert political influence. Prior to the Weimar hyperinflation, Stinnes borrowed vast sums of money in reichsmarks.

When the hyperinflation hit, Stinnes was perfectly positioned. The coal, steel and shipping retained their value. It didn't matter what happened to the German currency, a hard asset is still a hard asset and does not go away even if the currency goes to zero.

Stinnes' international holdings also served him well because they produced profits in hard currencies, not worthless reichsmarks. Some of these profits were kept offshore in the form of gold held in Swiss vaults. That way he could escape both hyperinflation and German taxation. Finally, he repaid his debts in worthless reichsmarks, making them disappear.

Not only was Stinnes not harmed by the Weimar hyperinflation, but his empire prospered and he made more money than ever. He expanded his holdings and bought out bankrupt competitors. Stinnes made so much money during the Weimar hyperinflation that his German nickname was *Inflationskönig*, which means Inflation King. When the dust settled and Germany returned to a new gold-backed currency, Stinnes was one of the richest men in the world, while the German middle classes were destroyed.

Interestingly, you see Warren Buffett using the same techniques today. It appears that Buffett has studied Stinnes carefully and is preparing for the same calamity that Stinnes saw — hyperinflation.

Buffett recently purchased major transportation assets in the form of the Burlington Northern Santa Fe Railroad. This railroad consists of hard assets in the form of rights of way, adjacent mining rights, rail and rolling stock. The railroad makes money moving hard assets such as ore and grains.

Buffett next purchased huge oil and natural gas assets in Canada in the form of Suncor (SU:NYSE). Buffett can now move his Suncor oil on his Burlington Northern railroad in exactly the same way that Stinnes moved his coal on his own ships in 1923. Buffett is also a major holder in Exxon Mobil, the largest energy company in the world.

For decades, Buffett owned one of the most powerful newspapers in the U.S.: *The Washington Post*. He sold that stake recently to Jeff Bezos of Amazon, but still retains communications assets. He's also purchased large offshore assets in China and elsewhere that produce nondollar profits that can be retained offshore tax-free.

A huge part of Buffett's portfolio is in financial stocks — particularly in banks and insurance companies — that are highly leveraged borrowers. Like Stinnes in the 1920s, Buffett can profit when the liabilities of these financial giants are wiped out by inflation, while they nimbly redeploy assets to hedge their own exposures.

In short, Buffett is borrowing from the Stinnes playbook. He's using leverage to diversify into hard assets in energy, transportation and foreign currencies. He's using his communications assets and prestige to stay informed on behind-the-scenes developments on the political landscape. Buffett is now positioned in much the same way that Stinnes was positioned in 1922.

If hyperinflation were to slam the U.S. today, Buffett's results would be the same as Stinnes'. His hard assets would explode in value, his debts would be eliminated and he would be in a position to buy out bankrupt competitors. Of course, the middle classes in the U.S. would be wiped out, as they were in Germany.

My advice to you when it comes to billionaires like Buffett is to watch what they do, not what they say. Stinnes saw the German hyperinflation coming and positioned accordingly. Buffett is following the Stinnes playbook. Perhaps Buffett sees the same hyperinflation in our future. It's not too late for you to take some of the same precautions as Stinnes and Buffett.

Should You Be Borrowing Money?

A common question I get from readers is, "Should I be borrowing money, given the threat of hyperinflation?"

My answer is that if you have a legitimate reason to borrow, such as to finance a house or something like that, and you can afford it without being overleveraged, that's fine.

But I would not advise you go out and borrow a lot of money right now to lever up. That strategy only works if we do, in fact, experience inflation. The trouble is that the inflation might not come right away. We might be faced with deflation. That's why I recommend having a balance of hard assets and cash.

When I say cash, I'm not talking about money market funds or bank CDs. Instead, I mean the highest-quality instruments you can get. If you're a U.S. investor, that would be U.S. Treasury bills or 1-year notes.

Then get hard assets to protect you from inflation. The cash protects you in deflation and reduces volatility. It's hard to know which one we're in for, so you should prepare for both.

CHAPTER 4

The Threat of Deflation

A Central Banker's Worst Nightmare

From a mathematical perspective, inflation and deflation are two sides of the same coin. Inflation is a period of generally rising prices. Deflation is a period of generally falling prices. Both are deviations from true price stability, and both distort the decisions of consumers and investors.

In inflation, consumers may accelerate purchases before the price goes up. In deflation, consumers may delay purchases in the expectation that prices are going down and things will be cheaper if they wait.

To investors, inflation and deflation are bad in equal, if opposite, measure. But, from a central banker's perspective, inflation and deflation are *not* equally bad. Inflation is something that central bankers consider to be a manageable problem and something that is occasionally desirable. Deflation is something central bankers consider unmanageable and potentially devastating. Understanding why central banks fear deflation more than inflation is the key to understanding central bank monetary policy today.

Central bankers believe they can control inflation by tightening monetary policy. Generally, monetary policy is tightened by raising interest rates. Since rates can be raised to infinity, there is not limit on this tool. Therefore, no matter how strong inflation is, central banks can always tame it with more rate increases.

The classic case is Paul Volcker in 1980 who raised interest rates to twenty percent in order to crush inflation that had reached thirteen percent. Central bankers feel that if the inflation genie escapes from the bottle, they can always coax it back in.

Central bankers also believe that inflation can be good for an economy. This is because of something called the Marginal Propensity to Consume or MPC. The MPC is a measure of how much an individual will spend out of an added dollar of income. The idea is that if you give a poor person a dollar they will spend all of it because they struggle to pay for food, housing and heath care. If you give a rich person a dollar, they will spend very little of it because their needs are already taken care of, so they are more likely to save or invest that dollar. Based on this, poorer people have a higher MPC.

Inflation can be understood as a wealth transfer from the rich to the poor. For the rich person, his savings are worth less, and his spending is about the same because he has a low MPC. By contrast, the poor person has no savings and may have debts that are reduced in real value during inflation. Poor people may also get wage increases in inflation, which they spend because of their higher MPC.

Therefore, inflation tends to increase total consumption because the wealth transfer from rich to poor increases the spending of the poor, but does *not* decrease spending by the rich who still buy whatever they want. The result is higher total spending or "aggregate demand" which helps the economy grow.

Deflation is not so benign and hurts the government in many ways. It increases the real value of the national debt making it harder to finance. Deficits continue to pile up even in deflation, but GDP growth may slow down when measured in nominal dollars. The result is that the debt-to-GDP ratio can skyrocket in periods of deflation. Something like this has been happening in Japan for decades. When the debt-to-GDP ratio gets too high, a sovereign debt crisis and collapse of confidence in the currency can result.

Deflation also destroys government tax collections. If a worker makes $100,000 per year and gets a $10,000 raise when prices are constant, that worker has a 10% increase in her standard of living. The problem is that the government takes $3,000 of the increase in taxes, so the worker only gets $7,000 of the raise after taxes.

But if the worker gets no raise, and prices drop ten percent, she still has a ten percent increase in her standard of living because everything she buys costs less. But now she keeps the *entire* gain because the government has no way to tax the benefits of deflation. In both cases, the worker has a $10,000 increase in her standard of living, but in inflation the government takes $3,000, while in deflation the government gets none of the gain.

For all of these reasons, governments favor inflation. It can increase consumption, decrease the value of government debt, and increase tax collections. Governments fear deflation because it causes people to save, not spend; it increases the burden of government debt, and in hurts tax collections.

But, what is good for government is often bad for investors. In deflation, investors can actually benefit from lower costs, lower taxes and an increase in the real value of savings. As a rule, inflation is good for government and bad for savers; while deflation is bad for government and good for savers.

There are many flaws in the way the government and economists think about inflation and deflation. The idea of MPC as a guide to economic growth is badly flawed. Even if poor people have a higher propensity to consume than rich people, there is more to economic growth than consumption. The real driver of long-term growth is not consumption, but investment. While inflation may help drive consumption, it destroys capital formation and hurts investment. A policy of favoring inflation over deflation may prompt consumption growth in the short run, but it retards investment led growth in the long run. Inflation is a case of a farmer eating his own seed-corn in the winter and having nothing left to plant in the spring. Later he will starve.

It is also not true that inflation is easy to control. Up to a certain point, inflation can be contained by interest rate increases, but the costs may be high, and the damage may already be done. Beyond that threshold, inflation can turn into hyperinflation. At that point, no amount of interest rate increases can stop the headlong dash to dump money and acquire hard assets such as gold, land, and natural resources. Hyperinflation is almost never brought under control. The typical outcome is to wipe out the existing currency system and start over after savings and retirement promises have been destroyed.

In a better world, central bankers would aim for true price stability that does not involve inflation or deflation. But given the flawed economic beliefs and government priorities described above, that is not the case. Central banks favor inflation over deflation because it increases tax collections, reduces the burden of government debt and gooses consumption. If savers and investors are the losers, that's just too bad.

The implications of this asymmetry are profound. In a period where deflationary forces are strong, such as the one we are now experiencing, central banks have to use every trick at their disposal to stop deflation and cause inflation. If one trick does not work, they must try another.

Since 2008 central banks have used interest rate cuts, quantitative easing, forward guidance, currency wars, nominal GDP targets, and operation twist to cause inflation. None of it has worked; deflation is still a strong tendency in the global economy. This is unlikely to change. The deflationary forces are not going away soon. Investors should expect more monetary experiments in the years ahead. A fourth round of quantitative easing, so-called "QE4," perhaps in late 2015 or early 2016 cannot be ruled out. If deflation is strong enough, central banks may even encourage an increase in the price of gold by 2017 in order to raise inflationary expectations.

Eventually the central banks will win and they will get the inflation they want. But it may take time and the inflation may turn into hyperinflation in ways the central banks do not expect or understand. This "tug-of-war" between inflation and deflation creates the most challenging investment climate in 80 years.

The best investment strategies involve a balanced portfolio of hard assets and cash so investors can be ready for both. These strategies are the focus of our research and will be highlighted in *Strategic Intelligence* in the months ahead.

Deflation's Winning the Tug of War

Deflation is one of the most confusing issues for investors today.

To illustrate the point at a speech I gave once, I asked a simple question: "Will anyone in the audience who is 90 years old please raise their hand?"

As I expected, no one did.

My point was simple and relevant to your investments today: You'd have to be at least 90 years old to have any recollection of deflation in the United States. There hasn't been a sustained deflation here since the stretch from 1927–1933. Even then, you'd probably have been about 5 years old.

The main fear for the last few decades or more has been of inflation as the Fed continually prints money. And as we discussed, that threat is very real, so you have to prepare. But the battle between inflation and deflation is not a short-term story.

After months or even years, either force can prevail, which is why it's imperative you be prepared for either outcome. Then, you watch for signposts along the way that will help you decide which force is more likely. Our portfolio is ready for either outcome, but we've promised to monitor which force is winning in the meantime.

As of early 2015, I believe deflation is winning in the short run, while inflation will prevail in the long run.

Both inflation and deflation are challenging to investors who have to guess future returns based on changes in price indexes in addition to navigating the normal business risks of an investment. In short, both inflation and deflation make your economic decisions more difficult by adding a wild card to the deck.

Inflation favors the debtor because the real value of his debts goes down as money becomes worth less. Deflation favors the creditor because the real value of amounts owed to him goes up as money becomes worth more.

But if you take the time to understand the phenomenon, you can profit handsomely from it while others are scratching their head.

"You Can't Always Get What You Want"

It's natural that we have deflation today because we're in a depression. But there are powers at work to make sure nature doesn't take its course.

Mick Jagger famously sang, "You can't always get what you want." This is exactly the situation facing central banks today. They want inflation and can't get it. This is highly unusual. If a central bank, such as the U.S. Federal Reserve, wants inflation, they can typically lower interest rates and print money, and the inflation is sure to follow (with a slight lag).

But the Fed has been pursuing these policies for the past five years and inflation is nowhere in sight. The reason is that the Fed's efforts have been blunted by a strong deflationary force, the strongest in 80 years. This deflationary force will not abate soon.

The Fed has an announced an inflation target of 2%, although in December 2012, they said a short-term goal of 2.5% expected inflation was reasonable. Privately, I was told by Charles Evans, president of the Federal Reserve Bank of Chicago, that he wouldn't mind seeing 3.5% inflation for a short period of time.

Evans is now a voting member of the Federal Open Market Committee, the group that sets Fed policy, so his views count. But whether they target 2%, 2.5% or 3.5%, the fact is that inflation as measured by the Fed has been about 1% — well below the Fed's targets. The Fed has tried rate cuts, quantitative easing, forward guidance, currency wars and Operation Twist over the past five years and none of it has worked. Mick Jagger was right.

The reasons the Fed wants inflation are straightforward. There is a stated reason and an unstated reason. The stated reason is that the Fed occasionally needs to cut rates to stimulate the economy. If rates are at zero, there's nothing to cut.

If you have 2% inflation, you can have normalized interest rates of 2.5% or higher. This gives the Fed something to cut when needed. This rationale is like someone saying they will steal your money so they can lend it back to you later, but the Fed hopes that 2% is low enough that investors won't notice the theft.

The unstated reason is that inflation reduces the real value of the U.S. debt. Right now, the U.S. has about $18 trillion of Treasury debt outstanding and the highest debt-to-GDP ratio since the end of the Second World War. With the economy near stall speed, the U.S. is moving closer to a sovereign debt crisis every day.

If the Fed can achieve, say, 3% inflation for about 20 years, the real value of the debt is cut in half, to about $9 trillion in today's dollars. The trick is to keep interest rates low while inflation does its dirty work. The Fed can do this through financial repression, bank regulation and quantitative easing. Of course, inflation of this slow, steady kind is a form of unseen theft from investors, but that's their problem. The Fed's job is to make the debt melt away, and inflation is the key.

As I said since 2008, central banks have used interest rate cuts, quantitative easing, forward guidance, currency wars, nominal GDP targets, and Operation Twist to cause inflation. None of it has worked.

But don't think that will discourage them. You should expect more monetary experiments in the years ahead. A fourth round of quantitative easing, so-called "QE4," perhaps in late 2015 or early 2016 cannot be ruled out. If deflation is strong enough, central banks may even encourage an increase in the price of gold by 2017 in order to raise inflationary expectations.

The world is not cooperating with the Fed's master plan. We are in a global depression, and the natural consequence of depression is deleveraging and deflation. Businesses in distress sell assets at fire sale prices.

This drives the price down and puts other businesses in distress, which then also sell assets to survive and so on. This is the famous debt-deflation theory of depression written about by economist Irving Fisher in the 1930s. That dynamic has now returned with a vengeance.

The Difference Between "Good" and "Bad" Deflation

We also live in a world of rapidly advancing technology, which is also deflationary because of improvements in efficiency. Larry Page, the co-founder of Google, recently gave an interview to the *Financial Times* in which he said, "Even if there's going to be a disruption on people's jobs, in the short term, that's likely to be made up by the decreasing cost of things we need, which I think is really important and not being talked about... I think the things you want to live a comfortable life could get much, much, much cheaper."

The Google CEO told the *Financial Times* that the average price of a home in Silicon Valley today is $1 million, but he sees no reason why it couldn't be $50,000 in the future. That would represent a 95% price decline, really a form of hyper-deflation.

These insights of Irving Fisher and Larry Page highlight the fact that deflation comes in two forms: what writer James Grant has called "good deflation" and "bad deflation."

Good deflation is the type Larry Page envisions. It comes from technology, efficiency, investment and innovation. If we are getting more efficient through technology, things should cost less.

We see this in personal computers, which have dropped in price from $4,000 to $800 in recent years. This is also the kind of deflation that prevailed from 1870 to 1914, when innovations in railroads, radio, steamships, harvesters and many other fields led to strong consistent growth with low or declining prices. Today, we see good deflation coming not only from information technology, but also from fracking and other aspects of the energy revolution.

Bad deflation is the kind Irving Fisher wrote about in 1933. In prevailed from 1927–1933, when prices dropped over 30%. It is associated with asset sales, liquidations, bankruptcy, unemployment and declining output. Once this kind of deflation takes hold, consumers will stop spending because they expect lower prices in the future and prefer to wait. Cash becomes more valuable in deflation, so consumers don't mind sitting on cash. Bad deflation feeds on itself and is very difficult for central banks to reverse.

Today, investors and policymakers are faced with two challenges as a result. The first is that we are experiencing good deflation and bad deflation *at the same time*. The good deflation is coming from technology, and the bad deflation is coming from deleveraging. This double-whammy makes the deflation train almost impossible to stop. The second dilemma is that the central banks *must cause inflation*. Without inflation, sovereign debts are impossible to service and the world will cascade into outright defaults.

This is extremely dangerous ground for your investments. On the one hand, you must be alert to *deflation*, because it's the natural state of the world. On the other hand, you have to be prepared for *inflation*, because central banks are out to cause it at any cost. We've already shown you how… and will continue to in the coming months.

The answer is to have a diversified portfolio with a selection of assets that will do well in all states of the world. We've written elsewhere about inflation hedges that include gold, land, fine art and hard asset plays such as transportation, energy and natural resource stocks. For a deflation hedge, you should have cash or cash equivalents including high-quality money market funds. But there are potential problems with money market funds, too.

Money Market Reform Regulation

Few people know about a regulation the SEC finalized in early August 2014. It allows money market funds to suspend redemptions under panic circumstances. That's always been true of hedge funds, but never before true of money market funds.

Money market funds are supposed to be as good as gold. You're supposed to be able to get your money back tomorrow if you want. This change means that during a crisis, you may call up your bank and say, "I'd like to redeem my money market fund."

And they'll say, "Hey, you and 10 million other people. We're suspending redemptions under a new SEC regulation. Didn't you see the brochure we slipped into an envelope a year ago?" You should be aware of the dangers to your money even in places conventionally thought of as safe.

CHAPTER 5

The Greatest Unwind in Economic History

Early signs indicate that the greatest unwind in modern economic history could begin this year in China. For many investors, the fallout will be painful. If you're properly positioned ahead of time, however, I believe you can profit.

To do so, it's important to understand the dynamics in play. Bubbles have three consistent characteristics: They are easy to spot; they persist longer than most investors expect (that's why they're bubbles in the first place); and they end badly with massive losses for investors who are still in at the top.

These three traits are related in terms of investor psychology and behavior. Even when investors see a bubble, they often cannot resist riding the wave, because they assume they'll be smart enough to get out at the right time. The fact that bubbles last longer than most analysts expect tends to validate this investor assumption. People waiting on the sidelines for bubbles to pop are routinely ridiculed by those reaping large gains as the bubble expands.

But in the end, the bubble profiteers tend to stay too long at the party and suffer massive losses, as bubble markets can easily lose 30% or more in a matter of months, sometimes weeks, as assets are dumped and investors head for the exits. Today, the greatest bubbles in modern economic history are in China.

China is at risk of seeing multiple markets in real estate,

stocks, corporate loans and commodities all crash at once. Chinese growth statistics have been overstated for years. This is not because the officials lie, but because 45% of Chinese GDP is investment and much of that is wasted on white elephant infrastructure that will either never be used or produce scant gains in productivity.

Adjusted for waste, real Chinese GDP growth is more like 4% than the 7.5% claimed until recently. Chinese growth is also slowing for other reasons having to do with demographics and declining marginal returns to factor inputs. Growth will no longer be sufficient to service the mountain of debt on which the growth was built.

The Chinese people have extremely high savings rates but limited choices as to how to invest their savings. They are generally prohibited from buying foreign assets. Local banks pay almost nothing on savings accounts. This has forced Chinese savers into real estate, local stocks and so-called "wealth management products" (WMPs). This has resulted in property and stock bubbles, which are just beginning to come down to Earth.

The WMPs seem safer because they are sold by banks and offer steady yields of 5% or more. But underneath, the WMP market is a giant Ponzi scheme. The WMPs may be sold by banks, but they are not guaranteed by the banks. The proceeds are diverted to wasted real estate projects and dubious loans to inefficient state-owned enterprises.

Chinese investors who try to cash in their WMPs receive proceeds not from profits on the loans but from new sales to new investors in an ever-expanding pool. This is the essence of a Ponzi scheme.

Almost all of the economic data coming from China lately suggest the greatest unwind in modern economic history could happen this year. Rail and sea cargo shipments are declining, producer prices are crashing and loan growth has hit the wall.

Chinese officials can see this house of cards collapsing but are determined to prop it up as long as they can. Like central banks everywhere, the People's Bank of China is using easy money to reflate asset bubbles.

Last November, China cut interest rates for the first time in two years. On Feb. 4, China cut its reserve requirements for banks, a technical move that allows banks to make more loans with the same amount of capital. Both of these moves are intended to ease credit conditions. Another rate cut is expected soon.

China is also likely to join the global currency wars now raging in Europe and Japan. A devaluation in the yuan will help Chinese exports relative to competition from Japan, Korea and Taiwan. Since 2012, China has been quiet in the currency while its Asian trading partners and competitors have engaged in repeated devaluations. Now China has had enough and is ready to shoot back.

If you're a U.S. investor and use dollars as a reference currency, China offers three ways to win. China has weak national fundamentals. Certain companies have weak sector fundamentals, especially those in financial services with large loan and investment portfolios. And the Chinese currency will weaken.

This means that a short position in the Chinese financial sector, including the purchase of put options, can produce profits from a slowing economy, cheapening currency and higher credit losses.

A Bigger Bubble Than the U.S.

China, believe it or not, has a bigger credit bubble than the United States does. The United States has lots and lots of problems and I could go on at length about them, but China is actually worse. That may be because they haven't experienced as many credit bubbles as we have.

China is coming out of four hundred years of decline and

decadence, one hundred years of chaos, starting with the Taiping Rebellion, all the way through the Boxer Rebellion, and then the Manchu, Qing Dynasty, the warlord period, the Japanese invasion, the Communist period, and the Cultural Revolution. For one hundred years, China has had something bad coming around the corner.

Their whole experience with panics and crises in markets is all very new. At least in the United States, if a crisis happens, there aren't too many people around who can say they haven't seen something like it before. Americans have seen crisis many times before — especially recently.

China seems to be naïve about how bad their credit bubble can get. They're also certainly over-relying on the ability of central party officials to keep a lid on it.

I remember when I was visiting the Chinese countryside, south of Nanjing, not too long ago. I witnessed of the so-called ghost cities. I was with some Communist Party and provincial officials who were behind all of the construction. There was, literally, construction as far as the eye could see. The buildings were magnificent, but all empty.

I remember turning to the officials, and saying, "This is all debt financed and all empty. You have no revenue. So, how are you going to pay the debt?"

One of them replied, "Oh, we can't. But Beijing's going to bail us out." That's what he said. To them, a default wasn't a possibility.

What they misunderstand is that Beijing has their own problems. When you look at their wealth management or products, shadow banking, real estate finance, crony capitalism you realize the true problems China faces.

They're also suffering from flight capital — oligarchs taking all they can, like pigs at the trough, and then funneling it out to Vancouver, Australia and Park Avenue. All of this is happening on a massive. It will collapse.

China is not anticipating this bust, and even if they were, they don't know how to deal with it. The Chinese government is very slow at making decisions. US policymakers are no better at seeing coming crises ahead of time. Once they show up at our doorstep, however, they are able to react quickly.

Query whether they had the right reaction, but Paulson, Geithner and Bernanke were up night and day for days on end, and patched the system together.

I've been through that. That's certainly what we did when LTCM collapsed. We were on the verge of destroying global markets, and we patched something together in five days. That involved fourteen equity banks; nineteen credit banks and untold trillion of dollars. Fast response time is a good American characteristic.

We have this can do attitude, work around the clock and get the job done. In China, they're just very slow. When the crisis hits them, they may have the capacity to deal with it but they don't have much experience and they're going to take their time.

That means that things can get a lot worse and maybe get away from them before they can put a lid on the crisis. That's when global contagion comes into play. China's great unwind is one big catalyst which I watch very closely.

CHAPTER 6

The Perfect Storm

I believe the perfect financial storm is brewing at this very moment. If you act now, however, you might not only sidestep the danger, but profit handsomely from it.

If you've ever read the book *The Perfect Storm* by Sebastian Junger or seen the film version starring George Clooney, you know that the perfect storm was not one storm but three; two Canadian fronts and the remnants of a hurricane from the south that all converged off the coast of New England. At the point of convergence, each storm amplified the effects of the other until, as portrayed in the film, a rogue wave 100 feet high sank the vessel *Andrea Gail*, resulting in the deaths of the crew.

Something similar is happening in financial markets today. Three head winds, any one of which would be challenging, have converged to create financial havoc. Some investments are safely in port and will survive the storm. Other investments are far out to sea and will suffer the effects of all three head winds. Those stocks at the point of convergence may be as helpless as the *Andrea Gail* when the storm intensifies. Investors buying long-dated put options on those stocks may have the most to gain.

The first storm is the continued currency wars. They have been ongoing since 2010, but the start of 2015 marks a more intense phase where beggar-thy-neighbor retaliation is happening daily. Any U.S. company with significant foreign earnings will see the value of those earnings reduced when translated to U.S. dollars as long as these competitive devaluations continue.

The second storm is the slowdown in energy production. Here the battle is being waged between Saudi Arabia and the frackers in North America. Saudi Arabia wants to maintain high production in the face of a global oil glut in order to force the frackers to stop drilling and even shut down some existing capacity. The cost of lifting oil from the ground in Saudi Arabia is less than $10 per barrel, whereas the cost of oil from fracking in North America averages over $70 per barrel. This is a war the frackers cannot win. The impact is already showing up in layoffs, cancelled orders for pipe and declining rig counts. This damage will get worse.

The third storm is the slowdown in global growth generally. Japan and parts of Europe are technically in recessions. China still has growth, but it is slowing rapidly. The U.S. growth engine seems to be slowing also, with GDP falling from 5% in the third quarter to 2.6% in the fourth quarter, and with initial signs indicating even weaker growth ahead.

The question for you as an investor is who is the *Andrea Gail* in this perfect storm scenario? Is there a single company that has exposure to the oil patch and overseas earnings streams and that is geared for growth at a time when growth is slowing? Which companies are most exposed to all three converging fronts in this financial perfect storm?

Once you know that, positioning yourself to profit is a matter of getting the timing right and then buying the right put options.

Bayes' Theorem

In my counterterrorism work for the CIA, we were constantly confronted with problems that could not be solved with the information available. That's the nature of intelligence work — you never have enough information.

After all, if you had all the information, you wouldn't need an intelligence service; a smart college kid could do the job. The reason you have intelligence analysts is to fill in the blanks and try to make sense of the puzzle even when a number of the pieces are missing.

The CIA is divided into two main branches — the clandestine service and the analytical branch. The clandestine service is the "collector." They recruit spies and gather information from hard-to-get places. The analytical branch takes the information provided by the collectors and tries to connect the dots and draw actionable conclusions to deliver to policymakers up to and including the president.

The same is true in financial analysis. You may have a lot of information, but you always need more. Some of the most important information is buried inside company management or the Federal Reserve boardroom and not easy to get to. As an investor, you can't afford to just throw up your hands. Guessing is usually a bad idea. You need an analytical method just as we do at the CIA.

One of the most powerful tools we use in the intelligence community goes by technical sounding names like "causal inference" or "inverse probability." These are methods based on a mathematical equation known as "Bayes' theorem."

Basically, you form a hypothesis based on experience, common sense and whatever data are available. Then you test the hypothesis not by what has happened before, but by what comes *after*.

Instead of reasoning from cause to effect, you reverse the process. You watch the effects to determine the cause. This will validate or invalidate the "cause" you have hypothesized.

Sometimes the effects contradict the hypothesis, in which case you modify or abandon it and adopt another. Often, the effects confirm the hypothesis, in which case you know you're on the right track and keep going.

Right now, my favorite hypothesis is that the world is facing a $2 trillion tsunami of bad debt coming from oil drilling, emerging markets and corporate junk bonds. This debt will not go bad until late 2015 or early 2016 and thereafter.

Even money-losing operations can keep up debt service for a while by using working capital and cash flow — at least until the cash runs out. Banks that hold some of the debt can also cover up the losses for a while with accounting games such as fiddling with what are called their loan loss reserves. If I'm right, bank stocks may take a hit by early 2016 as these losses come home to roost.

Using the language of Bayes' theorem, bad debts will be the "cause" of a decline in financial stocks. What "effects" am I looking out for to test the validity of my hypothesis? There are many.

For energy junk debt, we can look at rig counts in the oil patch and layoffs among energy exploration companies. For emerging-market debt, we can look at the strong dollar and dwindling hard currency reserves in countries like Russia, Turkey, Mexico and Brazil.

In short, we can work backward from these visible causes to test the validity of the original hypothesis. Right now, the idea that financial stocks will suffer due to write-offs by this time next year looks like a good one.

Junk Bond Meltdown

Over the coming months, I believe we could see an economic meltdown at least six times the size of the 2007 subprime mortgage meltdown.

Circumstances lead me to believe it could play out like the meltdown I experienced in 1998 after Long-Term Capital Management (LTCM) failed.

This time, however, there will be several crucial differences that will leave investors and regulators unprepared.

To understand what market outcome is likely, we start with something we know and extrapolate from it.

In the national defense community, military commanders are known for fighting the last war. They study their prior failures in preparation for the next conflict. The problem is that each war inevitably involves new tactics for which they're completely unprepared.

The most famous case was the backward-looking Maginot Line in the 1930s.

In response to Germany's rapid advances in WWI, France built a line of concrete and steel fortifications and obstacles on their border to buy time to mobilize if Germany tried to invade again.

Hitler made the Maginot Line irrelevant by outflanking it and invading France through neutral Belgium. The French were unprepared. A few weeks later, German forces occupied Paris.

The same mistake is made in financial circles. Financial regulators are no different than military commanders. They fight the last war. The last two global meltdowns, in 1998 and 2008, are cases in point.

In 1998, a financial panic almost destroyed global capital markets. It started in Thailand in June 1997 and then spread to Indonesia and Korea. By the summer of 1998, Russia had defaulted on its debt and its currency collapsed. The resulting liquidity crisis caused massive losses at hedge fund Long-Term Capital Management.

I know about the losses because I was there. As LTCM's lead counsel, I was at every executive committee meeting during the height of the crisis that August and September. We were losing hundreds of millions of dollars per day. Total losses over the two-month span were almost $4 billion. But that wasn't the most dangerous part.

Our losses were trivial compared with to the *$1 trillion* of derivatives trades we had on our books with the biggest Wall Street banks. If LTCM failed, those trillion dollars of trades would not have paid off and the Wall Street banks would have fallen like dominoes. Global markets would have completely collapsed.

I negotiated a bailout with the leaders of the 14 biggest banks including Goldman Sachs, JPMorgan and Citibank. Eventually, we got $4 billion of new capital from Wall Street, the Federal Reserve cut interest rates and the situation stabilized. But it was a close call, something no one ever wanted to repeat.

It was a valuable lesson for me, because soon after, regulators set out to make hedge fund lending safer. They ordered banks to monitor their hedge fund exposures more closely, improve their legal documentation and require more collateral to secure the performance on open trades.

Regulators believed this would prevent the next crisis. When the panic of 2008 hit, however, they were surprised that problems were not in hedge funds but in something new — subprime mortgages. The mortgage market collapse quickly spun out of control and once again brought global capital markets to the brink of collapse.

After the 2008 debacle, regulators *again* set out to fight the last war. This is the setup for the crisis I'm forecasting. They made mortgage lending much safer by requiring larger down payments, better documentation, proof of income, proof of employment and higher credit scores before a home loan could be made. But once again, regulators today are fixing the last problem and totally ignoring the next one.

The next financial collapse, already on our radar screen, will not come from hedge funds or home mortgages. It will come from junk bonds, especially energy-related and emerging-market corporate debt.

The Financial Times recently estimated that the total amount of energy-related corporate debt issued from 2009–2014 for exploration and development is over *$5 trillion*. Meanwhile, the Bank for International Settlements recently estimated that the total amount of emerging-market dollar-denominated corporate debt is over *$9 trillion.*

Energy-sector debt has been called into question because of the collapse of oil prices. And emerging markets debt has been called into question because of a global growth slowdown, global deflation, and the strong dollar.

The result is a $14 trillion pile of corporate debt that cannot possibly be repaid or rolled over under current economic conditions. Not all of this debt will default, but a lot of it will. Most of the energy related debt was issued in the expectation that oil would remain in the $80 to $130 dollar per barrel range.

Most of the emerging markets debt was issued with the expectation that the dollar would remain at its weak 2011 levels. Instead, at writing, oil is down, and the dollar is up, which capsizes these expectations. The moves have been swift and dramatic.

If default rates are only 10% — a conservative assumption — this corporate debt fiasco will be *six times larger than the subprime losses in 2007*. The world is looking at a debt catastrophe much larger than LTCM in 1998 and the mortgage market in 2008. Regulators are completely unprepared for this because they have been busy fighting the last war.

The good news for investors is that this fiasco will not happen overnight. It will take a year or two to play out. The panic of September 1998 started a year earlier, in Thailand in June 1997. The panic of September 2008 also started a year earlier, in August 2007, when CNBC commentator Jim Cramer screamed, "They know nothing!!" on live television in reference to the Federal Reserve.

This new junk debt fiasco started in the summer of 2014 but will not reach its peak until 2016 or later. Even companies and countries with dim prospects often have enough cash on hand to make payments for a while before they actually default. In the meantime, you can profit.

The bond defaults have not happened yet, but the signs are already visible in the form of lower oil prices and the strong dollar. In intelligence analysis, we don't wait for disasters to happen. We look at today's information, what are called "indications and warnings," and use inferential techniques such as inverse probability to see the future.

The strong dollar is deflationary. If it persists, it means oil prices will likely remain low. This means much of the energy-sector debt cannot be paid off and will default. The defaults have not happened yet, but you can see them coming. There is still an opportunity for you to profit from the coming collapse in junk bonds, but the time to act is now.

The Coming Bust

The drop in the price of oil from approximately $100 a barrel to the $40-60 range roughly constitutes a 40 percent decline or more. That's extreme. That's only happened in that short a period of time three times in the past seventy years.

Oil and other commodities are volatile, but don't think for one minute that this is a normal fluctuation. It's not. This would be like the equivalent, if you were talking about Dow points, of an 8,000 point drop. We're talking about extreme territory.

The question, of course, is what are the implications of that?

Our job is to figure out what they are and figure out what that means for investors. This is a bit of a shock and no one expected it, other than maybe a handful of people who were plotting it behind the scenes.

I think we're looking at the possibility of a floor, at least a temporary price range around $60 per barrel.

A lot of investors tend to extrapolate from whatever is going on. Behavioral psychologists have a name for this. It's called "recency bias".

We tend to be over influenced by whatever happened recently, and forget about the bigger picture. When the price of oil goes from $100 to $60, which as I said is extreme, people say: "Now it's going to go to $50, then it's going to go to $40 and then, soon after, to $30.

You can't rule anything out, but it does look as if oil is going to oscillate around $60. That's still a big deal and will cause damage to junk bonds and a lot of other markets.

Why do I say $60? It's not because I think I'm smarter than a lot of other analysts. And I don't have a crystal ball. But I did have the opportunity to speak to various people in the industry.

There are no guarantees; of course. I want to be clear about that. I suppose the price of could go below $60, but it does look like it's going to settle around $60.

I want to explain the reasons why, because I don't like to write things that have a categorical tone without providing the backup. This didn't just come out of the blue.

Obviously, Saudi Arabia is the marginal supplier. They can dial up the supply or dial it down. They're well aware of what's going on in the rest of the world. They see the fracking and US oil output.

They also see that the US is now the world's largest energy producer and is close to becoming a net oil exporter. Yet, even if we give the US credit for being a stronger than some of the other economies, there's no question about the global slowdown. Therefore, Saudi Arabia sees demand slowing down. It's something you learned the first day in economics: supply is up because of fracking technology, and the demand is down because of a slowing economy.

When supply is up and demand is down, you get lower prices. That's Econ 101. But the question is: how much lower and what does Saudi Arabia want to do about it?

If they can't make fracking go away, they at least want to bankrupt a lot of the fracking companies and make them slam on the brakes. To do that, Saudi Arabia wants to get the price low enough to hurt the frackers. That's because frackers have higher costs.

The power of Saudi Arabia comes from the fact that they have the lowest marginal cost of producing oil. It only costs them a couple of bucks to lift the oil out of the ground. That oil was discovered, explored, drilled when their entire infrastructure was put in place decades ago.

Because their marginal cost of production is just a few dollars, they can still make money — even at $40 and $30 per barrel. The question is, what is the number that hurts the frackers but doesn't hurt Saudi Arabia? Because obviously, the lower the oil price, the more money that's taken out of of Saudi Arabia's profit.

In theory, there's a number that's low enough to hurt the frackers, but high enough so that Saudi Arabia still maximizes their revenues.

It's what's called an optimization or a linear programming problem. That number, again from very good sourcing, is about $60 a barrel. It's not a number I made up or pulled out of a hat.

Think of $60 per barrel as the sweet spot where we have all the bad stuff in terms of fracking — corporate bonds and junk bond defaults — but not so low that the Arabs hurt themselves more than necessary.

Oil below $60 is more than low enough to do an enormous amount of damage in financial markets. Losses are all over the place. We don't know necessarily where they are right now. But I guarantee there are major losers out there and they're going to start to merge and crop up in unexpected places.

The first place losses will appear are in junk bonds. There are about $5.4 trillion — that's trillion — of costs incurred in the last five years for exploration drilling and infrastructure in the alternative energy sector. When I say alternative I mean in the fracking sector.

A lot of it's in the Bakken and North Dakota, but also in Texas and Pennsylvania. That's a lot of money. It's been largely financed with corporate and bank debt. These companies issued some equity, but it's mostly debt.

Here's how it works. Suppose I'm an oil exploration company. Let's say I borrowed a couple hundred million dollars to drill for oil using fracking technology. The bank -- the lender, bond investor or whoever — says: "Well, Jim, you just borrowed $200 million. How are you going to pay me back?"

And I'd say: "Well, I'm going to sell my oil at $80 a barrel."

To which the bank says: "How do I know that's true?"

So, I go to Morgan Stanley, JP Morgan or Citibank and I buy what's called a "swap contract." It's a kind of derivative.

Citibank or whoever basically agrees to pay me the difference between $80 and the actual price of oil. If oil goes to $50 and I have a swap contract with Citibank that guarantees me $80, they have to pay me the $30 difference. That way, I've locked in the $80 price.

That's not a free lunch. Oil producers give away the upside. If crude prices go to $150 they might have to pay the lenders the difference. But oil companies try to protect their downside.

Oil companies are protected because when oil goes to $50 because they can call up the bank and say: "Hey, bank, send me the other $30 a barrel because we have a deal." And the bank will have to send it to them.

Through the derivative contract the loss now moves over to the bank. It's not the oil company that suffers the loss. This is the case with the global financial system today — you never know where the risks end up.

So the first iteration is that some of the oil companies — not all of them — have shifted their risk over to the banks by doing these derivative contracts.

You might be saying to yourself: "Aha, so the banks are going to have all the losses."

Not necessarily. The banks are just middlemen. They might have written that guarantee to an oil company and have to pay the $30 difference in my example. But the bank may have also gone out and sold the contract to somebody else. Then it's somebody else's responsibility to pay the oil company.

Who could that somebody else be? It could be an ETF. And that ETF could be in your portfolio. This is where it gets scary because the risk just keeps getting moved around broken up into little pieces.

Citibank, for example, might write $5 billion of these derivatives contracts to a whole bunch of oil producers. But then, they may take that $5 billion and break it into thousands of smaller one or ten million dollar chunks and spread that risk around in a bunch of junk bond funds, ETFs or other smaller banks.

When many oil producers went for loans, the industry's models showed oil prices between $80 and $150. $80 is the low end for maybe the most efficient projects, and $150 is of course the high end. But no oil company went out and borrowed money on the assumption that they could make money at $50 a barrel.

So suddenly, there's a bunch of debt out there that producers will not be able to pay back with the money they make at $50 a barrel. That means those debts will need to be written off.

How much? That's a little bit more speculative.

I think maybe 50 percent of it has to be written off. But let's be conservative and assume only 20 percent will be written-off. That's a trillion dollars of losses that have not been absorbed or been priced into the market.

Go back to 2007. The total amount of subprime and Alt-A loans was about a trillion. The losses in that sector ticked well above 20 percent. There, you had a $1 trillion market with $200 billion of losses.

Here we're talking about a $5 trillion market with $1 trillion of losses from unpaid debt — not counting derivatives. This fiasco is bigger than the subprime crisis that took down the economy in 2007.

I'm not saying we're going to have another panic of that magnitude tomorrow; I'm just trying to make the point that the losses are already out there. Even at $60 per barrel the losses are significantly larger than the subprime meltdown of 2007. We're looking at a disaster.

On top of those bad loans, there are derivatives. Right now, some of the producers are kind of shrugging, saying: "We went out and borrowed all this money on the assumption of $80, $90, $100 oil. But we also sold our oil production forward for a couple of years at $90. So we're fine."

That's not true in every case, but it is true in a lot of the cases.

The problem with derivatives, however, is that you don't know where the risk ends up. I don't know where it is, the Federal Reserve doesn't know where it is and neither do the bank regulators. The banks might know their piece of it, but they don't know the whole picture. That means we have to keep digging and digging.

The losses out there are larger, potentially, than the subprime crisis. The losses could actually be bigger than the sector's borrowings because you can create derivatives out of thin air. And as I say, they could be in your portfolios.

There's still time to call your investment advisors or broker to see whether you have any of this risk buried in your portfolio. You might not, but even if you don't it may be time to take a little more defensive posture. That could be a little more cash or other hedges. That way when things start to collapse around you — even if you're not taking a direct hit — you're not collateral damage.

Going back to my first point, the losses out there are larger, potentially, than the subprime crisis. The losses could actually be bigger than the borrowings because you can create derivatives out of thin air. And as I say, they could be in your portfolios.

I was talking to an investor recently about shifting some investments, and he said: "Well, you know, my broker took care of me I got some cash, money market funds, I got some stocks, and I got this bond fund."

And I said: "Do you know what's in your bond fund?"

He answered: "No, the broker recommended it." And I answered: "Well, let's get out the documents."

We dug inside. It was a municipal bond fund. We found bonds from Puerto Rico, we found the bonds from city of Detroit — absolute garbage. This is the kind of danger you're in.

Some of these fracking companies are going to go bankrupt. That means you may have equity losses on some of the companies if they didn't hedge.

Then, many frackers issued debt which is going to default. It doesn't necessarily mean the company goes into bankruptcy, although it might; they might have to restructure. That debt, however, whether it's bank debt or junk bond debt, is going to default.

Some other companies are going to be fine because they bought the derivatives. But then, where did those derivatives go?

Think back to the housing bust. We now know that a lot of the derivatives ended up at AIG.

AIG was a 100-year-old traditional insurance company who knew that they were betting that house prices would not go down. Goldman Sachs and a lot of other institutions were taking that bets too.

When house prices did go down, everyone turned to AIG and said: "Hey, pay me."

It's just like if you win at roulette in the casino, you expect the house to pay you. But AIG of course couldn't pay and had to be bailed out by the United States government to the tune of over $100 billion. That's the kind of thing we're looking at now. These bets are all over the place, because nobody thought oil was going to go to $60.

The losses are going to start to roll in, but they'll come in slowly. I'm not suggesting that tomorrow morning we're going to wake up and find the financial system collapsed. This is the beginning of a disaster.

Here's How to Protect Yourself

The two most specific ways investors will lose is, first, on the equity side of their portfolios. To protect yourself, check to see if you have any second tier or mid-tier drilling and exploration companies in your portfolio.

Exxon Mobil is not going go bankrupt. They might cut back their capital expenditures or maybe their earnings will go down a little bit. But a company the size of Exxon Mobil is not going away and they're not going to go bankrupt. In fact, the largest companies sometimes benefit from situations like this because it flushes out the competition, gives them more flexibility and they can buy up some of these assets on the cheap.

The fracking sector is more vulnerable than the traditional oil sector because that technology is a little more expensive. So much of it is new and was financed with debt. They are a lot of small, mid sized companies. They are the ones you should look out for because you could lose on the equity if they go bankrupt.

You also have to look at the bond part of your portfolio and look to see if you have any debt from these companies. There are investors who are sick of getting no interest from the bank, no interest from Treasury bonds or other safe investments. I like gold, but gold doesn't pay any dividends or interest. You have to have a view that it's a wealth preservation mechanism. Gold, cash, and Treasury bills pay you nothing.

That means people are chasing yield. Perhaps an investor says to himself, "Hey, I'm retired, I worked hard all my life, I've got this amount of savings; and I'm counting on five, six or seven percent out of my portfolio to enjoy a comfortable retirement."

Good luck getting that out of Treasury bills.

But what a broker will come along and say, is: "I've got a fund right here; it's a bond fund and it's paying five or six percent." And the investor says: "Well, I'll take some of that."

But often, investors don't look at what's inside.

When times are good and everyone's rocking and rolling, the economy's growing, new oil is being discovered and the price of oil seems strong; those funds do pay five or six percent. I'm not saying you can't make that.

But when all of a sudden losses come rolling in you may find that your five percent dividend doesn't compensate you for twenty percent portfolio losses when these things start going belly up.

Look at the equity names in your portfolio, but also look in the bond part of the portfolio to see if inside any of these funds they're holding notes issued by, or bonds issued by some of these.

They're not too hard to find. Simply screen for small, mid-sized oil exploration and production companies, especially those in the fracking industry. Again, North Dakota, Pennsylvania and Texas are among the main centers.

The Oil Price: The Good, Bad and the Ugly

Everyday Americans have good reason to celebrate and fear the recent collapse in oil prices. This is the fastest, steepest decline in oil prices since the mid-1980s. Results are already showing up at the gas pump. The price of regular gasoline has collapsed from almost $4.00 a gallon to $1.99 a gallon in some places.

For a driver who uses 50 gallons per week, that's an extra $100 per week in your pocket: enough to buy a new dress or take your family out to a nice dinner. If that new low price sticks, the savings keep coming, and it adds up to a $5,000 per year raise. Best of all, the government can't tax that $5,000. If you got a pay raise, they would tax it, but if the cost of things you buy is lower, they can't tax the savings. What's not to like? That's the good news.

Economists assume this extra money in your pocket will immediately be spent. That extra spending might put some money in someone else's pocket. For example, if you spend your $100 weekly savings from gasoline going out to dinner, you might tip the waiter $15, at which point the waiter has an extra $15 (maybe more if your neighbors are doing the same thing), and he can spend more, and so on.

This is the famous "multiplier" effect at work, where an extra amount of spending leads to more spending by the recipients so that the total economic growth, what economists call "aggregate demand," is higher than the initial spending. More good news. At least that's what you'll hear on television.

When you look beneath the surface, however, you'll see some things that are not so good, are maybe even bad, for your portfolio.

For example, just because someone has an extra $100 in his pocket does not mean he'll run out and spend it in knee-jerk fashion like Pavlov's dog. Many people may use the money to pay down debt including credit cards, student loans, auto loans, home equity loans and other forms of credit.

That can be a prudent thing to do, but it adds nothing to GDP. It's just a form of deleveraging. Both sides of your personal balance sheet, cash and debt, are reduced. There's nothing wrong with that, but there is no increase in aggregate demand and no mystic multiplier.

Also, when you spend $2 per gallon less at the pump, that means someone else — the oil company — is getting $2 less. Your gain is their loss. None of us needs to shed a tear for Big Oil, but the practical effects of greatly reduced oil prices and energy company revenues show up in damaging ways. The low price of oil causes new projects to be delayed and existing high-cost fields to be shut in. That means layoffs and reduced capital expenditure for pipes, equipment and transportation. Jobs in the oil field are high-paying jobs. Jobs waiting in a restaurant are not. If we gain restaurant jobs and lose oil field jobs, it's not clear the economy is better off.

That's the bad news.

From there, things start to get ugly. The price of oil is low both because demand has slowed down along with slower global growth and because supply is up due to fracking. But all of that fracking output costs money to develop, and a lot of that money was raised in the form of junk bonds. When those junk bonds were issued, the projects behind them assumed oil would be priced in a range from $80–130 per barrel.

With oil in the $45–55 per barrel range, those projects are no longer profitable and that debt will begin to default in late 2015 or early 2016. Who holds that debt? Some of it might be in your 401(k) buried inside a "high yield" fund sold to you by your broker. That's something you might want to take a look at. Whether it's owned by you, your neighbor or the bank across the street, the point is someone owns it and those holders are looking at a tidal wave of write-offs coming their way.

Finally, we should consider the impact of rapidly falling oil prices on the Federal Reserve and U.S. monetary policy. The Fed has a stated policy of achieving 2% inflation. Right now, inflation is below that target and falling fast. Recent price indexes have shown outright deflation, the opposite of what the Fed wants.

When the Fed looks at price data, they focus on "core" inflation, which excludes the impact of food and energy prices. The basis for this is that food and energy prices are highly volatile and tend to track core inflation over long periods of time. You can ignore the spikes and dips of energy prices because they tend to be monthly noise, which evens out over the course of a year.

There is actually good empirical evidence to support this approach, which is why the Fed uses it.

But what if this energy price drop is not just noise? What if it lasts for years because it's driven by geopolitical and macroeconomic forces that are not going away anytime soon?

If that's the case, then the standard Fed approach would miss the significance of the move and underestimate the impact of the price drop and the deflation that comes with it. In that case, the Fed might raise interest rates in 2015 — as it has indicated it will — just as persistent price drops are creating deflationary expectations and driving the economy into a recession. An interest rates increase on the verge of a recession is the worst possible medicine. But the Fed's flawed models may be setting us up for just such an outcome.

In the long run, lower oil prices are good for consumers and good for real growth. But in the short run, they are bad for producers, disastrous for junk bond holders and possibly misleading for Fed policy. The next year could be a rough ride as the layoffs pile up and the bad debts roll in. It would be even worse if the Fed misread the tea leaves and raised rates as they have threatened to do.

You should scour your portfolios and sell any bond funds that are stuffed with junk debt. Then, use the proceeds to build cash positions and buy high-quality U.S. Treasury notes. The cash will preserve wealth, and the notes will produce gains in the deflationary times ahead. When visibility about Fed policy improves, the cash can be deployed to buy distressed assets on the cheap. We'll have more to say about what those bargains might be in the months ahead.

Spill-Over Effects and Contagion

In 1933, during the depths of the Great Depression, famed economist Irving Fisher wrote a work that became a classic of economics and is still widely read and cited today. The book was titled *The Debt-Deflation Theory of Great Depressions.*

Fisher was the most famous U.S. economist of the first half of the 20th century and made many intellectual contributions to economics, including work on monetary policy and equilibrium analysis that led to later contributions by contemporary economists including Milton Friedman and Ben Bernanke. Yet Fisher's work on debt and deflation is his best-known and most important effort.

His thesis was straightforward. Depressions are the inevitable aftermath of credit booms and extreme overindebtedness. During the expansion phase of a cycle, easy credit allows debtors to bid up asset prices.

The higher asset prices then serve as collateral for further debt, which is used to invest in other assets, causing those prices to rise also. At some stage, valuations become stretched. Creditors refuse to extend more credit and demand repayment or require more collateral from the debtors.

At this point, the entire process goes rapidly into reverse. Now debtors have to sell assets to repay creditors. This forced selling causes asset prices to drop. The lower asset prices reduce the collateral values on other loans, which cause those loans to be called by the creditors also.

Now the forced liquidation of assets becomes widespread, businesses fail, layoffs increase, unemployed workers cannot afford to spend, more businesses fail as a result and so on until the entire economy is thrown into recession or, even worse, depression.

This process played out in the period 1929–1933, and again from 2007–2009. The latest episode is usually known as the Great Recession, but is more accurately called the New Depression. It is still with us in the form of below-trend growth, threats of deflation and low labor force participation. This new episode has led to a revival of interest in Fisher's theory.

Investors today can see Fisher's thesis at work in the field of shale oil production. From 2009–2014, several trillion dollars of debt was issued to support shale oil exploration and drilling using a method called hydraulic fracturing, or "fracking."

Most of this debt was issued on the assumption that oil prices would remain above $70 per barrel. With oil now trading in a range of $50–60 dollars per barrel, much of this debt is unpayable, and defaults can be expected in early 2016 if oil prices do not recover. This has caused new exploration and new credit in the shale industry to dry up.

The next stage, exactly as Fisher predicted, will consist of the bankruptcy of the smaller producers and the forced liquidation of assets. This causes existing wells to be pumped even faster to generate what revenues they can to maintain cash flows in the face of falling prices. This pumping, a kind of asset liquidation, puts more downward pressure on prices, making the situation even worse.

Unfortunately, the process has far to run. Eventually, a new equilibrium of supply and demand will be achieved, but for now, the debt-deflation story has just started. There are many ways to "liquidate" in the oil patch.

These include laying off workers, cancelling new orders for pipe and drilling rigs and shutting in existing shale reserves until prices recover. This liquidation stage affects not only the drillers, but also oilfield suppliers, labor, landowners who lease their properties for drilling, equipment leasing companies and municipalities that will see declining tax revenues.

Fisher also pointed out that once deflation begins in one economic sector, it spreads rapidly to others. When debtors are in distress, they don't sell what they want — they sell what they can. A debtor involved in one sector of the economy who needs to raise cash will sell assets from an unrelated sector to meet his obligations.

Today, this behavior that Fisher identified in the 1930s is

called a "spillover effect" or "contagion." Distress can rapidly spread from the oil patch to commercial real estate and beyond.

Some of this debt-deflation spiral has already shown up in the stock prices of affected companies. More stocks like them may be heading for a fall as the Fisher debt-deflation cycle runs its course.

The System is Now Even More Unstable

Our job is to figure out how unstable the global financial system is or how big is the unstable snowpack is. We knew something about the risks derivatives, bank balance sheets, sovereign debt and currency imbalances posed.

Now the oil price drop has revealed that the snowpack is even bigger than we thought — $5.4 trillion of oil debt suddenly seems to be in jeopardy.

Will that be the snowflake that causes the financial avalanche?

At the risk of sounding like a broken record, I advise readers to focus on instability.

How big is the snowpack?

How much damage is it going to cause when the avalanche comes tumbling down?

Those are the relevant questions. Now we have both at once — a bigger, more unstable mountainside and more snow falling harder from the sky. That means we have more snowflakes to take account of.

One Oil Snowflake to Watch

One snowflake that I've been looking at more closely is Algeria.

We've heard so much about the Islamic State in Libya and Syria, Iran, Iraq, Afghanistan and Turkey. Those are all important issues and none of them are going away. But keep an eye on Algeria.

Algeria is a major energy producer. It has a very powerful Al Qaeda type Islamic extremist movement that has recently declared allegiance to the Islamic State. They're the same bad guys but they've hitched their wagon to the leadership of the Islamic State. They're gaining strength and it may just be a matter of time before they topple the Algerian government.

At that point, the Islamic State would stretch from Iran almost to Morocco. It would begin to look more and more like the real caliphate. When I say the real one, I mean that the Islamic State has declared a caliphate, and that they think what they have is a real caliphate.

If you go back in history and look at the caliphates that have existed, the biggest ones went from Spain to Indonesia and everything in between. There were smaller ones in North Africa and the Middle East too.

What's interesting is that when the Islamic State gets control of these oil fields, they don't shut them down. They keep pumping because they need the money. That's something that a lot of investors misunderstand. They see geopolitical turmoil in the oil patch and they think it's going to cut production and send the price of oil higher. Actually, history shows the opposite is true.

The Islamic State will produce oil like crazy because they want the money, and they're not bound by OPEC casts. That's going to make OPEC's job a little more difficult. We saw this in 1986 during the Iran-Iraq war.

Iran and Iraq are two of the largest oil producers in the world. When they got into a war — when Saddam Hussein and Ayatollah Khomeini were still around — a lot of people thought the price of oil was going to go to the moon because of supply disruptions. The opposite happened.

Both countries pumped like crazy and the oil price went down to $12 a barrel. And to think, so far, we've been talking about distress at $60 per barrel.

You could have the worst of both worlds if the Islamic State takes over Algeria because there would be no oil production disruption. Then you may see embargos and seizing of tankers. It could get very messy.

With these geopolitical and domestic energy trends, the biggest question is what the most powerful central bank will do in 2015?

The Federal Reserve has hinted, teased and implied that they're going to raise rates in 2015. The market believes that to be true, based on some strong data in the US economy recently. If they do that, you're going to see a massive emerging markets crisis and debt defaults for the reasons we mentioned.

You're going to also see massive deflation. The US may even go into a recession. That's what happens if the Fed stays the course.

If the Fed blinks, which I think they will, and decides not to raise rates, people will realize the Fed is doing more easing than expected.

You can look at the dynamics, use complexity theory, observe the interactions between players, and see the problems before they happen. The one thing I think you can count on, though, is a lot of volatility and a lot of danger.

CHAPTER 7

Inside The Federal Reserve

Now, More than Ever Before, You Should Know the Players

The Federal Reserve is the central bank of America.

Why don't they call it the Central Bank of America? Because they know Americans hate central banks. We've rejected two central banks in the past in the 18th and 19th centuries. So, they gave it the funny name "Federal Reserve". That way people wouldn't understand what it is.

Today, investors use the name "Fed" as shorthand for the U.S. Federal Reserve System. Shorthand is convenient, but sometimes it hides as much as it reveals. A one-size-fits-all description for an institution is easy, but highly misleading. In fact, the Federal Reserve is a complicated, multifaceted structure with diverse parts and personalities that few investors follow.

Usually, this doesn't matter, because the Fed speaks with one voice and is of one mind. Most people are familiar with Janet Yellen in her role as chairwoman of the Federal Reserve, and know that Ben Bernanke and Alan Greenspan were her predecessors. Familiarity with the views of the chairwoman is enough most of the time. But this is not one of those times.

Today, it is critical for you to know the players while Fed-watching. Understanding Fed structure and the predilections of the players is the key to understanding interest rate policy over the next year and beyond. And your success or failure as an investor will depend on that understanding.

One reader recently emailed me saying, "Who owns the Federal Reserve? I've heard that it is owned by the Rothschilds and Rockefellers plus a few other banks."

The Fed is actually a system of 12 regional reserve banks that are privately owned by the commercial banks in each district. The most powerful of these is the Federal Reserve Bank of New York. It actually carries out the money market operations needed to implement interest rate policy.

The New York Fed also has custody of the largest gold vault in the world, holding about 7,000 tons of gold, more than Fort Knox. But other regional reserve banks in Chicago, Philadelphia, Boston and San Francisco also have a strong voice in policy.

The president of each regional reserve bank is selected by the private board of directors of each bank. In turn, the directors are elected by the stockholders, who are private banks in the region.

These 12 regional reserve banks are overseen by a Board of Governors in Washington, D.C.

There are seven governors selected by the president of the United States and confirmed by the U.S. Senate. So the Fed is a strange hybrid of private ownership in the 12 regions with oversight from a politically appointed board in Washington. The structure is even stranger when it comes to interest rate policy.

Rate policy is set not by the board or the regions but by the Federal Open Market Committee, FOMC. The FOMC has 12 members, composed of the seven governors and five regional reserve bank presidents. The president of the Federal Reserve Bank of New York has a permanent seat on the FOMC and the other four seats are taken on a one-year rotation among the remaining 11 regions.

This rotation is important because the regional reserve bank presidents are divided into "hawks," who favor tight money, and "doves," who favor easy money. The composition of the FOMC changes every January when four presidents leave and four new ones join the committee.

This Rubik's Cube arrangement is temporarily even more complicated by the fact that there are two vacancies on the Board of Governors awaiting appointment from President Obama or confirmation by the Senate. Instead of 12 members on the FOMC, there are only 10 for the time being, consisting of five governors and five regional bank presidents. It takes a majority of the FOMC — six votes for the time being — to implement policy.

Even the meeting calendar is convoluted. Meetings are not monthly, but eight times per year, and the dates and months are not exactly the same from year to year.

Normally, none of this complexity in organization matters much. All of the FOMC members take their economic guidance from the Fed staff and work hard to build a consensus view. The Fed chair is often a dominant personality and has no difficulty rounding up the votes to pursue his or her desired policies. The whole process comes down to the wishes of the chairman.

But these are not ordinary times. The composition of the FOMC and personalities of the individual members matter much more to you than usual. The December 2014 meeting of the FOMC produced a 7-3 vote in favor of its policy statement — just one vote more than the bare minimum needed to pass. The FOMC is far from united at this critical juncture. It is a house divided.

Two of the December dissents came from Richard Fisher of Dallas and Charles Plosser of Philadelphia, both super-hawks unhappy with the Fed's easy money policies. But Fisher and Plosser are both gone from the FOMC as of January. They have been replaced by two super-doves: Charles Evans of the

Chicago Fed and John Williams of the San Francisco Fed.

Evans and Williams are joined in the new FOMC by Dennis Lockhart of Atlanta and Jeffrey Lacker of Richmond. Lockhart is known as a moderate, but he has voted with the doves in the past and is often in sync with the dovish Evans. Lacker is less ideological and more data driven. He will vote with the doves if the data are weak.

As for the governors on the FOMC, they are a more cohesive group and are all reliably in Janet Yellen's camp if she wants to steer policy in a particular direction. Yellen herself is data driven but has dovish inclinations. She's revealed her strong support for quantitative easing (QE) in her public speeches, emphasizing slack in labor markets as a rationale for not raising rates.

This Fed background is crucial for assessing market expectations about policy and whether those expectations are well-grounded. Wall Street economists have been excessively optimistic in their growth forecasts for five consecutive years. This is a dismal track record, and you'd be right to be skeptical about any rosy scenarios for 2015.

Right now, markets are priced for a Fed interest rate increase in mid-2015. Lately, some analysts have been pushing back the expected date for an increase to the fourth quarter. But a rate increase in 2015 is not a foregone conclusion.

Preliminary data for the fourth quarter of 2014 show weaker growth, and this weakness appears to be carrying over into 2015. The FOMC has emphasized inflation in its guidance on the timing of rate increases, but the inflation signs have been weak. Deflation may be the greater concern for the foreseeable future. Labor force participation continues near an all-time low.

Janet Yellen has already said that the Fed will not raise rates before the April 2015 FOMC meeting, but even that meeting is an unlikely turning point. In fact, the Fed is caught in a conundrum of its own making. Talk about raising rates has made the dollar stronger because of money that has flowed into the U.S. from around the world in search of yield. But the strong dollar is deflationary because imports cost less in dollar terms. This deflation moves the Fed away from its inflation targets and makes the rate hike less likely.

Taking into account deflationary trends, the strong dollar, weak labor markets and the dovish composition of the new FOMC, it seems likely that no interest rate hike will be forthcoming in 2015. In fact, if the economy remains weak, another round of QE could be in the works by early 2016.

If this scenario plays out as expected, it could be extremely bullish for U.S. equity markets. Right now, equity markets are priced for a rate hike in mid-2015. When markets realized that easy money policies will continue into 2016, another upward thrust of the bull market would commence and a level of 2,200 or higher on the S&P 500 index would not be surprising.

You should never go "all in" on stocks. Certain bubble dynamics are at work, and a substantial stock market collapse in the years ahead is foreseeable. This is why I have always recommended a substantial cash component for your portfolio to reduce volatility and preserve your wealth in case a crash comes sooner than expected.

But for 2015, the Fed still rules the roost, and a decision to delay rate hikes until at least 2016 could be just the tonic needed to keep this long equity bull market alive for another year.

"We don't know what we're doing"

Don't ever think for a minute that the central bankers know what they're doing. They don't.

That's not only my own view, but I've heard as much from the mouths of a couple central bankers. I recently spent some time with one member of the FOMC, the Federal Open Market Committee, and another member of the Monetary Policy

Committee of the Bank of England, which is the equivalent of their FOMC.

They both said the same thing, "We don't know what we're doing. This is a massive experiment. We've never done this before. We try something. If it works, maybe we do a little more; if it doesn't work, we pull it away, and we'll try something else."

The evidence of this — besides hearing as much firsthand — is that there have been fifteen separate Federal Reserve policies in the last five years.

If you think about it, they started with forward guidance, which was, "We will keep rates low for an extended period of time."

Then they said, "Oh, extended means all the way to 2013."

Then they said, "All the way to 2014."

Then they said, "All the way to 2015,".

Then, "Wait a second. The dates don't work. Let's use some numeric concepts."

That's when they started nominal GDP targeting. They changed their tune to, "We have this threshold of 2.5 percent inflation, not based on actual inflation, but based on projected inflation, as projected by the Fed". Essentially, that meant it could be whatever they wanted it to be. They also set a target of 6.5 percent unemployment, but when they got down to that level, they said, "Oh, just kidding. We're not going to apply that."

They've had currency wars. They've had Operation Twist. Not to mention QE1, QE2, QE3 — except QE3 came in two flavors, $45 billion a month and $85 billion a month.

And now they've tapered. But the taper isn't the first taper because at the end of QE1 they tapered one hundred percent and at the end of QE2 they tapered one hundred percent. We have two data points to say tapering doesn't work. I expect this will fail as well.

Just How Nasty a Rate Increase Can Be

It's unfortunate that we have to be spending so much time on the Federal Reserve. It's the place to start if you want to understand a lot of what's going on in the markets. In fact, nothing is more important — but I wish that weren't true.

I wish the central banks could go back to just being boring, opaque, marginal institutions that took care of money supply and acted as a lender of last resort instead of monstrosities that seem to manipulate and invade every corner of every market in the world. But unfortunately, that is what we have today.

When the Fed manipulates the dollar and dollar interest rates, they are directly and indirectly affecting every market in the world — equities, gold, real estate, other commodities, junk bonds, corporate debt, etc. So even though I wish it wasn't the case, understanding what the Fed will do next is the big question.

Let's take two scenarios: What if they raise rates? And what if they don't?

I'll address both of those directly but first, I'd like to give you some background to help you understand what's behind the debate. The Fed has certainly signaled that they intend to raise rates and it's what the markets expect.

Securities around the world are priced as if the Fed were going to raise rates. I've never seen anything more trumpeted and more advertised in my career. There's good reason for that. The last time the Fed raised rates was 2006.

In terms of cutting rates, they hit bottom in late 2008 when they got to zero — and they've been at zero ever since. It's been six and a half years at zero. But you have to go back two years before that to find the last time they raised rates, so it's going on nine years at this point. That's a long time without a rate increase and people may forget how nasty they can be.

I was in the markets in 1994 when the Fed raised rates, and it was a wipe out. That's when we had the bankruptcy of

Orange County, California, and other dealers went out of business. There was a bond market massacre.

The same thing happened in 1987. A lot of people recall the crash of October 1987 when the stock market dropped 22% in a single day. In today's market, that would be the equivalent of over 3,000 Dow points. Imagine the market dropping not 300 points, which would get everyone's attention, but *3,000 points.* That's what happened in October 1987. But before that, in March of 1987, there was a bond market crash. The bond market crash preceded the stock market crash by about six months.

These things can get nasty and I could say it's been a long time since the last one. That's why the Fed is talking so much about it. You have to go all the way back to May 2013 when the Fed was still printing money and buying bonds (long-term asset purchases as they call it) when Ben Bernanke first started talking about maybe beginning the taper.

They didn't do anything. They didn't cut purchases and they didn't raise rates — they just talked about it — and still the market threw a taper tantrum fit. We had the actual taper through the course of 2014. Now the taper is over, QE3 is officially over, so this thing has been really advertised for two years.

The reason rates were at zero in the first place is because the Fed was trying to pump up assets. They wanted banks and other borrowers to go out, borrow cheap money, buy houses and stocks, bid up the price of assets, and create the wealth effect. Hopefully, that would make people feel richer, they would spend more money, and the economy would get on a self-sustaining path.

That didn't happen. The asset prices did go up, but the wealth effect did not kick in and the economy is still very weak. The Fed did not get the kind of 3.5–4% growth they were really hoping for when they started all this. I think if the Fed had it to do it over, they never would have gone down this path or at least not stayed on it this long.

They had encouraged everyone to borrow money and lever up and do maturity mismatches (borrow overnight in the repo market and go out and buy some risky asset like stocks or other assets). Because of that, they wanted to give people lots of warning that they're going to raise rates.

If I'm a dealer, I can borrow money overnight in the repo market and go out and buy a 10-year note, which until recently was about 2%. I have zero cost to funds and I make 2% of my 10-year note, but I can leverage that trade 10-to-1 because I can get more than 90% margin in the repo market.

A 2% profit levered 10:1 is a 20% return on equity, so with a government security as my asset, it's not like I have to go buy some junk bond. As long as rates were at zero, it was pretty easy to make 10%, 20%, or even 30% returns on equity with a highly leveraged trade.

You might be saying to yourself, "That sounds a little too easy; what's the risk in the trade?" Well, there's no credit risk in the trade because you've got a treasury note as your asset. The risk is that they may raise short-term rates while you're sitting there with overnight money holding a 10-year note.

All of a sudden the overnight money gets to be more expensive, the trade is upside-down, and you're losing money. The Fed was saying we encourage everyone to do these crazy carry trades, do these maturity mismatches, make a lot of money, and rebuild the bank balance sheet. The time will come when we're going to raise rates, but we're going to give you years, literally, to get out of the trade or wind it down or hedge it. Anybody who's caught out, shame on them, as you can't say you weren't warned.

The Fed wants to raise rates to normalize things. They've been talking about it for almost two years because they want to give people plenty of warning, but the markets don't listen so well, at least there's always somebody who doesn't get the message.

As I look around, there's still a lot of leverage in the system, enormous leverage in the stock market, enormous leverage in various carry trades around the world. Chuck Prince, then CEO of Citicorp, said prior to the last world financial calamity that you have to keep dancing as long as the music's playing. There are some people who literally either won't listen to the Fed or don't believe them, etc. and are still going to be in these trades.

The short answer is I expect a lot of market disruption. I think this might throw the U.S. economy into a recession because the economy is fundamentally weak. Some people have been smart enough to get out of these carry trades, at least based on the Fed's warnings, but some people have not and will get a rude awakening.

They may have to unwind those trades quickly, and we may see a lot of liquidity pressure. We're seeing it anyway based just on the Fed's talk. Imagine the reality of the Fed actually raising rates for the first time in eight years.

I think we'll have a very bumpy ride and it won't be soft landing. Beyond that, the whole idea that the Fed would raise rates was based on a forecast that the economy was getting stronger and we sort of achieved self-sustaining growth.

Nobody in economics, nobody on Wall Street, nobody on the buy side, nobody in academia, nobody I've seen anywhere has a worse forecasting record than the Fed. I don't say that out of spite or to try to embarrass anyone; it's just a fact. Year after year after year they produce these very high growth forecasts, and every year they're wrong. They're not just wrong by a little bit; they're wrong by orders of magnitude.

So when the Fed says, well, we think the economy is healthy enough for a rate increase, that's the first sign that it's not. Now besides that, there's a lot of data. We're seeing auto loan defaults go up, real wages are stagnant to down, labor force participation continues to be very low, our trade deficit is getting worse partly because of the strong dollar, emerging markets are slowing down, and China and Europe are slowing down.

I think it's nonsense to believe that we would be closely coupled on the way up but somehow the rest of the world is going to go down and the U.S. won't be affected by that.

Growth is weak, so not only would I expect some disruption from the rate increase simply because people don't listen or they're greedy or they stay in the trade too long, but I would say the Fed's got the economy wrong and they're going to increase rates into a very weak economy.

I would expect probably for the U.S. economy to come close to a recession, more deflation, and probably some disruption in equity markets. The one market that might rally actually is the bond market. Ten-year notes are still pretty attractive based on everything we see.

Now, that's if they raise rates. Let's flip that around and talk about what happens if they don't raise rates, because that's the other scenario. Very few people expect this outcome, but I actually don't think they will raise rates. I've been saying that for about six months, and more people are jumping on board that bandwagon recently.

I did a bunch of interviews in the fall where I said I did not think the Fed would raise rates in 2015. We can debate 2016 — that's still pretty far away — but let's just talk about 2015.

If you go back six months just to last summer, the debate was the Fed's definitely going to raise rates in 2015. The only question was: would it be March or June? I was one of those saying they won't do it. Well, here we are and nobody is talking about March.

Even Janet Yellen said they weren't going to raise them in March, so now you have your April people and your June, July people, but you're hearing more and more people say maybe it won't be until September. Bill Gross recently said he expects it in December. What's the difference between December 2015 and January 2016? Not much.

We're starting to hear a lot of doubt about whether they

will, in fact, raise rates. My view that they won't is based on what I expect the data to show. I don't have a crystal ball and I'm not sitting inside the Fed boardroom overhearing the chit-chat. I'm basing this on what the Fed itself says.

They say that the decision is data-dependent. If you look at the data, it's coming in weak. I know we had this gangbuster third-quarter 2014 GDP, but there's a lot of noise around that and it doesn't appear to be sustained. The fourth quarter came in a lot weaker yesterday and the first quarter 2015 may be weaker yet. We're still not seeing any pulse in the thing that Janet Yellen pays so much attention to, which is real wages. Real wages are stagnant.

Remember that the Fed has a dual mandate that consists of trying to reduce unemployment (or create employment, depending on how you want to put it) and price stability. Sometimes those things are in conflict and they have to roll the dice on inflation a little bit in order to create jobs or other times they have to stifle job growth in order to damp down inflation.

You can't always do both of them at once, but sometimes you can. What's the one piece of data where both parts of the dual mandate come together? One thing you can look at that tells you something about both is real wages. If real wages are going up, that's a leading indicator of inflation, but it also tells you that the labor market's pretty healthy because employees cannot get a raise or demand a raise from their bosses or their companies unless the labor market's tight.

Real wages is the number one thing Janet Yellen is looking at. Guess what? They went down; they're still going down. There doesn't seem to be anything indicating, at least as far as the data is concerned, that they should raise rates. I think this is just the result of bad forecasting. They always forecast stronger growth than we actually get, and by the time they catch up to the reality of their forecast, they find out that we're nowhere near what they expected.

This is interesting because the market is set up for a rate increase. What if they don't? I think we'll get to the summer, the data will be lousy, the Fed will make it clear that they're not going to raise rates anytime soon, and "patience" will just turn into "more patience," using their new favorite buzzword. (They seem to come up with new buzzwords every six months or so!)

The Fed did QE1, QE2, QE3 part 1, QE3 part 2, then they promised to raise rates. Once it becomes clear that they're not going to raise rates, I think the markets might think that they can never raise rates.

It wouldn't surprise me to see QE4 in early 2016. What may happen then will be very interesting, because the stock market could actually rally on that. It won't be rallying on fundamentals; it will be rallying on cheap money.

The market's expecting tightening. If they get ease, at least no rate increase and the possibility of reasons to launch QE4, markets might even rally. I'm not a big stock market bull, but if the Fed doesn't raise rates — and my expectation is they won't — you might actually see stocks higher at the end of the year than they are now based on more free money.

I think by then the inflationary expectations will start to ratchet up, and that's probably good for gold as well. It could be one of those periods in the second half of this year when gold and stocks go up together for the same reason, that it's apparent the Fed has no way out of this dilemma.

Outlook for 2015

If you're going to do an outlook, it's always good to know where you're starting from and then project from there. I think the biggest surprise in 2015 may be that the Fed does not raise interest rates.

Right now, the markets fully expect an interest rate increase coming from the Federal Reserve. The only debate is when.

You have people who say March and other people say June or July. Some of them think it might be a little later. I don't see anyone, however, saying that they won't do it at all in 2015. That's what I expect.

We might not even see an interest rate increase 2016, but that's another story. For now, let's just look at 2015 and explain why they won't raise rates.

The Fed is saying a couple of things at present. They say the U.S. economy is getting stronger; and that they want to normalize interest rates. They've also hinted with a nod and a wink and tweaked their language to imply they're going to raise rates 2015. That's what the market is set up for.

This explains why the dollar is so strong. People expect Europe is going to continue to print money and that the Fed is going to raise interest rates or tighten. If you are an investor, you'd rather be in the dollar because you are going to get a higher return.

I think a lot of investors are missing that the data is coming very weak. We've actually been losing full-time jobs and gaining part-time jobs. If you have a $25 per-hour job at forty hours per-week, you earn $50,000 each year.

But if you have a $10 per-hour job, twenty hours per-week, you earn $10,000 each year. That's a big difference. We're losing $50,000 jobs, gaining $10,000 jobs. There's' nothing wrong with those $10,000 jobs. I'm sure people are glad to have them, but this is not going to drive the economy forward.

The other problem is the strong dollar. The dollar is up because people think the Fed is going to raise rates, but a strong dollar is deflationary. The Fed has said over and over they want inflation.

They've told us that. They say 2%... sometimes they say 2.5%... and privately, central bank officials have told me they wouldn't mind seeing 3–3.5%.

But inflation is actually coming in at zero or negative.

We're seeing signs of deflation.

The setup is as follows. The Fed says they want to raise rates but they also say they want inflation. Meanwhile, deflation is stronger which means if the Fed raises rates, they will get more deflation.

How can raising rates work? The answer is, it won't work. You can't reconcile those three things.

There are only two ways out. One is that the Fed does raise rates — of course, that's what the market expects. If they do, watch out below — the U.S. is going to have a major recession because the deflationary powers are too strong. Raising rates strengthens the dollar and makes the deflation worse.

I think the Fed will see that — perhaps by the first quarter of 2015. They will back away and not raise rates. My expectation, contrary to what most people on the market say, I don't think they're going to raise rates in 2015 at all.

Right now the market thinks they will, however, so that sets up a shock. If by March or April — somewhere in there — the data is weak and the Fed starts to signal they're not going to raise rates, all of a sudden everything could flip.

That could be very bullish for oil, gold, and hard assets. You could see the euro strengthened and the dollar go down. Right now it is set up for the opposite. We are looking at a strong dollar, weak gold, weak oil. But that's because everyone thinks the Feds is going to raise rates. But if they don't, which is why I expect, that's going to flip.

CHAPTER 8

Today's Currency and Financial Wars

Currency Wars are one of the most important dynamics in the global financial system today. Of course, I started talking about this year ago in my first book, *Currency Wars*. My point then is the same today: The world is not always in a currency war, but when we are, they can last for five or ten, fifteen and even twenty years. They can last for a very long time. There have been three currency wars in the past one hundred years.

Currency War One covered the period from 1921 to 1936. It really started with the Weimar hyperinflation. There was period of successive currency devaluation.

In 1921, Germany destroyed its currency. In 1925, France, Belgium and others did the same thing. What was going on at that time prior to World War I in 1914? For a long time before that, the world had been on what's called the classical gold standard.

If you had a balance of payments, your deficit, you paid for it in gold. If you had a balance of payment surplus, you acquired gold.

Gold was the regulator of expansion or contraction of individual economies. You had to be productive, pursue your comparative advantage and have a good business environment to actually get some gold in the system — or at least avoid losing the gold you had. It was a very stable system that promoted enormous growth and low inflation.

That system was torn up in 1914 because countries needed to print money to fight World War I. When World War I was over and the world entered the early 1920s, countries wanted to go back to the gold standard but they didn't quite know how to do it.

There was a conference in Genoa, Italy, in 1922 where the problem was discussed. The world started out before World War I with the parity.

There was a certain amount of gold and a certain amount of paper money backed by gold. Then, the paper money supply was doubled.

That left only two choices if countries wanted to go back to a gold standard. They could've doubled the price of gold — basically cut the value of their currency in half — or they could've cut the money supply in half. They could've done either one but they had to get to the parity either at the new level or the old level.

The French said, "This is easy. We're going to cut the value of the currency in half." They did that.

If you saw the Woody Allen movie *Midnight in Paris*, it shows U.S. ex-patriots living a very high lifestyle in France in mid-1920s. That was true because of the hyperinflation of France.

It wasn't as bad as the Weimar hyperinflation in Germany, but it was pretty bad. If you had a modest amount of dollars, you could go to France and live like a king.

The UK had the same decision to make but they made it differently than France did. There, instead of doubling the price of gold, they cut their money supply in half. They went back to the pre-World War I parity. That was a decision made by Winston Churchill who was Chancellor of Exchequer at that time. It was extremely deflationary.

The point is, when you've doubled the money supply, you might not like it but you did it and you have to own up to that and recognize that you've trashed your currency.

Churchill felt duty-bound to live up to the old value. He cut the money supply in half and that threw the UK into a depression three years ahead of the rest of the world. While the rest of the world ran into the depression in 1929, the UK it started in 1926.

I mention that story because to go back to gold at a much higher price measured in sterling would have been the right way to do it. Choosing the wrong price was a contributor to the great depression.

Economists today say, "We could never have a gold standard. Don't you know that the gold standard caused the great depression?"

I do know that — it was a contributor to the great depression, but it was not because of gold, it was because of the price. Churchill picked the wrong price and that was deflationary.

The lesson of the 1920's is not that you can't have a gold standard, but that a country needs to get the price right.

They continued down that path until, finally, it was unbearable for the UK, and they devalued in 1931. Soon after, the US devalued in 1933. Then France and the UK devalued again in 1936.

You had a period of successive currency devaluations and so-called "beggar-thy-neighbor" policies. The result was, of course, one of the worst depressions in world history. There was skyrocketing unemployment and crushed industrial production that created a long period of very weak to negative growth.

Currency War One was not resolved until World War II and then, finally, at the Bretton Woods conference. That's when the world was put on a new monetary standard.

Currency War Two raged from 1967 to 1987. The seminal event in the middle of this war was Nixon's taking the US, and ultimately the world, off the gold standard on August 15th, 1971.

He did this to create jobs and promote exports to help the US economy. What actually happened instead?

We had three recessions back to back, in 1974, 1979, 1980. Our stock market crashed in 1974. Unemployment skyrocketed, inflation flew out of control between 1977 and 1981 (US inflation in that five-year period was 50%) and the value of the dollar was cut in half.

Again, the lesson of currency wars is that they don't produce the results you expect which are increased exports and jobs and some growth. What they produce is extreme deflation, extreme inflation, recession, depression or economic catastrophe.

This brings us to Currency War Three, which began in 2010.

Notice I jumped over that whole period from 1985 to 2010, that 35-year period? What was going on then?

That was the age of what we call "King dollar" or the "strong dollar" policy. It was a period of very good growth, very good price stability and good economic performance around the world.

It was not a gold standard system nor was it rules-based. The Fed did look at the price of gold as a thermometer to see how they were doing.

Basically, what the United States said to the world is, "We're not on a gold standard, we're on a dollar standard. We, the United States, agree to maintain the purchasing power of the dollar and, you, our trading partners, can link to the dollar or plan your economies around some peg to the dollar. That will give us a stable system."

That actually worked up until 2010 when the US tore up the deal and basically declared Currency War Three. President Obama did this in his State of the Union address in January 2010.

Here we are going in 2015 and they're still continuing. That comes as no surprise to me. A lot of journalists will see, say, the weak yen, and they'll say, "Oh, my goodness. We're in a currency war."

And I'll say, "Well, of course we are. We've been in one for five years. And we'll probably be in one for five more years, even longer."

Currency wars are like a see saw — they go back and forth and back and forth. In 2011, for example, we saw a very weak dollar. We also saw a very high price of gold. That was the all-time high — about $1,900 per ounce. Since then, the dollar has gotten much stronger and gold has come down a lot.

It's a very simple correlation. If you want to understand gold, the dollar price of gold is just the inverse of the dollar. It's simple, but many investors don't understand the dynamic.

If we have a weak dollar, gold's going to go up. If we have a strong dollar, gold's going to go down.

If you're interested in gold or other hard assets you need to pay attention to the dollar. Many investors ask me "What's the dollar really worth?" I always reply, "Compared to what?"

Everything is a cross rate. There's a dollar/euro cross rate. There's a dollar/yen cross rate. There's a dollar/yuan cross rate, a dollar/franc cross rate and so on. They're very dynamic because the dollar could be going up against the euro, which at writing, it has been, but at the same time it could be going down against the Chinese yuan.

Investors can profit from these dynamics if they can understand them. Any two currencies are part of a zero sum game. That's another thing that confuses investors. They say, "Oh, the euro's falling apart. The euro's got to go down."

That may or may not be true. But what investors miss is that the Fed wants the dollar to go down too. But the dollar and the euro cannot both go down against each other at the same time.

Lately the dollar's been going up and the euro's been going down. But if you know the Fed wants a weak dollar and you're seeing a strong dollar, what does that mean? It means the Fed has to do something to make the dollar go down. That, in turn, means the euro *must* go up.

In other words, the dollar and the euro can't go down against each other at the same time. It doesn't work. Once you understand the cross rates are a zero sum game, then you can look at all of the cross rates effectively. I think of gold as money, too, so I put gold into the cross rate mix. It's just another currency.

The difference between when we're in a currency war and when we're not is that normally there's stability. I don't mean that we have fixed exchange rates. We don't, we have floating exchange rates. But the central banks agree to keep their currencies within a certain range when the currency wars are off. When the currency wars are on, however, all bets are off. Anything can happen.

They're very dynamic, very complicated and we watch them very closely in *Strategic Intelligence*. There are a lot of ways for investors to win.

The Difference Between Currency Wars and Financial Wars

People sometimes conflate currency wars with financial wars — but they are not the same things.

A currency war is a battle, but it's primarily economic. It's about economic policy. The basic idea is that countries want to cheapen their currency. Now, they say they want to cheapen their currency to promote exports. Maybe it makes a Boeing more competitive internationally with Airbus.

But the real reason, the one that's less talked about, is that countries actually want to import inflation. Take the United States for example. We have a trade deficit, not a surplus. If the dollar's cheaper it may make our exports slightly more attractive. But it's going to increase the price of the goods we buy — whether it's manufactured good, textiles, electronics, etc. — and that inflation then feeds into the supply chain in the U.S.

So, currency wars are actually a way of creating monetary ease and importing inflation. It's part of why Japan is doing Abenomics.

The problem is, once one country tries to cheapen their currency, another country cheapens its currency, and so on causing a race to the bottom. It's a kind of struggle that's primarily economic.

Financial wars are different. Financial war is just the continuation of traditional war by different means. Instead of using missiles or ships or drones, you use stocks, bonds and derivatives. Another difference is that the goal isn't economic gain; it's economic advantage or political gain.

That means the goals of financial war include damaging your enemies' infrastructure, impairing their markets, increase their costs or interest rates. In other words, the goal is to damage your opponent's economy.

What does warfare do? It damages the enemy's' economy. You transfer wealth from them to you. Financial war is no different. If another nation or group wanted to defeat the United States, they can't do it militarily. But they might do it economically.

Financial Wars Are Coming to the Fore

Financial warfare is not a metaphor — it's real. There's real financial warfare going on now. It has been for years and will continue in the future.

If you think of a traditional Venn diagram: one big circle is the world of national security, intelligence and defense. Another big circle is the world of capital markets, stocks, bonds, commodities, derivatives, etc. Think of the intersection of the two, that's what we're talking about.

That intersection is getting bigger, more important, and there are very few people standing in the middle. There are brilliant practitioners on both sides — on the military side and on the financial side. But the number of people who are really conversing with both worlds is few. That's going to be more and more important to you as an investor on a going-forward basis.

I was fortunate enough to participate in a financial war game that was conducted in 2009. I was invited by the Pentagon to be a facilitator and a planner for it. Of course, the Pentagon, our Defense Department, had been doing war games forever. They didn't need any help from me in terms of a traditional war game.

But this was the first financial war game ever done. The weapons were non-kinetic meaning nothing that would shoot or explode. We could only use stocks, bonds, currencies, derivatives and commodities. We had some of the usual teams as you might imagine.

There was a U.S. team, a Russian team, a Chinese team and so forth. We also had a team of banks and hedge funds because they're very important players in the space as well.

We spent days, months really, designing this and played it out over a couple of days in March 2009, at a top secret weapons laboratory outside of Washington — the applied physics laboratory.

What was interesting was one of the scenarios that I introduced myself. Some colleagues, who were playing as the Russian and Chinese teams would get together, pool their gold and issue a new currency backed by that gold. Of course, we had the gold in a Swiss vault and the currency issued by a UK bank because nobody would trust a Russian or a Chinese bank per se.

Using those safe jurisdictions to issue this new currency, Russia and China would then say, henceforth, any Russian natural resource exports or any Chinese manufactured exports could only be paid for in this new currency. If you wanted some, you could trade and earn it or you could deposit your gold and they would issue the currency and then you could use this for transactions with them.

Obviously, this was a stretch. This is not anything that was going to happen tomorrow. But at that time, we were actually ridiculed. We had uniformed military and intelligence experts, and people from the Fed, people from the United States Treasury, think tanks, universities actually ridicule us saying, "This is ridiculous. Don't you know gold has no place in the monetary system? It's obsolete. Why are you doing this? This just seems like a waste of time."

Be that as it may, we played it out.

I won't take you through every move, it's all described in my first book *Currency Wars*. Since 2009, Russia has increased its gold reserves by 70%. China has increased its gold reserves several hundreds of percent. No one knows the exact number because they're not transparent about it.

As of 2009, they now stay at 1,054 tons. Whether today they have 3,000 tons or 4,000 tons, no one knows exactly. But that's the right order of magnitude and they seem to be determined about acquiring more.

Their actions were actually playing out as we modeled it for the Defense Department in 2009. China is a very robust actor in financial warfare.

In the United States, we've been in a financial war with Iran since 2011. The United States did a couple of things. This was, of course, because of Iran's uranium enrichment efforts and a drive to get nuclear weapons.

The U.S. first kicked Iran out of the dollar payment system, that's called Fedwire. It's a clearance system run by the Federal Reserve. We said, "You're out and your banks are out. Any Swiss or other foreign banks that do business with Iran, you're out too."

That's the way the U.S. forces other banks to follow their policy — by telling them they can't do business in the U.S. unless they comply.

Iran said, "Fine, we'll just ship our oil and price it in Euros. We don't need your dollars and we don't need your dollar payment system."

There's another, even larger, payment system in Europe

called SWIFT — Society for Worldwide Interbank Funds Transfers — and you can pay in Euros, Yen, Australian dollars or any other reserve currency.

The U.S. then got together with its allies and prevailed on them to kick Iran out of SWIFT. Now Iran was stuck. They could ship oil but they couldn't get paid for it, at least not in any currency that you would want. They began to do a number of workarounds, acquiring massive amounts of gold from Turkey so they could arrange gold for import swaps. They were selling oil to India, for example.

India could pay Iran in rupees, deposit it in an Indian bank account for them that was outside the payment system I described. But then Iran has rupees, and what can you do with those?

You can buy things in India, but I'm not sure how much curry the Iranians actually needed. Indian merchants were very inventive because the rupee is a convertible currency they got dollars, imported goods to India and then sent them to Iran for Rupees, converting them back to dollars and taking spreads all along the way. It was very costly to Iran, but it worked.

As a result of this, the Iranians themselves tried to take their money out of the bank because there was a black market for dollars — some of which were smuggled in from Iraq, which can get dollars. They could pay the smugglers in Dubai to bring the computers and the cellphones and the printers and all the things we enjoy, across from Dubai.

That caused a run on the bank because people were taking the little currency they had out to go to the black markets. In response, the Iranian government raised interest rates to try to keep the money in the bank, and inflation broke out.

We really came close to destroying the Iranian economy with, as I say, financial weapons. No boots on the ground, no missiles and a little bit of sabotage here and there but not much more than that.

We caused high inflation, a run on the bank, contracted their economy and had very powerful impacts on the Iranian economy. It was moving on a direction of regime change.

President Obama lifted a lot of these sanctions because the Iranians made some promises. We'll see how that plays out as there are talks going on.

Don't think that Vladimir Putin wasn't watching when the US backed away from those financial sanctions because we have another financial war brewing — a couple of them actually — out in the nations in the Middle East.

I gave you the Iranian example just to show that these financial weapons are very powerful. The United States uses them aggressively to destabilize countries. Of course, the U.S. works hand-in-glove with the IMF to do the same thing.

Financial warfare is real. It's going on, and if you're an investor and you're not aware of it, you're occasionally going to get blindsided.

I can't tell you how many very good fundamental stock analysts and bond analysts I've met who've spent, in some case, decades learning their craft and understanding how to analyze markets on to get slammed every now and then because Angela Merkel got out of the wrong side of the bed, and decided to have a fight with the Greek finance minister.

You can't ignore global macro events if you are a fundamental investor making fundamental decisions because these things are not going away; in fact they're getting worse.

The Petrodollar

Of course, there have been a couple of new developments. I mentioned that in December of 2013 President Obama shook hands with Iran and entered into negotiations — direct talks for the first time since 1979.

In effect, Obama anointed Iran as the regional hegemon in the

Persian Gulf. This was taken by Saudi Arabia as a stab in the back.

The Saudi-US relationship goes back to the late 1940s. But in particular, in the mid-1970s, there was a very famous deal, if you will, struck between Henry Kissinger — who was President Nixon, and later, President Ford's leading national security adviser and Secretary of State — and the Saudi King.

In this deal they said that Saudis agreed to price oil in dollars. They didn't have to do that. They could have said, "We'll take gold." There were other currencies at that time like the Deutschemark, French francs and Japanese Yen. But they said, "We will only take dollars for oil." That put a prop under the dollar.

The United States agreed a guarantee on their national security to protect them. We made good on that guarantee in 1991 when Saddam Hussein invaded Kuwait and threatened Saudi Arabia — the U.S. did respond to that forcefully.

That deal was in place for over 40 years. That was torn up in December of 2013. Again, the Saudis took it as a stab in the back. Here's the United States saying to Iran, "Not only are you the regional power, but we're going to let you continue on your path to nuclear weapons." Imagine what that feels like from the perspective of Saudi Arabia.

They haven't done anything drastic yet but they are reevaluating this "petrodollar" relationship. If the Saudis decide, "Okay, if you don't have our back, if you're not protecting our national security why should we support your currency and not decide to start pricing oil in, either Euros or perhaps Yuan or other currencies to the parties who are actually buying the Saudi oil?" That removes a very significant prop under the U.S. dollar.

This financial warfare, as I say, is more and more pervasive. Of course, the last event I want to call attention to what's going on in Ukraine.

Russia has taken over Crimea. I think that's a *fait accompli,* they're not leaving anytime soon. No one in the United States, left to right or center, thinks that the United States should have a military response to this, a traditional military response. No boots on the ground, we're not going to put the 82nd airborne division into Sevastopol.

What do you do? You can't just shrug and ignore it. So, of course, the US immediately used economic sanctions, which are a form of financial warfare. I said at the time this happened — I've been saying ever since — these financial sanctions are not going to go very far. Why is that?

It takes us back to the 1960s and the 1970s to a doctrine called "mutual assured destruction" — MAD — or the MAD doctrine. You may recall it.

This is actually still true, although it's much less talked about today. At the time, the United States had enough nuclear missiles to destroy Russia. Russia, or the Soviet Union also had enough nuclear missiles to destroy the United States.

There was an enormous temptation to shoot first. If you could fire your missiles and destroy the other side, you won. Both sides were aware of that so they said, "What we need is the so-called second strike capability. That way, if the other side shoots their missiles and devastates our country, we're going to have enough missiles left to shoot back and destroy their country." Therefore, both sides developed a second strike capability.

This is what the 1960s and 1970s was all about. You can analogize this to two scorpions in a bottle. One scorpion can sting and kill the other, but the victim has just enough strength left to sting back and they both die.

Russia, Ukraine and the Future of Sanctions

In early February 2015, I traveled to Washington DC for a private meeting with top national security, defense and intelligence professionals. Our meeting was focused on a specific aspect of threat finance — the Russian invasion of eastern Ukraine, and the behind-the-scenes financial war that has been going on in response.

Our group of about a dozen experts met behind closed doors at a think tank on M Street in downtown Washington. We operated under Chatham House Rules, which means that participants cannot be mentioned or quoted by name. But, it is permitted to describe the tone and substance of the conversation. Included around the table were subject matter experts and former officials from the State Department, Defense Department, U.S. Treasury, White House National Security Council, and CIA.

It was the perfect mix of defense, diplomacy, finance and intelligence. Our mission was to evaluate the economic sanctions currently in place against Russia and to develop recommendations for changes in sanctions policy if needed. These recommendations would later be made public with a view to influencing sanctions policy either in the current or next White House administration.

This is the kind of work that has enormous implications for investors and their portfolios, but which is too often unknown to the Wall Street analysts on whom investors rely. At *Strategic Intelligence*, our goal is to synthesize geopolitics with capital markets expertise so that investors are not blindsided by geopolitical earthquakes that seem far removed from the quotidian concerns of finance.

Our discussion began on a note of frustration from the assembled experts that U.S. economic sanctions had not produced any change in Russian behavior. The U.S. and most of its allies were unhappy with the Russian takeover of Crimea, but were prepared to live with that outcome for various historic and strategic reasons. Crimea has historically been part of Russia and the Russia Black Sea Fleet, the only warm-water fleet in Russia, was based there. Putin's methods in securing Russian interests in Crimea were blunt, but effective, and NATO seemed willing to treat it as a *fait accompli*. But Russian support for rebel forces in Eastern Ukraine, including the use of Russian troops and heavy weapons, was seen as completely unacceptable. It was a blatant breach of international law and territorial integrity that could not be rationalized in the way that Crimea could.

Despite the egregious nature of Russia involvement in Eastern Ukraine, there was no consensus that a NATO military response should result. That battle would be up to the main Ukrainian forces directed by Kiev. But the U.S. and its Western allies did agree to impose economic sanctions. These were mild at first, involving travel bans and asset freezes on certain Russian oligarchs and officials. When these sanctions failed to modify Russian behavior, they were enhanced to prohibit financing activity of many important Russian companies by Western banks.

The economic impact of the sanctions was severe and undeniable. Russia's GDP dropped precipitously and the exchange value of the Russian ruble collapsed. There was a drain on Russia's foreign reserves. These were used to prop up Russian companies that could no longer access dollar markets to refinance their debts. Of course, these sanctions came at the same time that global oil prices crashed in late 2014, which made the Russian dilemma even worse. It was in response to these developments that President Obama claimed that the sanctions were "working."

Importantly, there was good evidence that the business interests of Russian oligarchs had been severely impacted. Their revenues were drying up, their stock valuations were down, and ultimately their companies could fail if they could not refinance their dollar denominated debts. This was important because it was believed that desperate oligarchs would put pressure on Putin to force him to seek a reasonable accommodation with the West.

But the sanctions were only working in terms of their economic impact; they were *not* working to alter Russia behavior. The conflict in Eastern Ukraine actually intensified in late 2014, and early 2015 with significant rebel gains against Ukrainian forces. It was this conundrum — sanctions were economically effective but politically impotent — that preoccupied my colleagues. Time and again they asked: What does Putin want? The implication was that Putin was an enigma but, if we could discern his hidden preferences a sanctions regime could be devised to frustrate those preferences and, in turn, alter his behavior.

When my turn came to address the group, I cut to the heart of our failed sanctions policy. The entire program was an example of a well-known intelligence failure called "mirror imaging." This arises when an analyst assumes the adversary thinks the way he does. Policies that might change the analyst's behavior are assumed to affect the adversary's behavior the same way. The mirror image assumption often proves false, and can result in failed policy.

For example, America has its own oligarchs including Warren Buffet, Bill Gates, and Larry Page. It is reasonable to assume that if harsh sanctions by others were to seriously impact the economic interests of Buffett, Gates and Page, they would find a way to pressure the White House for sanctions relief, including changes in U.S. policy if needed.

But the process does not work in reverse. Pressure on Russian oligarchs is easy to apply, but their ability to influence Putin's behavior is nil. In fact, Putin would not hesitate to imprison or kill them if they were too outspoken. One cannot imagine the White House throwing Warren Buffett in prison for being a policy critic, but that outcome is easy to imagine in Russia. Unfortunately, U.S. policy makers had fallen prey to mirror imaging and did not realize that pressuring Russian oligarchs, versus U.S. oligarchs, would produce different outcomes.

The other area where U.S. policymakers were guilty of mirror imaging is assessing the impact of economic costs. Declining GDP and a crashing currency would send most U.S. politicians running for cover and looking for ways to undo the damage. But Russians were accustomed to adversity and used the Western economic assault as a rallying cry. Rather than looking for a way out of the sanctions, Russians took pride in adversity, and were more determined than ever to support the Russian-speaking peoples of Eastern Ukraine.

As for the question, "What does Putin want?" I said the answer was easy. I explained that Putin wants Georgia, Ukraine and Moldova firmly in the Russian orbit, and he's prepared to use military force to accomplish that. Later he will decide what he wants next.

My question for the group was more difficult: What does the U.S. want? The failure of economic sanctions was not only due to mirror imaging, but also to a lack of U.S. strategy. The U.S. did not have an endgame in Ukraine apart from wishful thinking about the impact of sanctions.

Henry Kissinger advised that countries couldn't formulate policy on a case-by-case basis, but need a firm vision of national interests as a context within which to consider policy. Only when goals are known can strategy and tactics be devised.

Kissinger said that countries not only needed to know what they wanted, but needed to know what they wouldn't allow. Would the U.S. allow Russian dominance in Eastern Ukraine? If the answer is "no" then the U.S. needs to pursue regime change in Russia. If the answer is "yes" then diplomacy, not sanctions, are the best path to a modus vivendi. The policy problem was that the U.S. had neither asked nor answered the question. We were lurching day-to-day with no vision, and no strategy.

Given the clarity of Russian ambitions, and lack of clarity on the part of U.S. strategists, investors should expect further confrontation in Ukraine. There will be good days and bad days. At times a truce may be in effect, but at other times truces will be broken, and hostilities resumed. The Ukrainian government is near bankruptcy, but will be propped up by IMF loans. The Ukrainian military appears ineffective against Russian heavy weapons, but may receive lethal aid from the U.S. and NATO.

The U.S. may consider economic sanctions a branch of diplomacy, but Russia considers them an act of war. So, war it is.

In the end, Russia will prevail because it has the will, the vision, and the physical proximity to pursue its interests, while the West does not even have a strong sense of what its interests are. Beyond that, Russia is the eighth largest economy in the world, and produces much of Europe's energy. The world economy is slowing down for reasons unrelated to Russia, but Russia's isolation makes things worse. The appetite for additional sanctions outside of Washington is slight. Russia has absorbed our best shot, and is still standing. Our will to escalate is not there, and Putin knows it.

For investors, this geopolitical dead end for the west creates a classic contrarian investment opportunity. Russian ETFs are among the best performing investments of 2015, so far, but have further to go as the situation in Ukraine is slowly resolved in Russia's favor.

The ETFs to consider are RSX (Market Vectors Russia ETF), and RBL (SPDR S&P Russia ETF), which are both up over 20% so far in 2015. For investors with more appetite for volatility, you can consider RUSL (Direxion Daily Russia Bull 3x Shares), which uses leverage to amplify returns. RUSL is up over 65% year to date, and is in position to perform well in the months ahead. Of course, leverage can amplify losses as well as gains, and RUSL is highly speculative. All of these investments should be added as a small slice of your portfolio — do not go all in. But, they can be an attractive, if volatile, addition to other more conservative investments.

The RSX, RBL and RUSL ETFs are all bets on the Ukraine situation moving toward a resolution and to sanctions gradually being lifted. Based on my meetings with the national security professionals, that seems the most likely path. The U.S. is not willing to go for the throat, so we will be forced to go for diplomacy. That can only favor Putin and Russia in the end.

The BOJ, Currency Wars and Money Printing Gone Wild

On Oct. 31, 2014, staffers at Japan's central bank were sweating bullets...

They'd worked past midnight, drafting a proposal to shift the Bank of Japan's dangerous yen-printing experiment into higher gear.

The staffers' boss, BOJ governor Haruhiko Kuroda, was concerned the Japanese public would maintain a deflationary mindset. The public was hoarding cash, expecting prices to drift lower forever. In Kuroda's view, this is a problem in need of fixing.

Kuroda wants to shock the public out of its deflationary mindset. Nothing short of a revolution in inflation expectations will suffice.

For the past two years, Kuroda had nudged the Japanese public into expecting higher prices. In anticipation of inflation, Kuroda's theory says, there would be a spending spree. The spending spree might be enough to revolutionize Japan's consumer psychology.

Ahead of the BOJ's Oct. 31 meeting, Kuroda must have been nervous his policy proposal wouldn't receive a majority vote. He proposed accelerating the yen-printing program begun in 2013. Previously, the Japanese monetary base was growing at an annual pace of about 60–70 trillion yen. Kuroda proposed an acceleration, to 80 trillion yen per year.

After a heated two-hour debate, it came down to a cliffhanger: Kuroda and his deputies were reliable "yes" votes; two skeptical board members, as expected, voted "no"; and the four other members split down the middle.

With a 5–4 vote, the BOJ launched a major new battle in the global currency war...

Immediately after the vote became public, the U.S. dollar jumped in value against the yen. Japanese stocks spiked. The BOJ is heading down a one-way path toward currency destruction…

My work on central banks and currency wars indicates that the yen will keep weakening against the U.S. dollar in the coming months.

Kuroda is a zealot in his belief that the can revolutionize inflationary psychology in Japan. He took the helm of the BOJ in early 2013, vowing to boost inflation and inflation expectations.

He immediately launched the largest quantitative easing program the world had ever seen — twice as big, in GDP terms, as the Federal Reserve's QE3 program. The BOJ pledged to purchase $1.4 trillion of Japanese government bonds over the course of 2013 and 2014 using printed money.

"[The] Bank of Japan was explicit about its goal to increase inflation in order to increase nominal, if not real, GDP," I wrote in *The Death of Money*. "The BOJ explicitly targeted an inflation rate of 2% 'at the earliest possible time.'"

Kuroda is increasingly desperate. The prior plan to inflate Japan's base money supply wasn't shocking enough to boost inflation expectations. So Kuroda sought an acceleration in yen printing, got the votes and announced the policy shift on Oct. 31.

The Bank of Japan is so far down the road to currency destruction that it's now the only sizeable bidder in the Japanese government bond (JGB) market. JGB trading volumes have collapsed. With Japan's shrinking workforce, declining competitiveness and a national debt that requires near-zero interest rates, more and more of the JGB market will be converted into cash deposits. The yen-based money supply will keep growing.

Why is Japan's debt a problem if the central bank stands ready to convert the entire stock of debt into yen?

Here's why: It's only a matter of time before the supply side of the Japanese economy starts viewing yen as hot potatoes to be traded for real assets — a spiraling inflation crisis that the BOJ won't have the flexibility to fight.

Currencies die quickly when producers lose confidence

they'll retain value and withhold supply from the market. In *The Death of Money,* I use the term "phase transition" to describe the process:

"When wood burns and turns to ash, that is a phase transition, but there is no easy way to turn ash back into wood. The Federal Reserve believes that it is managing a reversible process. It believes that deflation can be turned to inflation, and then to disinflation, with the right quantity of money and the passage of time. In this, it is mistaken."

Like the Federal Reserve, the BOJ believes it can dial up inflation and dial it back down. But confidence is fragile and will get even weaker with each surge of yen emitted from the BOJ.

Many central banks, including the BOJ, are squandering their reputational credibility on wealth effect experiments. These experiments are leaving central banks with huge balance sheets that cannot be allowed to shrink.

A Currency Wars "Pearl Harbor"

The most dramatic battle yet in the currency wars took place on January 15, 2015. It was the financial equivalent of a Pearl Harbor sneak attack...

"I find it a bit surprising that he did not contact me," IMF director Christine Lagarde told CNBC's Steve Liesman that day, "but you know, we'll check on that."

You can almost imagine the conversation afterward between Mario Draghi of the European Central Bank (ECB) and Swiss National Bank (SNB) President Thomas Jordan...

Mario Draghi: "Did you tell Christine?"

Thomas Jordan: "I thought you were going to tell her..."

Mario Draghi: "Wait, I thought you were!"

Switzerland had just abandoned its peg of the Swiss franc to the euro. The result was mayhem, with an immediate 30% drop in the value of the euro against the franc and billions of dollars of trading losses by banks and investors around the world.

Several foreign exchange brokers went bankrupt because their customers could not settle their losing trades. The Swiss operated in total secrecy.

Currency wars resemble real wars in the sense that they do not involve continuous fighting all the time. At certain times, there are intense battles, followed by lulls, followed by more intense battles.

But there is nothing new about the Swiss National Bank's move. It's the latest salvo in the currency war that President Obama started in 2010, and it won't be the last. It was in 2010 that the president announced his National Export Initiative designed to double U.S. exports in five years.

The only way to do that was with a cheaper dollar, so the president's policy amounted to a declaration to the world that the U.S. wanted other countries to let their currencies go up so the dollar could go down. Ten months later, the Brazilian finance minister, Guido Mantega, shocked global financial elites by publicly proclaiming what everyone knew but no one would say — that the world was in a new currency war.

The problem with currency wars is they last a long time — sometimes even 15 or 20 years. The reason is they have no logical conclusion, just back-and-forth devaluations and revaluations as countries retaliate against each other.

We have seen this seesaw pattern re-emerge. The weak dollar of 2011 has turned into the strong dollar of 2015. Countries that complained the weak dollar was hurting their exports in 2011 now complain that the strong dollar is hurting their capital markets in 2015.

That's the other problem with currency wars — no one wins, and everyone loses. Currency wars don't create growth; they just steal growth temporarily from trading partners until the trading partners steal it back with their own devaluations.

The surprise revaluation of the Swiss franc on Jan. 15 will

not be the last such surprise. There are many important pegs left in the international monetary system vulnerable to being broken. Right now, the Hong Kong dollar and the major Arab currencies are all tightly pegged to the U.S. dollar.

The Chinese Yuan is loosely pegged to the U.S. dollar too. If the U.S. raises interest rates this year as the Fed has warned, the stronger dollar may force those countries to break their pegs, because their own currencies would become too strong and hurt their exports.

If the Fed does not raise interest rates, the result could be a violent reversal of current trends and a weaker dollar as the "risk on" mantra causes capital to flow out of the U.S. and back to the emerging markets. Either way, volatility is the one certainty.

The other problem with the currency wars is what the IMF calls "spillover" effects, also known as financial contagion. Many mortgages in Poland, Hungary and other parts of Central and Eastern Europe are made not in local currency but in Swiss francs. The stronger Swiss franc means those borrowers need more local currency to pay off their mortgages.

This could lead to a wave of mortgage defaults and a mortgage market meltdown similar to what the U.S. experienced in 2007. This shows how a decision made in Zurich can wipe out a homeowner in Budapest. Financial contagion works just like Ebola. Once an outbreak begins, it can be difficult to contain. It may not be long before the Swiss franc sneak attack infects investor portfolios in the U.S.

Financial contagion can also be a two-way street. It not only creates dangers, it creates opportunities for investors who can connect the dots in the currency wars. The easiest conclusion you can draw and act on is this simple truth: Do not believe government and central bank lies.

This maxim is not without historical precedent. You've probably heard about Franklin Roosevelt's own sneak currency attack. In 1933, President Roosevelt devised a plan to increase the price of gold in dollars, effectively a dollar devaluation. But he had a problem. If he increased the price of gold while Americans owned it, the profit would go to the citizens, not the U.S. Treasury. He knew that he had to lie to the American people about his intentions in order to pull off the theft of the century.

So Roosevelt issued an emergency executive order confiscating the gold at about $20.00 per ounce and then revalued it to $35.00 per ounce, with the Treasury getting the profits.

On Jan. 15, the Swiss National Bank pulled a similar stunt. Last November, the Swiss citizens voted on a referendum to require an informal link of the Swiss franc to gold. The Swiss National Bank argued against the referendum on the ground that it would cause them to break the peg of the Swiss franc to the euro.

The people believed them and voted "no" on the referendum. But now the Swiss National Bank has broken the peg anyway. The price of gold is spiking as a result, but the Swiss citizens have lost the benefit of that because the referendum is now a dead letter. The Swiss National Bank lied to the Swiss people about their intentions with regard to the peg.

The lesson of history is that citizens should own some gold, store it safely and not believe government and central bank lies. In fact, we could see more investors fleeing to the safety of gold in the coming months as trust in central bankers wanes.

CHAPTER 9

Gold's Bull Market Isn't Over

A Win-Win Scenario for Gold Owners

Volatility and price drops may be nerve wracking, but the bull market in gold is far from over. In fact, it has barely begun.

To understand why, it helps to look at two prior episodes in the relationship of gold and money that are most relevant to today. These episodes were a period of extreme deflation, the 1930s, and a period of extreme inflation, the 1970s. History shows that gold does well in both conditions.

Commentators frequently observe that we are experiencing "price stability" or "low inflation" based on the fact that the consumer price index has averaged 2% over the past 12 months. However, this average hides more that it reveals.

The economy is experiencing strong deflationary forces as a result of weak employment and deleveraging associated with the depression that began in 2007. Simultaneously the economy is experiencing strong inflationary forces as a result of Fed money printing.

The deflationary and inflationary forces offset each other to produce a seemingly benign average. But below the surface the forces struggle to prevail with some likelihood that one or the other will emerge victorious sooner than later.

Inflationary forces often appear only with significant lags relative to the expansion of the money supply. This was the case in the late 1960s and early 1970s. The Fed began to expand the money supply to pay for Lyndon Johnson's "guns and butter" policy in 1965. The first sign of trouble was when inflation increased from 3.1% in 1967 to 5.5% in 1969.

But there was worse to come. Inflation rose further to 11% in 1974 and then topped off at 11.3% in 1979, 13.5% in 1980 and 10.3% in 1981, an astounding 35% cumulative inflation in three years. During this time period, gold rose from $35 per ounce to over $800 per ounce, a 2,300% increase.

The point is that neither the inflation nor the gold price spike happened overnight. It took 15 years to play out from start to finish. The Fed's current experiments in extreme money printing only began in 2008. Given the lags in monetary policy and the offsetting deflationary forces, we should not be surprised if it takes another year or two for serious inflation to appear on the scene.

Another instructive episode is the Great Depression. The problem then was not inflation but deflation. It first appeared in 1927 but really took hold in 1930. From 1930–1933, cumulative deflation was 26%. The U.S. became desperate for inflation. It could not cheapen its currency because other countries were cheapening their currencies even faster in the "beggar-thy-neighbor" currency wars of the time.

Finally, the U.S. decided to devalue the dollar against gold. In 1933, the price of gold in dollars was increased from $20 per ounce to $35 dollar per ounce, a 75% increase at a time when all other prices were decreasing. This shock therapy for the dollar worked, and by 1934 inflation was back at 3.1%, a massive turnaround from the 5.1% deflation of 1933. In short, when all other methods fail to defeat deflation, devaluing the dollar against gold works without fail because gold can't fight back.

It is unclear if the world will tip into inflation or deflation, but one or the other is almost certain. The good news for gold investors is that gold goes up in either case as shown in the 1930s and 1970s. Yet patience is required.

These trends take years to play out and policies work with a lag. Meanwhile, investors can use recent setbacks to acquire gold at more attractive prices while waiting for the inevitable price increase to occur.

The Long-Term Gold Outlook

My long term forecast for gold — meaning, over a three-year horizon — is much higher based on fundamentals, the amount of paper money in the world and the fact that we're in a global depression.

Money printing by itself won't do any good, but the central banks think it will. That alone should drive gold higher over the longer term because the central banks will keep printing and risk destroying confidence in the paper currencies.

If they had to restore that confidence, that might also mean going back to some kind of gold standard, or at least use the price gold reference point. If deflation is a problem, how do you get inflation? One way to get inflation is to depreciate your currency relative to the gold.

You might say to yourself, "What, hypothetically, is the non-deflationary price of gold if there was a gold standard implemented?" That's not a matter of making a prediction, it's an analytical question. You can do the math on that using available data. The answer is $7,000 to $9,000.

There's no central bank in the world that wants a gold standard. But if we were going to have one and wanted to avoid deflation of the kind we had in the Great Depression, the price of gold would have to at least be $7,000 per ounce, probably higher. It's closer to $9,000 per ounce. I call that the "implied non-deflationary price of gold." That part's easy, actually.

You can do that math because we know how much gold there is, how much paper money there is, and we can make some assumptions about the ratios and confidence levels.

The question then becomes, what would cause central

banks to want to go back to some kind of gold standard?

Obviously, it would take a collapse of confidence in paper money. The gold standard would be a desperate move to restore confidence in the system. Then, you have to figure out what the likelihood of that happening?

The more money central banks print, the closer we get to that confidence boundary and the point where we might actually have to implement a gold standard. That's the kind of instability built into the system. Confidence is fragile. It's something that can be lost very quickly.

How can confidence be destroyed quickly?

Think of a bank run. You wake up in the morning and the bank is on sound financial footing, but some people, for whatever reason, hear a rumor that the bank is actually not sound. So, they run down to withdraw all of their money immediately.

Their neighbors, seeing them lined up in front of the bank say, "I don't know what's going on, but I better get my money before they run out," and they get in line too.

The line gets longer and the buzz increase causing even more people get in line. Next thing you know, the bank is bankrupt even though it started out the morning perfectly fine. That's the classic scenario of a run on the bank.

We don't have that dynamic today. People don't line up at the bank anymore. They do everything digitally. Plus, we have deposit insurance and other things that mitigate that risk. But the fact of the matter is that psychology hasn't changed at all. A little rumor, even if it's false, or some person getting in line, could start the run on the bank.

Gold, right now, looks like the floor is around $1,100 an ounce. It's been smashed down to that level four times in the recent years.

That said, I did have a conversation recently with Jim Rogers. I think we all know Jim Rogers is one of the greatest commodity investors in history. He said that no commodity is ever going to its final destination without a 50 percent retracement, meaning even if you believe that gold could end up at $7,000 an ounce, which I do, if you see it at $1,900, a 50 percent retracement would take it down to $950.

In other words, it would go all the way down to $950 and then it would bounce back. So what Jim said, he said, "I have a lot of gold. I'm not selling it. I'm sitting on it. I'm a buyer at $1,000, but I'm not necessarily a buyer at $1,100 because I kind of look for that 50 percent retracement."

That said, if you go back over a four-year period, gold has been much higher. In August 2011, it was about $1,900 an ounce. It's made its way down to around $1,100 an ounce on four separate occasions, and each time, it rallied back. Now, it's never got back to the $1,900 level, but it has gone up to the $1,350 range.

That tells me is that there's a physical demand out there. Forget about gold futures and paper gold. There's physical demand. When gold gets up to those levels, people do line up. They don't line up to get their money out of the bank; they line up to buy physical gold.

You see this in Asia — in Hong Kong, Thailand, Malaysia and in mainland China. You see it even in Australia and other places around the world. I've been to many of those places and spoken to people there, and this is something they tell me about all the time.

This what's called a "recursive function." The plain English name for that is the feedback loop where something happens; A happens and that causes B to happen, but B gives you more A, and A gives more B, and B gives you more A, and A gives you more B, and it goes around and around and the behavior keeps amplifying based on that feedback loop.

Gold is Money (Once Again)

One of my favorite quotes on the topic of gold is attributed to Lord Nathan Rothschild, a legendary nineteenth century banker, and gold broker to the Bank of England. He said, "I only know of two men who really understand the true value of gold — an obscure clerk in the basement vault of the Banque de Paris and one of the directors of the Bank of England. Unfortunately, they disagree."

Another favorite quote, even more succinct, is from J. Pierpont Morgan who said in 1912: "Money is gold, and nothing else."

We also have a modern take on the meaning and value of gold from none other than Ben Bernanke, former Chairman of the Federal Reserve. On July 18, 2013, Bernanke said, "Nobody really understands gold prices, and I don't pretend to understand them either."

These quotes illustrate the perennial challenge that investors face in deciding what role gold should play in their portfolios. Few understand how to value gold, and even fewer understand that gold is not really an investment — it is money. Of course, if you want a portfolio that preserves wealth, money is a good place to start.

Saying gold is not an investment may seem strange, especially since I recommend some gold in an investor's portfolio. To illustrate this point, you can reach into your purse or wallet and pull out a dollar bill. You think of the dollar as "money" but you do not think of it as an investment. An investment has some element of risk, and typically has some yield in the form of interest, dividends or rent. Money can be turned into an investment by using it to buy stocks, bonds or real estate. But as a dollar bill, it is just money; it has no yield and will still be a dollar tomorrow or next year.

Gold is the same. It has no yield. An ounce of gold today will be an ounce of gold next year and the year after that. It will not mysteriously turn into two ounces. It will not rust or change shape or color. It is just gold. Yet, it is money.

It's true that the value of gold may change when measured

in dollars. It is also true that the value of a dollar may change when measured in euros or ounces of gold. But these changes in relative value do not turn these units into investments; they just reflect supply and demand for different forms of money.

If holders of euros have a preference for dollars, the euro may fall relative to the dollar. If holders of dollars or euros have a preference for gold, then the value of gold may rise relative to both. Still, these changes reflect changing preferences for different forms of money, not a return on investment. While gold is money investors frequently ignore the fact.

Gold often trades like an investment and is said to be "up" or "down" in dollar value, the same as a stock is said to be going up or down. Gold also trades like a commodity; in fact the primary trading venue for paper contracts in gold is the Commodity Exchange or COMEX. In that context, gold typically goes up in dollar terms during inflation, and down in dollar terms during deflation, just like other commodities including oil and copper.

That's why the chart below is so fascinating. It compares the price of gold to the Continuous Commodity Index, an index of major commodities that has been maintained consistently since 1957. The index includes gold, copper, cotton, crude oil, natural gas and twelve other widely traded commodities.

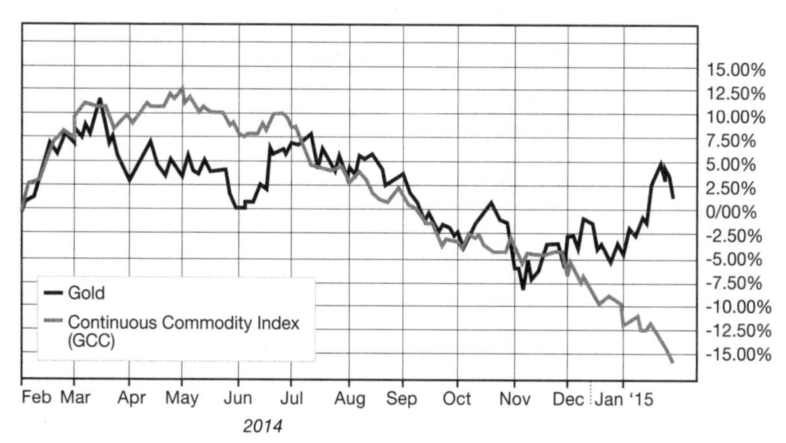

Throughout 2014 the gold price closely tracked the commodity index as might be expected. The price trend of both was downward, which reflected the strong deflationary trends that began to prevail last year. But in November, this correlation broke down and gold began to diverge sharply from the overall index.

In Tonnes	FRBNY Total Foreign Gold Deposits	Change
Jan-14	6195.60	0.00
Feb-14	6185.29	-10.31
Mar-14	6175.71	-9.58
Apr-14	6175.71	-5.16
Jun-14	6165.39	-5.16
Jul-14	6141.08	-24.31
Aug-14	6125.61	-15.47
Sep-14	6118.25	-7.37
Oct-14	6076.25	-41.99
Nov-14	6029.11	-47.15
Dec-14	6018.79	-10.31
	Total:	-176.81

Source: Bullion Star

That was not the only significant development in gold late last year. As this chart shows, the pace of gold shipments out of the Federal Reserve Bank of New York increased sharply in October and November. Over 90 tons of gold were shipped out of the Fed to their rightful owners abroad in those two months alone. That was more than half the total amount of gold shipped out for the entire year. Bear in mind that prior to 2012 almost no gold had been shipped from the Federal Reserve Bank of New York since the 1970s.

It's a mistake to read too much into short-time series of data such as the Gold/GCC correlation or the gold shipments from the Fed. Every analyst knows that correlation of factors does not prove causation. But these two charts do suggest that suddenly late last year, gold stop trading like an investment or a commodity, and started behaving like what it has always been — money.

Late 2014 was a period when commodities generally declined because of deflation, and currencies generally fell against the dollar as part of the currency wars. The declining currencies were also a symptom of deflation because currency devaluation is a way to import inflation from trading partners in order to stave off domestic deflation.

Only three major assets went up strongly in the past six months: U.S. dollars, Swiss francs and gold. The dollar/gold correlation was most striking because they had been inversely correlated since 2011 with the dollar getting stronger, and gold getting weaker. Suddenly gold and dollars were gaining strength together against commodities, euros, yen, Yuan and most other measures of wealth.

Using our causal inference models, our tentative conclusion is that gold is behaving like money again. This could be an early warning of a breakdown in the international monetary system as a result of persistent deflation and currency wars. Investors were moving to safe havens, and dollars, gold, and Swiss francs are at the top of the list.

However, our intelligence collections and inferential models suggest that something even more profound may be going on. Russian and Chinese gold acquisition programs have been going on for years; that story is well known to our readers.

But those acquisitions have now passed the point that Russia and China need to have a seat at the table in any new international monetary conference. Both countries have caught up to the U.S. in terms of the all-important Gold-to-GDP ratio. Yet massive gold acquisitions by Russia and China continue. Can something else be going on?

At a minimum, Russia and China are using gold to hedge the dollar value of their primary assets. In the case of China, those assets consist of $3 trillion of U.S. Treasury and other dollar-denominated debt. In the case of Russia, those assets consist of oil and natural gas, both of which are priced in dollars on world markets.

For China, the hedge is simple. If the U.S. inflates the value of the dollar, China will lose on its debt holdings, but will make large gains on its gold. Converting some portion of its dollar reserves to gold is a good way for China to hedge its exposure to dollars.

For Russia, the case is more convoluted. In the short run, Saudi Arabia is suppressing the dollar value of oil, which hurts Russian receipts since Russian oil is also priced in dollars at the world price. But this deflation has also tended to keep gold prices low in recent years.

When Russia sells oil at a low dollar price, it immediately converts the dollars to gold, also at a relatively low dollar price. When inflation returns, the dollar price of Russia's gold will soar, thereby compensating it for the "lost dollars" or the earlier sales of oil.

What China and Russia have in common is they are both protecting themselves against dollar and oil price manipulation by converting their export sales into gold. While investors may have missed this development, other central banks have not. The withdrawals from the Federal Reserve represent efforts by central banks in Germany, Netherlands, and elsewhere to take physical possession of their gold in advance of a systemic monetary breakdown.

The correlation of dollars and gold, the divergence of gold from commodities, the repatriation of gold from the Fed, and continued large acquisitions of gold by China and Russia are all visible from the data. The conclusion that gold is beginning to behave like money, rather than a commodity, and that Russia and China are using gold to hedge dollar exposures in oil and Treasury securities respectively, are reasonable inferences using our models.

But is something else going on; something that is not apparent in the data and for which the inference would be less certain? Could Russia and China be trying to corner the market in gold?

Leaving aside blatant government intervention such as FDR's 1933 gold confiscation, there has not been a successful effort to corner the gold market since Jay Gould and "Big Jim" Fisk tried it in 1869. Even that corner was broken when the U.S. Treasury unexpectedly sold large quantities of gold after Fisk and insiders had assured Gould that the Treasury would not do so.

The Hunt Brothers infamously tried to corner the silver market in 1979 and 1980. That corner was broken by a combination of scrap silver flooding the market in the form of tea sets and silverware, and changes in exchange regulations that increased margin requirements and hurt the Hunt's ability to maintain their leveraged futures positions.

A Russian corner of the gold market would not be leveraged on futures exchanges because Russia is a cash buyer of physical gold. Russia is also immune from U.S. regulation; the U.S. has no enforcement powers in Russia. As in the cases of Gould, Fisk, and the Hunt Brothers, patience and stealth are needed at the beginning of a successful corner. Russia has both.

Gold Manipulation

A lot of people think about gold as a percentage of a country's total reserves. They are surprised to learn that the United States has 70 percent of its reserves in gold. Meanwhile, China only has about 1 percent of its reserves in gold. People look at that and think that's an imbalance. But those are not very meaningful figures in my view.

The reason being that a country's reserves are a mixture of gold and hard currencies, and the currencies can be in bonds or other assets. The United States doesn't need other currencies. We print dollars, so why would we hold euros and yen?

The U.S. doesn't need them, so it makes sense that the country would have a very large percentage of its reserves in gold. China, on the other hand, has greater need for other currencies.

A better metric, in my opinion, is to look at a country's gold holdings as a percentage of GDP. GDP is a representation of how big a country's economy is. It's the gross value of all the goods and services.

There are different measures of money supply — M3, M2, M1, and M0. In a money economy, however, you can say that the country's gold holdings are the real money. That's why I call gold M-subzero.

The IMF officially demonetized gold in 1975. The U.S. ended the convertibility of gold in 1971. Gold disappeared officially in stages in the mid-1970s. But the gold never went away.

Today, the US has about 8,000 tons. We haven't sold a significant amount of gold since 1980. We dumped a lot of gold in the late 1970s to suppress the price, but none after that. So one of my questions for central bankers is, if it's such a ridiculous thing to have, why are we hanging onto it? But that's a separate question.

Right now, China does not have enough gold to have a "seat at the table" with other world leaders. Think of global politics as a game of Texas Hold'em.

What do want in a poker game? You want a big pile of chips.

Gold serves as political chips on the world's financial stage. It doesn't mean that you automatically have a gold standard, but that the gold you have will give you a voice among major national players sitting at the table.

For example, Russia has one-eighth the gold of the United States. It sounds like they're a small gold power — but their economy's only one-eighth as big. So, they have about the right amount of gold.

U.S. gold reserve's at the market rate is about 2.7 percent of GDP. That number varies because the price of gold varies — but it's around 2.7 percent. For Russia, it's about 2.7 percent. For Europe, it's even higher — over 4 percent.

In China, that number is 0.7 percent officially. Unofficially, if you give them credit for having, let's say, 4,000 tons, it raises them up to the US and Russian level, but they want to actually get higher than that because their economy is growing.

Here's the problem: If you took the lid off of gold, ended the price manipulation and let gold find its level, China would be left in the dust. It wouldn't have enough gold relative to the other countries, and because their economy's growing faster and because the price of gold would be skyrocketing, they could never acquire it fast enough. They could never catch up. All the other countries would be on the bus while the Chinese would be off.

When you have this reset, and when everyone sits down around the table, China's the second largest economy in the world. They have to be on the bus. That's why the global effort has been to keep the lid on the price of gold through manipulation. I tell people, if I were running the manipulation, I'd be embarrassed because it's so obvious at this point.

The price is being suppressed until China gets the gold that they need. Once China gets the right amount of gold, then the cap on gold's price can come off. If it doesn't matter where gold is because all the countries will be in the same boat. As of right now, however, they're not, so China has though catch-up.

There is statistical, anecdotal and forensic evidence piling up for this. All of it is very clear. I've also spoken to members of Congress, the intelligence community, the defense community and very senior people at the IMF about it.

What's in it for the United States?

China is our largest trading partner. It's the second largest economy in the world. The US would like to maintain the dollar standard.

I've described some catastrophic scenarios where the world switches to SDRs or goes to a gold scenario, but at least for the time being, the US would like to maintain a dollar standard. Meanwhile, China feels extremely vulnerable to the dollar. If we devalue the dollar, that's an enormous loss to them.

That's why, behind the scenes, the U.S. needs to keep China happy. One way to do that is to let China get the gold. That way, China feels comfortable. If China has all paper and no gold, and we inflate the paper, they lose. But if they have a mix of paper and gold, and we inflate the paper, they'll make it up on the gold. So they have to get to that hedge position.

Gold is liquid, but it's a fairly thin market. If I call JP Morgan and say, "Hey, I want to buy 500 tons of gold," I can't do it. That would be a huge order. An order like that has to be worked between countries and central banks behind the scenes.

It's done at the BIS, the Bank for International Settlements, in Basel, Switzerland. They're the acknowledged intermediary for gold transactions among major central banks and private commercial banks.

That's not speculation. It's in the footnotes of the annual BIS report. I understand it's geeky, but it's there. They have to acknowledge that because they actually get audited. Unlike the Fed and unlike Fort Knox, the BIS gets audited, and they have to disclose those kinds of things.

The evidence is there. China is saying, "We're not comfortable holding all these dollars unless we can have gold. But if we are transparent about the gold acquisition, the price will go up too quickly. So we need the western powers to keep the lid on the price and help us get the gold, until we reach a hedged position. At that point, maybe we'll still have a stable dollar."

The point is that is that there is so much instability in the system with derivatives and leverage that we're not going to get from here to there. We're not going to have a happy ending. The system's going to collapse before we get from here to there. At that point, it's going to be a mad scramble to get gold.

The Threat of Paper Gold Default

So much of the gold market today is paper gold. We all know dozens of different ways to get involved in paper gold. So much of it is manipulated, which we no longer have to speculate about. It's very well documented. But the whole paper gold market rests on some physical gold. It's like an inverted period with a little tiny bit of gold at the bottom, and a whole big inverted pyramid of paper gold resting on top of that.

What's happening is that the physical gold at the bottom of that inverse pyramid is getting smaller. You would say, "Gee, there's two thousand tons of mining output per year, maybe a little more, and the gold that exists doesn't go anywhere, so why isn't that little brick getting bigger instead of smaller?" The answer is that investors have to distinguish between the total supply, and the floating supply.

The total supply gets bigger every year by about two thousand tons. People don't throw gold to the bottom of the sea. They don't blow it up with explosives. They hoard it. That means all the gold that's been mined is still around, and new gold keeps coming into the system.

The total supply grows every year, and when you move gold bars from the GLD warehouse in London to the Chinese warehouse in Shanghai, the impact on the total supply is zero. A lot of people say that, and they're right. But the floating supply shrinks. Now, what do I mean by the floating supply?

The floating supply is the gold — the physical gold that is available for paper transactions. Re-hypothecation, collateral, et cetera, which supports the paper transactions. The floating supply can be leased, it can be in a warehouse and it can be sold forward on an unallocated basis.

When you take gold from the GLD warehouse and put it in Shanghai, there's no impact on the total supply, but you have shrunk the floating supply. I've seen this firsthand.

I was in Switzerland not long ago, and I met with VIA MAT, which is one of the big four secure logistics firms in the world — as well as G4S, Brinks and Dunbar.

These are the firms that handle physical gold. They're not dealers or bankers. They bring in armored cars and freight planes and use vaults. These are the people handling the actual stuff.

I met with the head of gold, precious metals and fine art for VIA MAT outside of Zurich. He told me that they're building vaults as fast as they can. They're actually negotiating with the Swiss Army. If you know anything about the Swiss Army, it's as if behind every rock in Switzerland there's hidden entrance to a cave or an artillery piece. The whole country is an armed camp.

Over the years, they've hollowed out some of these mountains in the Alps, and built these extensive warehouses, storage facilities and tunnels. All can withstand nuclear attack. Some of them are obsolete and they're getting to the point where they don't think they need as many.

So, VIA MAT is in negotiation with the army to lease these nuclear bomb proofed mountains. He told me that they're building vault space as fast as we can because they're running out of capacity.

I asked him, "where's the gold coming from?" to which he replied, "UBS, Deutsche Bank, Credit Suisse and customers are taking it out of the banks, and giving it to us."

Now, there's another example where the total gold supply is unchanged. Let's say, I have four thousand ounces of gold with UBS, and I them up and say, "please send the gold to VIA MAT".

In that case you have to send an armored car, pick the gold

up, drive it down the street, drop it off with VIA MAT, and get a receipt. It's the same four thousand ounces, but I've now reduced the floating supply because VIA MAT is not doing anything with it. They're not a bank and don't lease the gold out like UBS might.

VIA MAT just watches the gold for you. UBS, on the other hand, is taking my gold and selling it ten times over as unallocated gold on an LBMA forward contract.

How does this end? It ends sooner rather than later when someone goes to a bank like UBS and says, "I want my gold, please," the bank is unable to give it to them. They're not going to be able to get their hands on it. This is happening a lot now in small ways.

There are stories are out there including from pretty well-known people, like Kyle Bass and others, where the bank tells them, "We're sorry, you have to come back in a few weeks. " Then you go back in a few weeks, and they say, "There's your gold. "

Obviously it took them a few weeks to get the gold; otherwise they would have let you in in the first place. So, there's a lot of that going on behind the scenes, but none of it has really broken the system. The quantities of gold haven't been particularly large.

People don't find it in their interest to talk much about this, but it is happening. But what if a there was a failure to deliver gold by a major dealer like HSBC or JPMorgan? That would be a shockwave.

Then I think it would set off panic buying in gold, inflation expectations would get out of control. That could be a catalyst for the next crisis.

There are linkages you must consider too. I talked to a top employee at Goldman Sachs last time I was in China, and he's anticipating what he calls a demand shock in China. He's anticipating a situation where 200 million people run out to buy all the gold they can.

We talked about that, and I said, "Well, that's interesting, because your firm is calling for $1,000 gold. You're the head of commodities trading. Why are you telling me you're expecting a demand shock when you're calling for $1,000 gold?"

That's when his associate said, "Well, that's our research department. We don't listen to them."

I found that revealing. Goldman Sachs research was telling every institution in the world at the time that gold's going to $1,000 dollars. Meanwhile, the head of commodities trading at Goldman Sachs is telling me he's positioning for a demand shock.

It sort of pulls the rug out from under the idea that firms like Goldman Sachs are evil, monolithic forces manipulating the world. I know that's not true because I've known a lot of these people very well. It's also revealing in the sense that here's a major dealer that doesn't listen to his own research department.

The main point however is that there are major risks in the market right now. A threat I've already described, like a Chinese credit shock, could start this gold demand shock that the guy described to me. Then, that could feed into a failure to deliver physical gold somewhere else in the system, maybe Switzerland or London, and then, quickly, the situation spins out of control.

Where does it go from there?

The first thing that would happen is people would start to panic buy gold. The price would start to run up and then, gap higher. Instead of increasing by $10 per ounce, it goes up $100 per ounce. At that point everyone on CNBC would say, "Well, that's a bubble," but it could continue increasing $100 the next day, $200 the day after that. Within a week or ten days, it's up $1,000, and now everyone's calling it a bubble, and it keeps going.

Then, people might start selling stocks, taking money out of the banks to go buy gold. What does that do? That starts to take the stock market down. Then that could start to blow out. From there, interest rates could start to go up.

In turn, maybe a bank like UBS is in a swap agreement with some hedge fund. It's a fixed income swap, liable versus fixed, and it has nothing to do with gold or stocks. But one's given the other some Treasury collateral, and, as interest rates are spiking, there's a margin call. Then the bank says, "You're supposed to have ten percent margin, and your collateral's worth less. Send us some money because you have to top up your margin."

So, the hedge fund sells what it can to meet the margin costs. At that point, the hedge fund is selling good stocks to raise cash to meet a margin call on a fixed income swap, none of which has anything to do with gold. That's how cascades unfold.

Like a earthquake that causes a tidal wave, the damage has moved out from the source, and its hitting communities all around the coastline that are very far removed from the original earthquake. But these are the ripple effects that you see in a highly interconnected system.

At that point, stocks would be crashing, gold would be spiking, the repo market would be drying up and the Fed would most likely be on the phone, trying to keep it all together. Soon after, there might be a run on money market funds.

These are all real world scenarios and real network effects. The problem spreads quickly to areas far removed from the source of the problem. The essence of contagion is that the problem is never confined to the catalyst. It just spreads and spreads and spreads, and finds different channels, all of which lead to dead ends.

Physical Gold Versus Gold Miners

I've always talked about owning physical gold. By that I mean gold bullion, not paper gold. I've also never recommended gold mining stocks — for two reasons. Number one, stocks are very idiosyncratic. Gold is generic — it's an element, but mining stocks are not.

Miners are anywhere from extremely well run companies to complete frauds. You can make money in the well-aligned companies and you can lose your shirt in the frauds. There are bad mining companies out there so you have to be very careful.

Having said that, if you're equipped to do the proper due diligence, it may be the right time to look at some high quality gold mining stocks. I would suggest looking at some of the larger players. The reason is because they've been beaten down so much. When you're down ninety percent, one of two things is going to happen. You're either going to go to zero, or you're going to bounce back big.

You've got to watch out for the companies that will go to zero. There is a predatory aspect to it, too. Many investors may say, "Gee, these stocks are down so far, why not buy them?"

The answer is: Why not wait until they go bankrupt and buy the assets even cheaper? That's the shark mentality. But you have to do the research, do the diligence, read the balance sheets and know what you're doing as an analyst.

CHAPTER 10

The Best Way to Understand the Global Financial System

Backstory

My background is fairly diverse or eclectic. Some people say I could never decide what I wanted to be when I grew up, but I started as a lawyer. But before I went to law school, I got a graduate degree in international economics from the School of Advanced International Studies in Washington.

The interesting thing about that is I was studying international economics at a time when the world was still on a gold standard so I was taught about gold in an academic context in an economics course.

That hasn't been true since. I was really the last generation, almost the last student, to learn about gold in the monetary sense. Literally a year after I left grad school, the IMF officially demonetized gold and so, for several generations since then, if you want to learn about gold, you have to go to mining college or else be self-taught.

After that, I went to law school then got a second graduate law degree in taxation. Soon after I started my career as an international tax counselor at Citibank. I had the opportunity to travel around the world at a fairly early stage in my career, which was a great experience and allowed me to apply what I had learned about international economics in a banking legal context.

Over the course of my career, I made a move to investment banking and later made a move to hedge funds. In those areas and in those firms I learned a lot about government securities. I worked for one of the so-called primary dealers.

The Federal Reserve conducts monetary policy by increasing or reducing the money supply. They do that by buying and selling bonds. If they buy bonds from dealers, they for it with printed money. If they want to reduce the money supply, they sell bonds and remove the money from the system. They need someone to trade those bonds with and the Fed has an approved list. They won't trade with just anybody.

There are about twenty banks in the world that they're willing to trade with. The firm I worked for at the time was one of the banks, a so-called primary dealer.

After that, I joined a hedge fund and learned about derivatives. My career has evolved along the industry from commercial banking to investment banking to hedge funds and derivatives, but all the while I kept my hand in international economics.

More recently, I was involved on the national security side, particularly in the aftermath of 9/11, which I talk about in my books.

In *The Death of Money*, I talk about a study of insider trading and events of the 9/11 attacks and in *Currency Wars*, I talk about a war game — the first financial war game ever done.

I've been able to combine both my background in international economics and law on the one hand with geopolitical expertise on the other to the benefit of *Strategic Intelligence* readers like you.

I've Lost Everything Twice

Other personal experiences — two in particular — have helped form the goal of *Strategic Intelligence*.

If there was a middle of the middle class that's what my family was when I was growing up. We weren't wealthy but we weren't poor either. We had Chevrolet cars, a split-level house in New Jersey and a very "Leave it to Beaver" kind of upbringing.

At the age of 12, my family had the rug pulled out from under us financially. My father always supported the family with a job on the railroad but he was also entrepreneurial and started a gas station. It was a partnership with his brother.

They borrowed some money to do join a franchise operation. Unfortunately, there were price wars going on at the time causing that business to fail and enter into bankruptcy. This was in the early 1960s. At the time, the bankruptcy laws were a lot tougher then than they are today and we lost everything. We lost our house and our car.

We had to pack up and move. If you can picture that scene from *The Grapes of Wrath* when the Joad family gets in their old Model A and heads west on Route 66 looking for better times in California after the Oklahoma Dust Bowl. That was like what we went through moving to a place eighty miles away that we could actually afford. The rent was $35 a month in a bungalow that my grandmother owns.

I was the oldest of six. We went from a very comfortable middle class existence to being on the edge of poverty. Financially it was devastating. Some people who have heard this story say, "How did you put eight people — six kids and two adults — in a two-bedroom bungalow?"

Well, it wasn't easy but we made it work. I ended up on a porch, very windswept, kind of drafty, in the winter freezing cold. And my closet was a nail in the wall. I would take my sweatshirt off at night and hang it on the nail.

I didn't blame anybody. I understood that there are circumstances beyond everyone's control. At the same time, my attitude was, "I need to take my life in my own hands". I had taken too much for granted; I had had a very comfortable existence thanks to my parents.

Suddenly things weren't so comfortable. I made a vow to myself that I was going to take charge and not let this thing happen to me again. I wasn't going to be a victim, in other words.

Again, I wasn't blaming anyone. I understood that things change, but I wanted to be more alert to financial circumstances and try to understand them. If I understood things I couldn't control, I reasoned, I wouldn't be caught off guard.

That was a very seminal experience for me. I decided that my ticket out or my way forward was education. I got my undergraduate degree, a graduate degree in economics and I mentioned two law degrees. That got me on my way and into financial services.

Long Term Capital Management

In the late 1990's I joined Long Term Capital Management as a lawyer. That was another very critical experience for me.

The firm made billions of dollars and I was one of the partners there so I shared in that. Here I was working with sixteen finance PhDs. We had two Nobel Prize winners there too.

We actually had complaints from business schools that we were hiring so many finance PhDs that there wasn't anyone left to teach in academia. Our firm had the founders of modern financial theory.

We had the former Vice Chairman of the Federal Reserve David Mullins, Jr.. We had two Nobel Prize winners Myron Scholes, and Bob Merton, who had invented the Black-Scholes options formula. There were many others, some of who were less well known, but one of them occupied the office next to Janet Yellen at Berkeley. It was the crème d' la crème of finance PhDs.

I invested my money in the fund. My thought was, "These guys know more about investing than I do. I could try to buy stocks on my own, but compared to these geniuses, what do I know?" So I put all of my money with them.

At the time I was making a million dollars a year. I was one of the highest paid lawyers on Wall Street. Well, you probably know how the story ended. In 1998 that fund went down ninety-two percent and we all got back eight cents on the dollar. I was wiped out financially for the second time in my life, first time when I was 12, second time when I was 47 years old.

I had to pick myself up again and rebuild things. Once again, I didn't blame anybody. I made the decision so I wasn't going to point fingers. But I was dissatisfied intellectually.

I felt I did my job, but the PhDs didn't do their jobs. They were the risk managers. They were the modelers. They were the inventors of modern finance. Why didn't their models work?

That's when I decided to set out on a kind of intellectual odyssey to understand what went wrong.

When Genius Failed

To be clear, LTCM was not just another hedge fund failure. We had $1.3 trillion of swaps when we were bailed out at the last minute. As I mentioned, we were given eight cents on the dollar for us.

Wall Street put in $4 billion of cash to take over our balance sheet. I like to tell people, they didn't bail us out. They bailed themselves out because the next step would've been when LTCM went to zero; all those trades would've gone back to the counterparties and would've been no good from their point of view. Then they would've failed too.

It's interesting; we all knew that Lehman Brothers was the next firm to fail in 1998. Then, it ultimately did fail in 2008. It was literally hours away from failing in 1998, though, along with Morgan Stanley and all the other banks.

It was sort of like a plane coming in for a nosedive and about to hit the ground, then somebody grabbed the joystick gets it back in the air at the last second. We were just hours away from closing every financial market in the world.

That's how severe it was to the world financial system. That's how devastating it was to me personally. From that experience I realized there something wrong with modern financial theory. I knew there was something wrong with risk management on Wall Street. If they knew what they were doing, LTCM never would've happened.

It took me ten years. I spent five years figuring out what was wrong in the existing models. Then it took me five more years to figure out what did work. I said, "Well, if those other models don't work, what is the model that does work? What is the way to approach financial markets?"

I spent time in taking courses in applied mathematics, physics, network theory, graph theory and complexity theory. It was good timing too, because by the time of the panic of 2008, I was able to see the crisis ahead of time.

I gave a series of lectures in 2005, 2006, 2007 warning about it very explicitly.

I said that the crisis is coming, that it will be bigger than 1998 and more devastating. I'm glad to say that thanks to my understanding of risk and complexity I did not lose any money in 2008. But I only saw it coming because of my experiences in 1998 when I did lose money and I had a disastrous outcome. I considered that paying tuition for an education that enabled me to see what was wrong with modern finance.

Complexity Theory

My use of complexity theory in understanding risk in capital markets arose as a direct consequence of my involvement with Long-Term Capital Management, LTCM, the hedge fund the collapsed in 1998 after derivatives trading strategies went catastrophically wrong.

After the collapse and rescue, I chatted with one of the LTCM partners who ran the firm about what went wrong. I was familiar with markets and trading strategies, but I was not expert in the highly technical applied mathematics that the management committee used to devise its strategies.

The partner I was chatting with was a true quant with advanced degrees in mathematics. I asked him how all of our trading strategies could have lost money at the same time, despite the fact that they had been uncorrelated in the past. He shook his head and said, "What happened was just incredible. *It was a seven-standard deviation event.*"

In statistics, a standard deviation is symbolized by the Greek letter sigma. Even non-statisticians would understand that a seven-sigma event sounds rare. But, I wanted to know how rare. I consulted some technical sources and discovered that for a daily occurrence, a seven-sigma event would happen less than once every billion years, or less that five times in the history of the planet Earth!

I knew that my quant partner had the math right. But it was obvious to me his model must be wrong. Extreme events had occurred in markets in 1987, 1994 and now 1998. They happened every four years or so.

Any model that tried to explain an event, as something that happened every billion years could not possibly be the right model for understanding the dynamics of something that occurred every four years.

From this encounter, I set out on a ten-year odyssey to discover the proper analytic method for understanding risk in capital markets. I studied, physics, network theory, graph theory, complexity theory, applied mathematics and many other fields that connected in various ways to the actual workings of capital markets.

In time, I saw that capital markets were complex systems and that complexity theory, a branch of physics, was the best way to understand and manage risk and to foresee market collapses. I began to lecture and write on the topic including several papers that were published in technical journals. I built systems with partners that used complexity theory and related disciplines to identify geopolitical events in capital markets before those events were known to the public.

Finally I received invitations to teach and consult at some of the leading universities and laboratories involved in complexity theory including The Johns Hopkins University, Northwestern University, The Los Alamos National Laboratory, Singularity University and the Applied Physics Laboratory.

In these venues, I continually promoted the idea of interdisciplinary efforts to solve the deepest mysteries of capital markets. I knew that no one field had all the answers, but a combination of expertise from various fields might produce insights and methods that could advance the art of financial risk management.

I proposed that a team consisting of physicists, computer modelers, applied mathematicians, lawyers, economists, sociologists and others could refine the theoretical models that I and others had developed, and could suggest a program of empirical research and experimentation to validate the theory.

These proposals were greeted warmly by the scientists with whom I worked, but were rejected and ignored by the economists. Invariably top economists took the view that they had nothing to learn from physics and that the standard economic and finance models were a good explanation of securities prices and capital markets dynamics.

Whenever prominent economists were confronted with a "seven-sigma" market event they dismissed it as an "outlier" and tweaked their models slightly without ever recognizing the fact that their models didn't work at all.

Physicists had a different problem. They wanted to collaborate on economic problems, but were not financial markets experts themselves. They had spent their careers learning theoretical physics and did not necessarily know more about capital markets than the everyday investor worried about her 401(k) plan.

I was an unusual participant in the field. Most of my collaborators were physicists trying to learn capital markets. I was a capital markets expert who had taken the time to learn physics. One of the team leaders at Los Alamos, an MIT-educated computer science engineer named David Izraelevitz, told me in 2009 that I was the only person he knew of with a deep working knowledge of finance *and* physics combined in a way that might unlock the mysteries of what caused financial markets to collapse.

I took this as a great compliment. I knew that a fully-developed and tested theory of financial complexity would take decades to create with contributions from many researchers, but I was gratified to know that I was making a contribution to the field with one foot in the physics lab and one foot planted firmly on Wall Street. My work on this project, and that of others, continues to this day.

Similarities Between Today and 1998

I think it's important to know that no two crises are ever exactly the same. But we can learn a lot from history, and there are some elements today that do resemble prior crises. Right now today, as we sit here in 2015, the damage of 2008 is still fresh in a lot of people's minds. It was seven years ago but there's nothing like the experience of being wiped out and a lot of people saw their 401(k)s erased.

It wasn't just stock prices but real estate, housing, unemployment and students graduating with loans that were not being able to get jobs. There was a lot of trauma and distress.

That's still clear in people's minds, even though it was, as I say, eight years ago. But what's going on right now, in my view, more closely resembles that 1997–1998 crisis than it does the one in 2007–2008.

Let's skip over the dotcom bubble in 2000 because that was clearly a bubble with an associated market crash but not a severe recession. We had a mild recession around that time, and then of course that played into the volatility due to 9/11. It was painful if you were in some of those dotcom stocks, but that wasn't a real global financial crisis of the kind we saw in 1998 and again in 2008.

What are some of the characteristics of 1998 that I think we are seeing now?

What was interesting about that time was that the crisis had started over a year earlier — July 1997 in Thailand. It ended up in my lap at LTCM in September 1998 in Greenwich, Connecticut. That was fifteen months later and about halfway around the world.

How did a little problem that started in 1997 in Thailand end up in Greenwich, Connecticut fifteen months later as ground zero?

The answer is because of contagion. Distress in one area of financial markets spread to other seemingly unrelated areas of financial markets.

It's also a good example of how crises take time to play out. I think that's very important because with financial news, the Internet, the web, and Twitter, Instagram, Facebook, chat and email, there's a tendency for people to focus on the instantaneous and ignore trends.

That's what I call the curse of the two-second attention span. If there is a crisis it's going to take twelve or fourteen or maybe eighteen months to play out. When people hear that they go to sleep, then they wake up the next day and say, "Well, nothing bad happened today, I guess everything's fine."

That could be a mistake. Don't expect the kinds of things in this book to turn around and bite us tomorrow morning. It might actually take a year. But a year is not that long a period of time. It's certainly not too soon to start thinking about it and start getting prepared.

What happened in 1997–1998 was that US interest rates were going up. A lot of people had borrowed dollars and invested in markets like Thailand. There were lots of projects — golf courses, hotels, a lot of real estate, Oriental projects, tours, projects, certain Thai corporate names — but not just Thailand but all over South Asia as well. You may remember the story of the Asian tigers. Some of those countries — Thailand was one of them — had pegged their local currency to the dollar.

If you were a dollar investor and you bought the Thai baht and made investments in the country, the government was promising you that the baht would still be worth the same amount of dollars.

So investors said: "That's pretty good; it takes away my exchange risk, I've got all this upside, I can borrow cheap money, put it to work in a faster growing market, take out my exchange risk, and make a lot of money."

That was an earlier version of what we call the carry trade today. What happened was as U.S. rates started to go up, there was capital flight. Investors wanted to get their money out of Thailand. Meanwhile, Thailand was trying to defend the baht.

That meant that Thailand sold dollars from their reserves and bought baht in order to maintain the peg. It was pretty apparent at a certain point that the Thai Central Bank couldn't keep doing that. The demand for getting dollars out of Thailand was so great it began to overwhelm their reserves.

Finally, Thailand broke the link to the dollar. Then, they devalued their currency, which meant that investors could still get dollars but fewer of them for each baht. That started a panic and everybody wanted to get out of Thailand.

The crisis didn't stay in Thailand, however. All of a sudden, investors looked around and they saw other countries in the region that had their currency pegged to the dollar, with some attractive investment opportunities but that looked unsustainable. Lo and behold, it was Indonesia.

Next thing you know, there was a run on the bank in Indonesia. Everybody wanted to get his or her money out. That led, of course, to unemployment, layoffs, busted projects, bankruptcies, and riots in the streets of Indonesia. This was a few months later but still, people were killed — there was literally blood in the streets. After that came South Korea.

This was happening over the course of June, July, August, September and well into the fall. It was playing out country by country — exactly like Ebola spreads.

In fact, the mathematics of financial contagion are exactly like the mathematics of disease or virus contagion. That's why they call it contagion. One resembles the other in terms of how it's spread.

That's when the International Monetary Fund, the IMF, got involved. The IMF started working up bailout projects. By December, it looked as if things had settled down. We at Long-Term Capital in Greenwich, were sitting around in the early part of 1998 making plans to expand our operations in Asia.

We said "hey, look at all this financial distress." We were looking at buying Asian Pulp and Paper, because we thought there were good bargains to be had in Indonesia. Far from thinking: "We're the next in line", we were thinking "With our $4 billion in cash, what a great opportunity to maybe pick up some deals in Asia." Needless to say, we didn't know what was coming.

Then, of course, by the spring, the crisis hit Russia. To this day, a lot of people say: "Oh, Long-Term Capital, I remember that story; those are the guys lost all their money in Russian debt."

That's not true. We did lose about $100 million because of Russia. But our total losses were *$4 billion*. Not to mention the

$1 trillion of swaps that we had with the rest of Wall Street. Russia was just a slice of that.

At this point, it was August of 1998, and there were a lot of Russian derivatives because a lot of people wanted to buy Russian securities. It wasn't easy to buy them directly and so Credit Suisse and others in particular started creating basket derivatives where the return would be indexed to the performance of certain Russian securities.

But of course when that's done, the leverage increases because there's a certain amount of those securities but if I start writing derivatives, I can write five, six or ten times the amount of securities in derivative from and let everybody make the same bet. So, when Russia went down in August of 1998 that was a shock.

They not only defaulted on their external debts — it's one thing when you default on your external dollar denominated debt, which they did — but they actually defaulted on their internal ruble denominated debt. In theory, there's no reason to do that because they could have printed rubles. Yet, they let their currency crash.

The recent collapse of the Russian ruble was the worst since that time in 1998 when it collapsed even more rapidly than it has recently. Then, that started a global financial panic. Everybody wanted his or her money back. People had to sell good securities to raise cash to meet margin calls on bad securities.

Then, all of a sudden, the good securities weren't so good anymore because everybody was dumping them, trying to raise cash.

I saw another example of this dynamic in the early stages of the 2007–2008 panic.

I was in Japan in September 2007, right after the mortgage crisis started. It was a full year before Lehman Brothers. Remember, Lehman Brothers and AIG didn't happen until

September of 2008. There I was in September 2007, a year earlier in Tokyo, and the Tokyo stock market was going down. I remember my Japanese friend said: "Wait a second, Jim, we don't understand what's happening. You Americans have a mortgage problem, but we don't understand why that should affect the Tokyo stock market."

The reason the Tokyo stock market was going down was because the two were linked. That is, when you're' in financial distress, when you're in trouble, you don't sell what you want; you sell what you can. In other words, you sell whatever you can to raise cash to quell the trouble.

What was happening was that U.S. hedge funds and U.S. investment banks were getting margin calls on their mortgage back securities position. They didn't want to sell those because there was no market or they would suffer enormous losses. Instead, they were selling Japanese stocks, which were pretty liquid. They were selling Japanese stocks to raise cash to meet the margin calls on the mortgages. That's how contagion works.

That's how all these markets are linked. It happened in 2007–2008, it happened in 1997–1998. By August, everybody was selling everything. Everybody wanted his or her money back. Credit spreads were widening. That's where Long-Term Capital lost its money because we were basically "the bank of volatility."

We would sell a security that looked a little rich, we would buy one that looked cheap, and there would be some spread between the two. You could be pretty confident that over time, the spread would come in. As those securities got closer to maturity the pricing would converge.

They were essentially two different flavors of the same security; you're two different maturities of the same security. There was a security swap that was denominated in the same currency.

Whatever it was, it was enough in common that your expectation was that any spread between the two instruments — the long and the short — would converge. Well, they didn't converge; they diverged. They widened. The more the panic grew, the worse the spreads widened and the more money we lost.

We were heading for a complete crackup until Wall Street injected the $4 billion in. They didn't do that to bail us out. They were bailing out themselves. They were, in effect, buying our balance sheets so that they didn't have to suffer the defaults, which would have happened if the company had actually filed for bankruptcy.

That's true of most bailouts. The people putting up the money are not doing a charitable act. They're really protecting their own interests because they're on the other side of some trade that they don't want to see go down.

The lesson is simple. Don't underestimate the power of contagion.

6 Major Flaws in the Fed's Economic Models

For now, the U.S. dollar is the dominant global reserve currency. All markets, including stocks; bonds, commodities, and foreign exchange are affected by the value of the dollar.

The value of the dollar, in effect, its "price", is determined by interest rates. When the Federal Reserve manipulates interest rates, it is manipulating, and therefore distorting, every market in the world.

The Fed may have some legitimate role as an emergency lender of last resort and as a force to use liquidity to maintain price stability. But, the lender of last resort function has morphed into an all-purpose bailout facility, and the liquidity function has morphed into massive manipulation of interest rates.

The original sin with regard to Fed powers was the Humphrey-Hawkins Full Employment Act of 1978 signed by President Carter. This created the "dual mandate" which allowed the Fed to consider employment as well as price stability in setting policy. The dual mandate allows the Fed to manage the U.S. jobs market and, by extension, the economy as a whole, instead of confining itself to straightforward liquidity operations.

Janet Yellen, the Fed chairwoman, is a strong advocate of the dual mandate and has emphasized employment targets in the setting of Fed policy. Through the dual mandate and her embrace of it, and using the dollar's unique role as leverage, she is a de facto central planner for the world.

Like all central planners, she will fail. Yellen's greatest deficiency is that she does not use practical rules. Instead she uses esoteric economic models that do not correspond to reality. This approach is highlighted in two Yellen speeches. In June 2012 she described her "optimal control" model and in April 2013 she described her model of "communications policy."

The theory of optimal control says that conventional monetary rules, such as the Taylor Rule or a commodity price standard, should be abandoned in current conditions in favor of a policy that will keep rates lower, longer than otherwise. Yellen favors use of communications policy to let individuals and markets know the Fed's intentions under optimal control.

The idea is that over time, individuals will "get the message" and begin to make borrowing, investment and spending decisions based on the promise of lower rates. This will then lead to increased aggregate demand, higher employment and stronger economic growth. At that point, the Fed can begin to withdraw policy support in order to prevent an outbreak of inflation.

The flaws in Yellen's models are numerous. Here are a few:

1. Under Yellen's own model, saying she will keep rates "lower, longer" is designed to improve the economy sooner than alternative policies. But if the economy improves sooner under her policy, she will raise rates sooner. So, the entire approach is a lie. Somehow people are supposed to play along with Yellen's low

rate promise even though they intuitively understand that if things get better the promise will be rescinded. This produces confusion.

2. People are not automatons who mindlessly do what Yellen wants. In the face of the embedded contradictions of Yellen's model, people prefer to hoard cash, stay on the sidelines and not get suckered by the bait-and-switch promise of optimal control theory. The resulting lack of investment and consumption is what is really hurting the economy. Economists call this "regime uncertainty" and it was a leading cause of the length, if not the origin, of the Great Depression of 1929–1941.

3. In order to make money under the Fed's zero interest rate policy, banks are engaging in hidden off-balance sheet transactions, including asset swaps, which substantially increase systemic risk. In an asset swap, a bank with weak collateral will "swap" that for good collateral with an institutional investor in a transaction that will be reversed at some point. The bank then takes the good collateral and uses it for margin in another swap with another bank. In effect, a two-party deal has been turned into a three-party deal with greater risk and credit exposure all around.

4. Yellen's zero interest rate policy constitutes massive theft from savers. Applying a normalized interest rate of about 2% to the entire savings pool in the U.S. banking system compared to the actual rate of zero, reveals a $400 billion per year wealth transfer from savers to the banks from the zero rates. This has continued for six years, so the cumulative subsidy to the banking system at the expense of everyday Americans is now over $2 trillion. This hurts investment, penalizes savers and forces retirees into inappropriate risk investments such as the stock market. Yellen supports this bank subsidy and theft from savers.

5. The Fed is now insolvent. By buying highly volatile long-term Treasury notes instead of safe short-term treasury bills, the Fed has wiped out its capital on a mark-to-market basis. Of course, the Fed carries these notes on its balance sheet "at cost" and does not mark to market, but if they did they would be broke. This fact will be more difficult to hide as interest rates are allowed to rise. The insolvency of the Fed will become a major political issue in the years ahead and may necessitate a financial bailout of the Fed by taxpayers. Yellen is a leading advocate of the policies that have resulted in the Fed's insolvency.

6. Market participants and policymakers rely on market prices to make decisions about economic policy. What happens when the price signals upon which policymakers rely are themselves distorted by prior policy manipulation? First you distort the price signal by market manipulation and then you rely on the "price" to guide your policy going forward. This is the blind leading the blind.

The Fed is trying to tip the psychology of the consumer toward spending through its communication policy and low rates. This is extremely difficult to do in the short run. But once you change the psychology, it is extremely difficult to change it back again.

If the Fed succeeds in raising inflationary expectations, those expectations may quickly get out of control as they did in the 1970's. This means that instead of inflation leveling off at 3%, inflation may quickly jump to 7% or higher. The Fed believes they can dial-down the thermostat if this happens, but they will discover that the psychology is not easy to reverse and inflation will run out of control.

The solution is for Congress to repeal the dual mandate and return the Fed to its original purpose as lender of last resort and short-term liquidity provider. Central planning failed for Stalin and Mao Zedong and it will fail for Janet Yellen too.

Self-Organized Criticality

Let's say I've got a thirty-five pound block of enriched uranium sitting in front of me that's shaped like a big cube. That's a complex system. At the subatomic level, neurons are firing off — but it's not dangerous. You'd actually have to eat it to get sick.

Say I were to take the same thirty-five pounds, however, and shape part of it into sort of a grapefruit, and take the rest of it and shape it into a bat. If I were to put them in a tube and fire them together with high explosives, I'd kill 300,000 people because I would've engineered an atomic bomb.

It's the same uranium in both cases. My point is, the same basic conditions arrayed in a different way — what physicists call self-organized criticality — can go critical, blow up, and destroy the world or the financial system.

That dynamic, which is the way the world works, is not understood by central bankers. And it's not just central bankers. I've talked to monetary economists and staffers. They look at me and can't even process what I'm saying.

They don't get complexity theory or the critical state dynamics going on behind the scenes because they're using equilibrium models.

An equilibrium model basically says that the world runs like a clock. Every now and then, according to the model, there's some perturbation, and the system gets knocked out of equilibrium. Then, all you do is you apply policy and push it back into equilibrium. It's like winding up the clock again. That's a shorthand way of describing what an equilibrium model is.

Unfortunately, that is not the way the world works. Complexity theory and complex dynamics tell us that a system can go into a critical state.

The Problem with Equilibrium Models

I've met any number of governors and senior staff at the

Federal Reserve. They're not dopes. A lot of people like to ridicule them and say they're idiots. They're not idiots, though. They've got the 160 IQs and the PhDs.

Every year, however, the Fed makes a one-year forward forecast. In 2009 they made a forecast for 2010. In 2010 they made a forecast for 2011 and so on. The Fed has been wrong five years in a row by orders of magnitude.

They'll say they project 3.5 percent growth and it actually comes in at 2 percent. Then they lower the forecast at 3 percent and it actually comes in at 1.9 percent.

It's the same thing with the IMF. The IMF forecasts have been wrong five years in a row too. When I hear these forecasts and I hear commentators say, "We're projecting 3 percent growth next year based on the IMF forecast," I just laugh. How many years in a row can you be wrong and still have any credibility?

But they're not dopes — they are really smart people. I don't believe they're evil geniuses trying to destroy the world. I think they're dealing in good faith. If they're so smart and they're dealing in good faith, though, how can they be so wrong for so long?

The answer is they've got the wrong model. If you've got the wrong model you're going to get the wrong result every single time. The Federal Reserve, policymakers, finance ministers and professors around the world use equilibrium models.

They treat the world like car engine that works fairly well until it gets a little bit out of sync. At that point you just need to tweak it and then it runs fine again. As I've said, unfortunately, the world is not an equilibrium system.

Now, we pay attention to those models because the Fed pays attention to them. If you're trying to figure out what the Fed is going to do, you need to know how they think. And they're using these equilibrium models.

I don't believe the models are accurate, but I do believe the Fed thinks they're accurate. So the second derivative of that is to watch them because it's a good guide to policy. My own view is that you can't use equilibrium models in a non-equilibrium world. The world is a complex system.

What are examples of the complexity? Well, there are lots of them.

One of my favorites is what I call the avalanche and the snowflake. It's a metaphor for the way the science actually works but I should be clear, they're not just metaphors. The science, the mathematics and the dynamics are actually the same as those that exist in financial markets.

Imagine you're on a mountainside. You can see a snowpack building up on the ridgeline while it continues snowing. You can tell just by looking at the scene that there's danger of an avalanche. It's windswept... it's unstable... and if you're an expert, you know it's going to collapse and kill skiers and wipe out the village below.

You see a snowflake fall from the sky onto the snowpack. It disturbs a few other snowflakes that lay there. Then, the snow starts to spread... then it starts to slide... then it gains momentum until, finally, it comes loose and the whole mountain comes down and buries the village.

Question: Whom do you blame? Do you blame the snowflake, or do you blame the unstable pack of snow?

I say the snowflake's irrelevant. If it wasn't one snowflake that caused the avalanche, it could have been the one before or the one after or the one tomorrow.

The instability of the system as a whole was a problem. So when I think about the risks in the financial system, I don't focus on the "snowflake" that will cause problems. The trigger doesn't matter.

A snowflake that falls harmlessly — the vast majority of all snowflakes — technically fails to start a chain reaction. Once a chain reaction begins it expands exponentially, can "go critical" (as in an atomic bomb) and release enough energy to destroy a city. However, most neutrons do not start nuclear chain reactions just as most snowflakes do not start avalanches.

In the end, it's not about the snowflakes or neutrons, it's about the initial critical state conditions that allow the possibility of a chain reaction or avalanche. These can be hypothesized and observed at large scale but the exact moment the chain reaction begins cannot be observed. That's because it happens at a minute scale relative to the system. This is why some people refer to these snowflakes as "black swans", because they are unexpected and come by surprise. But they're actually not a surprise if you understand the system's dynamics and can estimate the system scale.

It's a metaphor but really the mathematics behind it are the same. Financial markets today are huge, unstable mountains of snow waiting to collapse. You see it in the gross notional value derivatives.

There are $700 trillion worth of swaps. These are derivatives off balance sheets, hidden liabilities in the banking system of the world. These numbers are not made up. Just go to the IS annual report and it's right there in the footnote.

Well, how do you put $700 trillion into perspective? It's ten times global GDP. Take all the goods and services in the entire world for an entire year. That's about $70 trillion when you add it all up. Well, take ten times that and that's how big the snow pile is. That's the avalanche that's waiting to come down.

What Backs the Dollar

All of your assets, whether they're stocks, bonds or other types of assets are denominated in dollars. A lot of people say the dollar is not backed by anything, but that's not true. The dollar is backed by one thing — confidence.

If confidence in the dollar is lost, that means that people almost simultaneously decide that the dollar is not a store of value. They want to get out of dollars and into other things. That's what I mean by a collapse in confidence in the dollar. When that happens, your dollars won't save you. You're going to need the other things, especially gold, fine art and land. There are some stocks that will preserve value too if the underlying assets themselves are tangible assets.

The problem I see is that the policymakers, the central bankers in particular, take confidence for granted. Using equilibrium models that have little relationship to the real world is bad enough, but if they us them them to pursue a certain policy that destroys confidence in the dollar then we have the kind of crisis I'm predicting.

Thomas Kuhn and Paradigm Shifts

The vast majority of the people working at the Federal Reserve are not uneducated they're mis-educated. They are very smart people who have worked very hard to learn the wrong things.

They've learned things that don't exist in reality. Let me back that up, because that's a big statement. When I lecture on complexity or on finance in general I include a digression on the history of science first.

There's a case study laid out in a book by Thomas Kuhn called *The Structure of Scientific Revolutions*. Kuhn coined the phrase "paradigm shift." I'm sure you've heard paradigm shift a million times. It's often misused or it's used as a cliché. Maybe somebody wears brown shoes instead of black shoes and a person says, "There's been a paradigm shift," when all that has really happened is somebody changed their shoes.

The way Thomas Kuhn intended it is that the paradigm is bigger than the model. We construct a model of reality as a tool kit for whatever kind of analysis we're doing. Your paradigm is the way you see the world, the big picture that forms the model that supposedly corresponds to the reality.

For about 1,500 years, from the first century A.D. to the sixteenth century A.D., all the smartest people in the world — or anybody who thought about it — believed that the sun revolved around the earth.

It was called the geocentric view. The church believed it, but you don't have to blame the church. This was science — because it was obvious. You woke up in the morning and the sun was over there, and then it moved across the sky and went down over there and then you went to bed. The next day it came up over there again. So clearly, the sun was revolving around the earth; that was very obvious.

They came up with a model that explained that the earth is the center of the universe, and that the sun, the planets, the moon and the starts revolve around the earth. They modeled concentric circles of the sun, moon, planet, and stars all revolving around the earth, which was the center of the universe. This was science for 1,500 years. People modeled it and wrote equations explaining it.

It wasn't mythology. They could write scientific equations to know what planet was going to be where on what day. Mathematicians, scientists and astronomers, were doing this for 1,500 years.

What happened, however, was, by the late 15th century, scientific data started to improve. This was around the time of Galileo and telescopes. Scientists and astronomers started to notice that the planets weren't exactly where the model said they were supposed to be. The data was coming in at odds with the model.

As a scientist, what you're supposed to do is question the model. But that's not what they did. What they did was embellish the model to account for the anomalies. They said "Well, there are big circles which are called cycles. But if the planet's off the cycle a little bit, then there must be what they called an epicycle or a little circle. So it's doing a big loop, but while it's doing a big loop it's also doing these little, counterclockwise loops." And they kept embellishing it. They wrote new equations for all of this. It is all well documented.

Finally, Copernicus came along and said, "Maybe the earth is not the center of the universe; maybe the sun is the center of at least the solar system. And maybe the planets — including the earth — revolve around the sun."

Then Kepler came along and said, "And maybe the orbits are not circular, maybe they're elliptical."

And after him came Tycho Brahe who uses his telescope to take observations. By the end of the 16th century, Copernicus, Brahe, and Kepler had created a new model, which is the heliocentric model where the sun is the center of the solar system and the planets and the moon revolve around it in elliptical orbits.

And guess what? It works. That's the model.

That's an example of how, for 1,500 years, all the smartest people in the world, using very good math, physics and astronomy, were completely wrong.

The men and women at the Federal Reserve and IMF have 170 IQs and advanced PhDs. But what good is all of that brainpower if you've got the paradigm wrong?

They're using equilibrium models, normally distributed risk, mean reversion, Monte Carlo simulations and other things that are the financial equivalent of thinking that the sun revolves around the earth.

What a small minority and I are doing is coming along saying, "no, the sun doesn't revolve around the earth; the earth revolves around the sun." The best model for understanding capital markets is complexity theory, physics, phase transitions, network theory, graph theory and other applied mathematics that go along with those.

Let's say you're a really smart 25-year-old, and you're trying to get a PhD in finance. Perhaps you're reading *Strategic Intelligence* or the *Daily Reckoning* and you say: you know, I think they're onto something. I think this complexity theory means something.

But your professor, your PhD thesis advisor, is a 55-year-old who spent the last 40 years learning about equilibrium models. They don't want to back away from it. It's very hard when you're 55, 60 years old to say: "Hey, everything I've been doing for the last 40 years is pretty much wrong."

If you, the smart 25-year-old PhD student ask your MIT professor if you can write your thesis on complexity theory, he'll say no. Instead of being the first student to write on complexity theory, you need to be the nine thousandth student doing some minute little tweak on the same equilibrium models that we've been doing for the last 50 years.

If you're the outlier who wants to pursue the new science, you're not going to get your PhD, or you're not going to get it from a prestigious school. You won't be taken under the wing of a prominent thesis advisor or get published either.

And, perhaps most important, you're not going to get a job. That's when the bright 25-year old gives up and writes something that the professor likes instead. That's how, even in the face of new ideas and new science, bad science perpetuates itself — all because of nostalgia. Fortunately, the old models are eventually replaced, but it takes time.

CHAPTER 11

The Beginning of the End for the Dollar

I talk a lot about the coming collapse of the international monetary system. It sounds a provocative, maybe even apocalyptic, but it's not meant to be. The international monetary system actually has collapsed three times in the past 100 years.

It collapsed in 1914 when the classical international gold standard was abandoned. It collapsed again in 1939 when something called the gold exchange standard was abandoned. And then it collapsed in 1971 when President Nixon abandoned the convertibility of dollars into gold. That's three collapses in 100 years. They happen about every 30 or 40 years and it's been about 40 years since the last one.

That doesn't mean the system is going to collapse tomorrow morning like clockwork. It does suggest, however, that the useful life of the international monetary system, if you will, is about 30 or 40 years. We're at the end of that period so we shouldn't be surprised if it collapses again.

I do make the point that when these collapses occur it's not the end of the world. It doesn't mean that we all go live in caves and eat canned goods. What it does mean is that the major financial trading powers of the world sit down around a table and they rewrite what are called the "rules of the game."

So far, I've laid out a four crisis scenarios thus far including: financial warfare, inflation, deflation and collapse. But there are also four different scenarios for the future of the international monetary system.

The Kumbaya Solution

One is the world of multiple reserve currencies where the dollar is still used. In the last ten years, the dollar has gone from 70 percent of global reserves to sixty percent. Imagine that continuing below fifty, down to forty-five. Maybe the Euro increases to thirty-five percent of global reserves and the roles of the Swiss Franc and the Japanese Yen as global reserve currencies increase as well. I call this the "kumbaya solution" — where all of these currencies get along.

I think that's extremely unstable because the system would not be anchored to anything. Instead of one central bank, like the Fed, behaving badly, we'd have five or six central banks behaving badly.

A New Gold Standard

The second scenario is a gold standard. There's not a central bank in the world that wants a gold standard, but they may be forced to do it to restore confidence. That's a possibility. If they go back to a gold standard, they have to get the price right and there is a calculation.

It is arranged depending on how much gold backing you want depending on if you're talking about M0, M1 or M2 and which countries are involved.

Special Drawing Rights

The third scenario is a world of SDRs. I believe this is the most likely outcome.

The SDR sounds geeky — it stands for Special Drawing Right. The name is by design. Global financial leaders pick strange names for what they're doing so people don't understand what it is.

Luckily, the SDR isn't complicated. It's very simple. The Fed has a printing press and can print dollars. The European Central Bank has a printing press and can print Euros. The IMF, the International Monetary Fund, has a printing press and can print Special Drawing Rights. The SDR is simply world money. They didn't want to call it world money because that sounds a little scary, but that's what it is.

They're not new; in fact, they've been around since 1969. The IMF can print them and in the next liquidity crisis, they will do so. In 2009, they printed hundreds of billions of dollars equivalent of SDRs. Not very many people noticed.

They'll be involved in a bigger way when the next crisis hits and we could see the SDR become the new global reserve currency. That doesn't mean the dollar goes away. It just means the dollar would be a local currency like a Mexican Peso or a Turkish Lira. We will have them for getting a taxicab or going out for drinks, but it won't be used for the big things.

When I say the big things, I mean the price of oil, the settlement or balance of payments between countries, probably the financial statements of the hundred or so largest corporations in the world. In the future, maybe you'll get your annual report from IBM or Volkswagen or General Electric and it'll be in SDRs.

Societal Collapse

The fourth scenario is simply collapse, as in, societal collapse. You'd see civilization falling apart.

You might see the president using executive orders to implement neofascist policies. Look at your local police force. When I was kid, cops would walk the beat and get kittens out of trees.

Today, they're wearing body armor, helmets, night vision goggles, flash bang grenades, battering rams, and automatic weapons. They drive around in armored personnel carriers. They're using drones, surveillance, etc.

We have a heavily militarized police force in every county and town in America. Under government direction, that militarization could be used to keep social order. These are the kinds of scenarios you're looking at if the system collapses.

Critical Thresholds for Quitting the Dollar

There is something called a "Hypersynchronous Ising Model" that illustrates how the dollar can collapse. It demonstrates how confidence can be lost and how tenuous and dangerous the dollar's situation is today contrary to what policymakers say.

Let me give you a very plain English explanation of it.

Imagine you're in a room of 300 people listening to a lecture on complexity theory. Everything is going smoothly until, suddenly, four people get up and run out of the room as fast as they could.

What would you do?

I dare say you would do nothing. You'd think that's odd or rude. Maybe you'd figure they got a text message or something urgent came up where they were late for something and had to go. Meanwhile, you'd stay in your seat to listen to the rest of the wonderful lecture.

Now, what if it was the same exact situation, except one hundred people suddenly got up and ran out of the room as fast as humanly possible. What would you and the people seated around you do? I dare say you'd be right behind them!

You wouldn't know why. Maybe you'd think that place is on fire, but you wouldn't stick around to find out. The collapse of the dollar will be no different.

The point of the illustration is to show what's called the

"T-Factor" or "critical threshold". The critical threshold is the point at which your behavior changes based on the behavior of others.

Where is it? It's probably different for every one of you.

Going back to our illustration, for some people, ten people running out of the room would be enough to convince them to run out right behind them.

For another person, maybe two hundred people running out wouldn't be enough to convince them there's a danger. The thresholds are all over the place. They change all the time.

Some days people are bolder and some days they're more fearful. Some days people are tired and other days they're energetic.

We all have different thresholds. Think of the complexity of just that room of two hundred people. Now, extrapolate that dynamic to the whole world and you get some idea of how complex systems work.

Take a look at this table:

Sub-Critical and Critical States

(Simplified Hypersynchronous Ising Model)

Assume 100 People repudiate the dollar in each casein total population of approximately 310,00,000 people.

T= Critical Threshold for each cohort

Case 1 Sub-critical State	Case 2 Critical State
1,000 people / T=500	1,000 people / T=100
1 million people / T=10,000	1 million people / T=1,000
10 million people / T= 100,000	10 million people / T= 100,000
100 million people / T=10 mil.	100 million people / T=10 mil.
200 million people / T=50 mil.	200 million people / T=50 mil.

In case 1, I'm assuming that the starting the place is that one hundred people will repudiate the dollar. What does that mean, "repudiate the dollar"? It means that they no longer want dollars. They no longer trust dollars as a store of value. They may get them because you got paid or you sold something. You dump the dollars and you buy some hard assets. It could be gold, other precious metals, fine art or land.

The next thousand people have a critical threshold of five hundred. That means five hundred people would have to quit the dollar before they're convinced to quit too.

The next million people have a critical threshold of ten thousand. In other words ten thousand people would have to quit the dollar before they quit.

These numbers on the right of the table are the thresholds at which the numbers on the left also repudiate the dollar.

In case one, one hundred people quit the dollar. What happens? The answer is nothing. Nothing happens because you haven't hit the threshold for the next thousand people.

A hundred people quitting the dollar are like four people running out of the room in my example. It's not enough to get anyone to do anything and so the dollar is stable.

If you move to case two, what I call the "critical state", you'll notice that I've lowered the threshold from five hundred to one hundred for the first group. I've also lowered the threshold from ten thousand to one thousand for the second group. All the rest is unchanged. I haven't changed the information for the other 310 million people. All I've changed are the preferences of three one thousandths of 1% of the population.

Now what happens?

When one hundred people quit the dollar the threshold for one thousand people to also quit is hit.

When those thousand people quit the dollar the threshold for one million people to quit also is hit.

At one million people quitting the dollar, you're way past the threshold for ten million more people to quit it too.

At ten million people quitting the dollar you've hit the threshold for a *one hundred* million people quitting the dollar.

You can see what happens. The dollar collapses because no one wants them.

Here's the point. If case one was stable, case two is a catastrophic collapse. The only difference was three one thousandths of 1% of the people. You didn't have to change three hundred million people's minds. You only had to change a tiny, tiny fraction. This is completely characteristic of complex systems.

Minute changes in initial conditions cause catastrophically different outcomes in the system as a whole. This is the world we live in.

This is an actual model that describes the economy — not the one the Fed is using. Are we at this point? Not yet and we won't know when we're there until it's too late.

I can tell you, however, we're getting closer with the Fed money-printing, bank derivative creation, increase in the scale of the system and the concentration of assets. We're getting closer to that critical state and the point at which the entire system collapses.

It's happening slowly and invisibly, but you can see the momentum. That momentum is going to build until suddenly we get to the point where there is a new global reserve currency, which, of course, is highly inflationary. Investors need to get out of the dollar system and there are a number of ways to do that.

You can buy gold, silver, land, fine art, carefully selected hedge funds, some mutual funds and select energy, transportation, natural resources, water and agriculture stocks. There are plenty of companies that have hard assets underneath that will survive the coming inflation.

It's a fairly dire forecast but it doesn't make me a "doom and gloomer". I'm just realistic about what I see. It doesn't mean you have to live in a cave. I don't. I wake up every day. I'm an investor, a writer, an advisor and an analyst. There are always things to do to protect your wealth.

I wouldn't discourage anyone from being an active investor, but just be smart about it and know what's coming.

CHAPTER 12

Protection and Wealth Building Strategies

Today's stock market is a bubble that's being propped up by zero interest rates.

There's nothing Wall Street doesn't like about free money. That's why leverage on the New York Stock Exchange is at an all time high. This is about the worst possible time for the everyday investor to get into the market because of new highs.

People like to say "Oh, well, the stock market has more than tripled since the low in March 2009". But, that was then and this is now. We're five years closer to the next collapse. Is this the time to be jumping in, or is it time to get out, at least on a selective basis? Besides, it has more than tripled with easy money, enormous leverage and very little participation. How long can that last? Volumes are low so you have a steeply rising stock market on very low volume with massive leverage. That is almost the definition of a bubble and that bubble will burst.

This is really the worst possible time to jump in. The everyday investor has to be very, very careful about stocks in here.

Use a "Barbell Strategy"

Not a day goes by without some pretty significant developments in the markets. You should not react or overreact in a knee jerk fashion to each piece of data that comes out. You'll just end up getting whipped around.

What you need to do — what analysts and investors need to do — is have a thesis to guide them. Don't pick one at random, but have a well thought out thesis. Then use the data to test that thesis. There's a name for this: it's called "inverse probability". You use subsequent data to test your original idea.

That method is different from a lot of science where you actually get a bunch of data and then you come up with an idea. Here, however, you have an idea and you come up with data to test it. There is no better way of approaching the markets because nobody has a crystal ball.

Our thesis has a number of elements. One of them is that there is a tug-of-war going on between inflation and deflation, which I've written about in these pages before (In the short-term, I believe deflation has the upper hand).

That confuses a lot of people because they understand one or the other, but it's challenging for them to keep both things in mind at the same time.

For your investment portfolio, that means taking a "barbell approach", which means have some protection at both ends. Have your deflation protection and your inflation protection, and some cash in the middle all at the same time because that's the best you can do with this kind of uncertainty.

The uncertainty is caused by central bank policy. We are in unprecedented times. And that's not just my opinion. If you listen to Janet Yellen or members of the FOMC or members of the Board of Governors of the Federal Reserve, leading economists and policy makers, they all say the same thing. They say these are completely unprecedented times.

I recently had occasion to spend two hours one-on-one with one of the ultimate Fed insiders. Sometimes, when you do these things, you agree not to mention names so, I won't mention any names here. But this was a guy who was in the room for every FOMC vote for the past two and a half years.

Nobody's closer to Bernanke and Yellen than this individual I spoke to.

He's a PhD economist, a very well regarded scholar but not a very well known name because he's not actually on the FOMC. Yet he's been invited into the room to help them figure these things out. And what he said was that we're not really going to know if the Fed's policies worked as intended for another fifty years. He said fifty years from now, there will be another young scholar like Ben Bernanke was in the 1980s who comes along and figures all this stuff out.

In other words, they're admitting that they don't know what they're doing. They're admitting this is kind of a big science experiment. What does that mean for us as investors, portfolio managers and people trying to make smart decisions?

It means that we have to be nimble, and we have to watch the data. We can't put a stake in the ground around one particular outcome because the chance of getting blindsided by something coming up from behind is pretty high.

At this writing, monthly jobs creation has ticked up a bit, with upward revisions for prior months. Even more jobs were created in November and December of 2014 than we knew at the time.

Importantly, real wages went up a little bit. Not a lot, but the fact that that time series even had a pulse is interesting. I've said before that that's one of the things Janet Yellen watches most closely because the Fed has this crazy dual mandate of creating jobs and maintaining price stability at the same time.

They're not really consistent goals; sometimes they run together, but sometimes they pull in opposite directions. Yellen's been putting the emphasis on job creation, but she wants some early warning about inflation. Seeing real wages going up is one indicator where the two wings of the plane, if you will, work together.

Because if real wages are going up, that's a sign that slack is being reduced in the labor market. If labor can get a raise that might be an early indicator of inflation and that might mean we're getting closer to the point where she needs to raise interest rates.

I look at data out so far in 2015, and I look at my thesis, which is that deflation has the upper hand. There's a tug-of-war, as we've described, but in a tug-of-war one team seems to get the upper hand on the other from time to time, and right now it does look like deflation's got the upper hand.

I've said a number of times — and it continues to be my view — that the Fed is not going to raise rates in 2015. And yet, when there's a rosy employment report you say: hold on. This would certainly push the Fed in the direction of raising rates when you have job creation and real wages going up.

Does that change the thesis?

I've spent considerable time thinking about that because we do have to be alert to these trends. To me, deflation still has the upper hand as of early 2015.

Look at the oil patch, for evidence. The US rig count is down, layoffs are going up, capital expenditure plans are being cut; you can see all those things happening.

But they don't happen overnight. It takes awhile to work through the supply chain and all of the places where oil is an input. It shows up at the gas pump pretty quickly and it shows up in airfares pretty quickly. But for some industrial processes, it takes awhile to filter through.

Those trends are still working their way through the economy — especially layoffs. They tend to come in waves. Companies start with some layoffs, and then do more the next month and more the month after that. They wait and see if things turn around, which I don't expect they will.

Compounding those problems is the big eight hundred pound gorilla in the deflation scenario — the currency wars. They're getting more and more intense. Between January

2015 and this writing we saw four rate cuts: from Denmark alone, and other cuts from Canada and Australia. Go around the world and you'll see they're popping up everywhere. And I think more are on the way.

I would expect another rate cut from Canada, and I think we'll see this continue as the currency wars rage on. And you can expect an even bigger announcement out of China. China hasn't cut rates since last November.

They've only adjusted what they call their reserve requirement ratio. That's how much in reserves they have to hold against their loan portfolio. They reduced it meaning they can expand lending with the same amount of reserves. It was meant as a form of easing.

China's growth is still coming in below our expectations, so I would look for a rate cut there. You still have these phenomena where every country in the world, including the European Central Bank, is easing — using quantitative easing, cutting rates, working around the edges to cheapen their currencies. All of that weight of adjustment is falling on the dollar, which continues to get strong, or at least maintains its strength at a very high level, which is, as we've said before, deflationary.

You should be nimble and prepare for both inflation and deflation. Your initial portfolio should have gold, fine art, raw land, cash, bonds, select stocks and some alternatives in strategies like global macro hedge funds and venture capital. Not all of those strategies will pay off in every scenario but some will do well enough to outperform others and preserve your wealth in the overall portfolio.

"Indications and Warnings"

There are investment techniques that I've learned working for the national security and intelligence communities that you can apply to understand the capital markets.

When you have a problem in the intelligence world, invariably, it's what mathematicians call "underdetermined." That's just a fancy way of saying you don't have enough information.

If you had enough information to solve the problem, a high school kid could do it. The reason it's a very hard problem to solve is because you don't have enough information.

What do you do when you don't have enough information?

Well, you can throw up your hands — that's not a good approach.

You can guess — also not a good approach. Or you can start to fill in the blanks and connect the dots.

You're still not sure how it's going to turn out but you can come up with three or four different scenarios. In all probability, the problem is going come out one of several ways. Maybe those ways are deflation, inflation or a market crash like we've discussed. Maybe there's a good outcome too.

A lot of analysts don't get that far. They put a stake in the ground and say, "This is what's going to happen."

The truth is, however, that there are several things that could happen. There could be three or four of outcomes. But even people who get that far start tagging probabilities on those outcomes. They say, "There's a 30 percent chance of deflation, 40 percent chance of inflation, etc."

I don't recommend doing that either. The way I think about these problems is that there's a 100 percent chance of one outcome happening and a zero percent chance of the rest. It's just that you don't know in advance which one it's going to be.

What are you supposed to do? In the intelligence community, we come up with what we call "indications and warnings", or I&W.

Indications and Warnings are the signposts or the milestones on the path to one of these outcomes. Say we have four outcomes — four paths — and you start down the path. You don't know which path you're on and you don't know what the outcome is. But you can come up with the indications and warnings — the signposts. When you see the signposts, then you can begin to know which way you're going.

Here's how I explain it to investors. I live in the New York area and it just so happens that if you drive to Boston all the roadside restaurants are McDonald's. And if you drive to Philadelphia, all the roadside restaurants are Burger King. So, if you blindfold me, put me in a car and don't tell me which way I'm going but you tell me there's a Burger King, I know I'm not going to Boston.

In other words, the Burger Kings and the McDonalds are my signposts.

The art of applying this technique to your investments requires, first of all, getting the possible outcomes correct. Then, instead of just assigning arbitrary probabilities to them, figure out the helpful indications and warnings. Then watch the data, watch geopolitical developments, watch strategic developments and when you see a particular signpost you know you're on your way.

It's an intelligence community technique that I've brought over to capital markets. Believe me, it works. I have years of experience using it. Now, you can use it too.

Preserve Your Wealth in the Face of Financial War

During the Cold War, the United States had enough nuclear missiles to destroy Russia and its economy and Russia had enough missiles to do the same to the United States.

Neither adversary used those missiles and the leaders were quite careful to avoid escalations that might lead in that direction. Proxy wars were fought in places like Vietnam, the Congo and Afghanistan, but direct confrontation between the United States and Russia was never allowed to come to a head.

The reason was that no matter how devastating a nuclear "first strike" might be, the country under attack would have enough surviving missiles to launch a massive "second strike" that would destroy the attacker. This is what was meant by "mutual assured destruction" or the balance of terror. Neither side could win and both sides would be destroyed, therefore they went to great lengths to avoid confrontation and escalation in the first place.

In financial warfare between the United States and Russia, a similar balance of terror exists. It is true that the United States has powerful financial weapons it can use against Russia. The United States can freeze the assets of Russian leaders and oligarchs that can be found both in United States banks and foreign banks that do business in dollars.

The United States can deny Russian access to the dollar payments system and work with allies to deny Russian access to the SWIFT system in Belgium that processes payments in all currencies, not just dollars. Many of these tactics have, in fact, been used against Iran and Syria in the financial war that has been going on in the Middle East and Persian Gulf since 2012.

But, Russia is not without financial weapons of its own. Russians could refuse to pay dollar-denominated debts to United States and multilateral lenders. Russia could dump the billions of dollars of United States Treasury notes they own thus driving up United States interest rates and hurting the United States stock and bond markets.

Most ominously, Russia could unleash its hackers, among the best in the world, to crash United States stock exchanges. On August 22, 2013 the NASDAQ stock market crashed for half a trading day and no credible explanation has yet been offered for the crash. Hacking by Syrian, Iranian or Russian cyber warriors cannot be ruled out. This may have been a warning to the United States about enemy capabilities.

In short, the United States has no interest in intervening in Ukraine militarily and even its economic response will be muted because of new fears of mutual assured financial destruction emanating from Russia and elsewhere. Putin has thought all of this through and has taken Crimea as his prize.

Russia's victory in Crimea may embolden China to assert territorial claims to certain islands in the South China Sea, which could increase tensions with Japan, Korea, Taiwan and the United States.

There is also always the possibility of a financial attack being launched by mistake or miscalculation, which could cause events to spin out of control in unintended ways.

Investors may not be able to change this dangerous state of the world, but they are not helpless when it comes to preserving wealth. A modest allocation of investable assets to physical gold will help to preserve wealth in the face of financial war or unexpected catastrophic outcomes.

Gold is not digital, cannot be wiped out by hackers, and is immune to crashing stock markets and bank failures. Russia has increased its gold reserves 70% in the past five years. China has increased its gold reserves over 200% in the same time period. Do they know something you don't?

A REIT to Protect Against 21st-Century Financial Wars

On Jan. 12, I traveled to Washington, D.C., to meet with an elite group of intelligence, counterterrorism and national security experts. It was the launch of a new think tank called the Center on Sanctions and Illicit Finance, CSIF.

After checking in at the Ritz-Carlton in the West End, my home away from home in D.C., I journeyed a few miles to a side street in Georgetown where our group gathered in a private dining room for our first joint session.

Included were several former officials of the White House National Security Council and advisers to the U.S. Treasury and U.S. Special Operations Command. It was an intriguing mix of seasoned professionals with roots in the military, intelligence and finance. It was exactly the kind of team needed to fight 21st-century financial wars.

Financial threats come in many forms. Some relate to criminal activities including money laundering related to drug smuggling and arms sales and hackers who steal credit card and other personal financial information. Other threats include efforts to end run economic sanctions. These threats involve countries such as North Korea and organizations such as Hamas that are the targets of U.S. and allied imposed sanctions.

The most serious threats, however, are strategic in nature. These involve rival states such as Iran, Russia and China that engage in clandestine financial warfare using everything from front companies in tax haven jurisdictions to cyber attacks that threaten to shut down stock exchanges and banks. All of these financial actors — from criminal gangs to strategic rivals — are within the scope of our group's efforts to help the United States understand and defeat their threats.

Since the 1980s, the key to military planning and war fighting has been the concept of "jointness." Prior to the 1980s, the Army, Navy, Marines and Air Force were not only separate branches of the military, but they utilized their own communications channels, equipment requirements and war fighting doctrine, among other attributes. The result was a lack of coordination and effectiveness.

These deficiencies came to a head in the darkly comical blunders surrounding "Operation Urgent Fury." That was the invasion of the tiny Caribbean island nation of Grenada in 1983. This was the first major combat operation conducted by the United States since the end of the Vietnam War, in 1975.

Intelligence was highly deficient to the point that invading forces were handed tourist maps of the island without military grid lines. U.S. Navy forces fired on and killed U.S. ground forces by mistake. Some invasion force members received maps on which the landing zone had to be drawn in by hand. Communications between the military branches broke down.

As a result, the Congress passed the Goldwater-Nichols Act in 1986, which enshrined the concept of joint operations and joint command. Today, it is not unusual to find an Army major general reporting to a Navy admiral who happens to be a combatant commander in one of the major commands such as Centcom. These reforms have made the U.S. military a far more effective and lethal force than it was in the 1980s.

A similar method is being used today in financial warfare. Major-threat finance initiatives typically involve participants from the Pentagon, CIA, U.S. Treasury, Federal Reserve and private-sector experts from Wall Street, major banks and the hedge fund community, all working together. Our CSIF team is using exactly such an approach to confront future financial threats.

Even as the United States and its allies are refining their ability to counteract financial threats, the bad guys and rival state actors are not standing still.

New technologies such as crypto currencies, Bitcoin being the best known, are being used by the Islamic State and other enemies to buy weapons and pay troops without interdiction by global bank regulators.

Large Russian and Chinese cyber brigades have been mustered to put those countries on the leading edge of cyber financial warfare. Wealth can also be moved around the world undetected using accounting games such as inflated transfer prices in the sale of mundane goods and services. Forensic expertise in law, accounting and taxation is needed to counter those threats.

Ironically, the most ancient financial techniques can be just as effective at avoiding sanctions as the most modern. Classic stores of wealth such as gold, silver, jewels, fine art and land are effective ways to transfer and hide wealth without moving assets through modern digital payments systems. Gold is scarce and valuable at about $1,300 per ounce.

But a Picasso painting, carefully rolled up and stashed in the lining of a suitcase, can be worth $500,000 per ounce. Better yet, a painting does not set off metal detectors in airports. Paintings are the best way to move wealth without detection.

In fact, enemies of the United States are using both the newest cyber techniques and the oldest wealth transfer techniques — such as gold and art — to bypass the major banking channels and payments systems. Meanwhile, conventional financial channels, such as stock exchanges and banks, are completely vulnerable to cyber attack, which can close venues and wipe out account balances with a few keystrokes. These types of cyber attacks are one of the 30 snowflakes that could cause the next financial avalanche.

My takeaway from the meeting with the CSIF financial threat team was that it is critical for you to keep at least part of your wealth in nondigital form. This can mean physical cash, physical gold, fine art or land. These are the assets than cannot be wiped out by digital warfare or attacks on the power grid.

When it comes to stocks, it is also useful to identify companies that have physical assets behind them. Even if banks and exchanges come under cyber attack, these stocks will retain value because they have tangible income-producing properties.

Real estate investment trusts, or "REITs," are ideal for this purpose. They have tangible property assets behind them, which are a good inflation hedge, and they pay attractive yields, which is a good deflation hedge. That's because tax law allows them to avoid corporate income tax as long as they distribute 90% of their earnings as dividends.

One Gold Stock That's Outperformed Bullion by Since 2007

There's one gold stock that's up over 200% since it starting trading in December 2007.

It's not an ETF or a gold miner. In fact, compared to bullion, a gold ETF or a gold miner, this play is a superior way to get exposure to gold.

As a rule of thumb, it's better to limit your portfolio to gold stocks with low financial risk. Many gold mining companies, for example, are poorly managed and expanded too aggressively in 2010–11. After sinking billions of dollars into exploration and mine development, most deliver disappointing returns.

That's why it's better to look for low-risk gold stock plays. Royalty companies tend to have the lowest financial risk. That's because they don't have the high costs that mine operators have.

A royalty company spends shareholders' money to finance gold miners' operations. In return, the royalty company gets a percentage, or "royalty," from the mine's revenue.

Franco-Nevada Corp. (FNV: NYSE) is an example of an expertly managed gold royalty company. Chairman Pierre Lassonde and CEO David Harquail lead FNV's executive team. They've delivered exceptional results for shareholders.

As you can see compared with bullion or a gold ETF, Franco-Nevada is a vastly superior vehicle to get exposure to gold. Franco-Nevada's business model benefits from rising commodity prices and new mining discoveries. At the same time, it limits your exposure to gold miners' large capital and operating costs.

FNV has lots of cash, no debt and rising cash flow. That means it has lots of dry powder to add to its long track record of smart business deals.

Since its 2007 initial public offering, Franco-Nevada has generated almost $1 billion in revenue. Over the same period, FNV also expanded its proven and probable gold reserves by more than 102%. Unlike a regular miner which must spend heavily to replace revenue with new mines, FNV only has to acquire new royalties.

In terms of revenues and number of gold assets, Franco-Nevada is the largest royalty company. Its 380 royalty interests include some of the largest gold development and exploration projects in the world. FNV's royalty portfolio is diversified geographically, with most exposure in safe mining districts: the U.S., Canada and Mexico.

The company also holds high-return interests in oil fields. In November 2012, it acquired an 11.7% net royalty interest in the Weyburn Oil Unit in Saskatchewan for C$400 million in cash, or just C$16.53 per proved and probable barrel of oil. Weyburn has performed well for shareholders.

By owning a business with such high profit margins and a high return on invested capital, you can enjoy a large, growing stream of future free cash flow. The higher gold, platinum and oil prices rise, the faster FNV's free cash flow will grow.

Capital is scarce in the gold mining business, right now. That puts FNV in a great position. Management has $1.8 billion to invest — putting them in the position to create lots of value for you, the shareholder. At current prices, I believe FNV offers an excellent way to boost your portfolio's exposure to gold.

One Safe Haven Where The Elites Hide Their Money

When elites and institutional investors see a catastrophe coming, the first things they look to buy are U.S. Treasury notes and bonds. Making money in the Treasury market is relatively straightforward, because there is minimal credit risk.

Imagine a seesaw. Bond prices are on one side of the seesaw, and bond yields are on the other side. Treasury bond prices rise when yields fall; prices fall when yields rise. The longer the maturity of the bond, the more its price will rise or fall in response to changes in interest rates.

During the last crisis in 2008, U.S. Treasuries soared. From Lehman Bros.' bankruptcy filing in September 2008 to the end of the year, the 30-year U.S. Treasury Bond Index rose 15%.

Over the same period, the S&P 500 stock index crashed 28%. Treasuries would likely strengthen again if we faced another crash. Investors' demand for liquid, safe instruments would overwhelm the supply of Treasuries, pushing up prices.

Conditions can change very rapidly in the bond market, however. That's why I believe an actively managed mutual fund is the best way for you to invest in Treasury bonds. Fund managers can adjust the mix of bond holdings in response to changing conditions.

Treasury Bonds Paid Off in the 2008 Crash

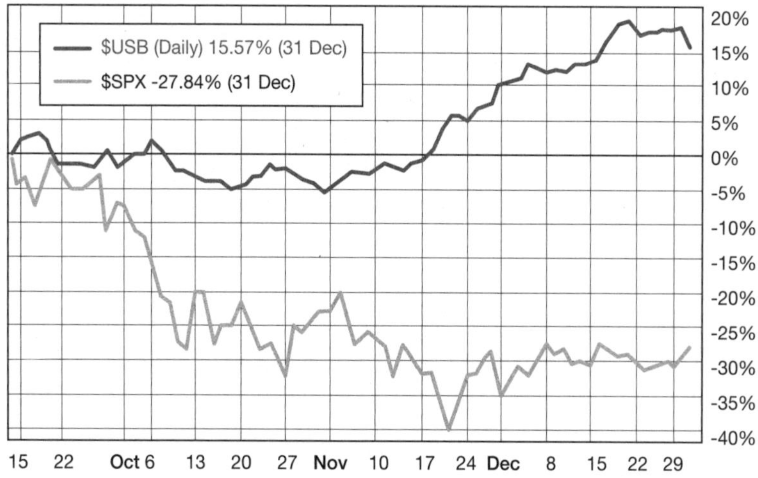

Van Hoisington at Hoisington Investment Management has one of the best long-term track records managing a Treasury-only mutual fund. He has managed the Wasatch Hoisington U.S. Treasury Fund (WHOSX) since 1996, delivering an impressive 8.1% compound annual return over the past decade.

Hoisington limits the risk of default by investing primarily in U.S. Treasuries. All Treasury bonds are direct obligations of the U.S. government and vary only in maturity and coupon. Hoisington wouldn't hesitate to concentrate assets into 30-year Treasury bonds — because the collapse would send their prices soaring.

Going back to our seesaw analogy, the longest-maturity Treasuries are at the far end of the seesaw. In response to falling rates, long-term Treasuries would rally much more than short-term Treasuries. In past deflation scares, Hoisington has positioned its investors to profit from sharp rallies in long-term Treasuries. WHOSX is an excellent deflation hedge for your portfolio.

It's a no-load fund with a $2,000 investment minimum and charges 0.71% per year in management fees. You can buy WHOSX through most discount brokerage platforms.

The Ultimate Form of "Cash" in Financial Markets

Aside from emergency cash held someplace safe, there are safe options for the cash portion of your portfolio. If you want to avoid interest rate risk and want intraday liquidity, the iShares 1–3 Year Treasury Bond ETF (SHY: NYSE) is a good alternative to money market funds. Money market funds invest in commercial paper, which became illiquid in the 2008 crisis.

Treasuries approaching maturity are generally liquid and in demand — even during crises. They're the closest thing to cash in the financial markets. SHY seeks to track the investment results of an index composed of U.S. Treasury securities with remaining maturities between one and three years. SHY won't offer any measurable return as long as the Fed keeps rates at zero, but it won't lose money, either.

How is this any different than the Wasatch-Hoisington U.S. Treasury Fund (WHOSX)?

The key difference is that WHOSX has more risk and more potential reward. It has interest rate risk. Interest rate risk simply refers to how much a bond price moves in reaction to changes in interest rates. Think of a seesaw; as bond yields go down, bond prices go up.

Once the deflation fear has passed, though, and interest rates rise, WHOSX is at risk of falling in value.

SHY, on the other hand is flat. It doesn't move and doesn't pay any measurable amount of yield. But that doesn't mean it's a frivolous recommendation. On the contrary, SHY is one of the safest places to park cash that you may want to use for buying stocks or bonds or real estate after the deflation panic has passed.

SHY is like the ultimate form of cash in your brokerage account.

Why You Should Consider Owning Both WHOSX and SHY

It's good to own both because WHOSX is more of a deflation "trade," with risk and reward, while SHY is more like a cash vault. Essentially, SHY is akin to "cash sitting in a safe" inside your brokerage account, ready at the click of a mouse to buy assets that others are panicking to sell.

If we continue to have mild inflation, soaring stocks and the Fed holding rates at zero, the risk is that you might hold back the potential performance of your portfolio. SHY will yield little (until the Fed starts raising interest rates).

Also, SHY steadily loses real value if inflation persists. But the other parts of your portfolio —inflation hedges like Franco-Nevada (NYSE: FNV) — should keep you ahead of inflation.

If the Fed surprises investors in 2015 and raises rates... both SHY and WHOSX will do well.

The biggest risk is the resumption of an inflationary environment. Interest rates would rise, which would depress the value of long-term Treasuries. The value of WHOSX would start falling, too.

In the early stages of an inflationary sea change, SHY would gain. It would not fall in value, while it would start reinvesting in Treasuries with short remaining maturities paying higher yields.

WHOSX will perform better during a deflation scare that is driving investors into long-term Treasuries. If this continues — and it should until the Fed cries uncle and starts printing again — WHOSX should continue outperforming.

Both SHY and WHOSX would perform badly if there were a repeat of the spring 2013 "taper tantrum." Back then, long-term bonds sold off violently for roughly a month after Ben Bernanke implied that the Fed would taper at some point in the future. At the same time, SHY just held its value, and held the promise that it wouldn't pay interest for as long as the Fed held rates at zero. But that episode was unusual and is unlikely to repeat anytime soon.

And if the Fed surprises us this year and raises rates, as it's indicated it will, both SHY and WHOSX will do well. As the Fed raises rates, the interest rate on SHY's newly purchased Treasuries with short maturities will rise… and the stock market could crash in response to the rate hike, thereby spreading a deflation panic into long-term Treasuries.

With SHY as a cash component in your portfolio, you can afford to wait. If deflation prevails, your cash will be worth more in real terms and you'll be positioned to pick up bargains when other investments start to crash.

If inflation takes off, you should pivot away from cash and catch the coming inflationary wave with your other investments. This tug of war between inflation and deflation is not close to being over and will be the prevailing investment paradigm for some time.

In the short run, deflation is more likely. In the long run, inflation is more likely. And the reason is that the government has to get to inflation. It's not working. They're trying to get inflation, and they're not getting it. We're getting deflation in the short run. But they're not going to quit trying.

So in the short run, bonds are going to rally on deflation. That said, I still like gold and hard assets for a slice; not the whole thing, but for a slice, because in the longer run, they'll do well when inflation comes in.

You may be surprised to learn that even in deflationary times, gold can perform well. From 1930–1933, for example, cumulative deflation was 26%. The U.S. became desperate for inflation. It could not cheapen its currency, because other countries were cheapening their currencies even faster in the "beggar thy neighbor" currency wars of the time.

Finally, the U.S. decided to devalue the dollar against gold. In 1933, the price of gold in dollars was increased from $20 to $35 per ounce, a 75% increase at a time when all other prices were decreasing.

This shock therapy for the dollar worked, and by 1934, inflation was back at 3.1%, a massive turnaround from the 5.1% deflation of 1933. In short, when all other methods fail to defeat deflation, devaluing the dollar against gold works without fail because gold can't fight back.

So don't think that because our portfolio is prepared for either inflation or deflation that you're bound to lose a portion of your investments.

That said, I recognize that volatility and price drops may be nerve-wracking. That's why I've found a new precious metals play I'd like to share with you…

Introducing the PMC Ounce: The Best of Precious Metals With Less Volatility

In a better world, central bankers would aim for true price stability that wouldn't involve inflation or deflation.

But whether you like it or not, central banks favor inflation over deflation. Inflation promotes the goals of the policy elite: It boosts tax collections, cuts the burden of government debt and gooses consumption. It also punishes both savers and cautious investors.

The elites' fondness for inflation isn't going to change. That's why I recommend owning a sleeve of physical gold — in addition to stocks, bonds, cash, land and fine art.

Even still, investors ask me: "What other precious metal inflation hedge can I buy? Does platinum or palladium have a place in an investor's portfolio?"

I'd like to introduce you to a little-known investment that helps you fight back against inflation's corrosive impact: the PMC Ounce. It's offered by precious metals dealer Neptune Global.

The PMC Ounce is a dynamic physical precious metals investment asset. It tracks the "PMC Index".

What is the PMC Index?

It's a fixed-weight index of the four primary precious metals expressed as a single ounce. It basically diversifies you across precious metals. Gold makes up roughly half of the PMC Ounce. The rest is split between silver, palladium and platinum.

The PMC Ounce is liquid and trades in real-time. Yet it also allows you to capture each metal's proven characteristics as a store of wealth, inflation hedge, currency hedge and industrial input.

Keep in mind that a PMC Ounce is not just a *claim* on physical metal; it's physical bullion stored in an insured, nonbank vault in Delaware. It's 100% bullion, it's not a fund, not a derivative and not "paper gold."

When you buy the PMC Ounce, there are no financial instruments between you and the bullion, thereby eliminating the counterparty risk associated with Wall Street-created financial instruments.

The metals are allocated in your name at a nonbank bullion depository and verified to you by them. With one day's notice, either the bullion or the bullion's cash equivalent can be delivered to you on demand. (The tax status for the PMC Ounce is the same as that for physical bullion.)

I like the PMC Ounce because it's a way to own four precious metals in a more diversified, stable manner.

For example, if gold is getting smashed, one of the other three metals may be rising. As the global monetary system experiences convulsions, the volatility of metals will spike. Most of the volatility will be to the upside, but there will be jarring corrections, too.

Over time, the PMC Ounce should yield a higher, smoother return than the return from each metal on its own.

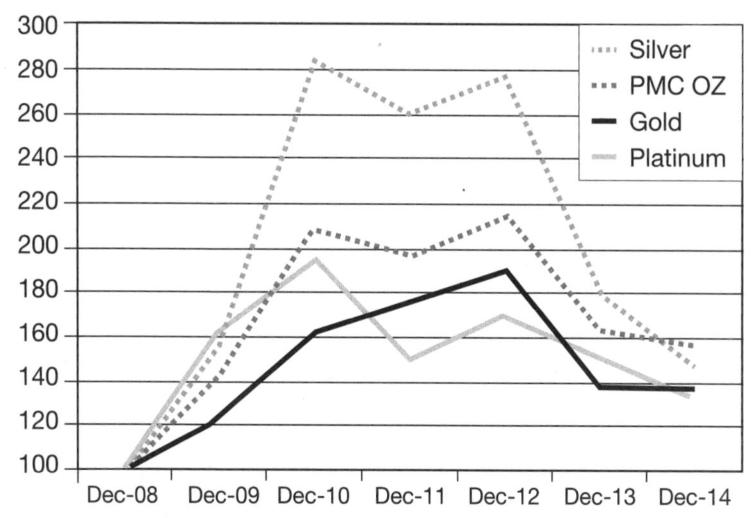

How would the PMC Ounce perform in a deflationary environment? We experienced a mild deflation stress test from late 2014 to the present. And the results were good.

Oil prices and stocks were weak and investors bid up Treasury bonds. Yet these four precious metals held their value. On several occasions throughout this deflation stress test, these metals rose, making them great instruments to diversify your investment portfolio. As 2015 unfolds, investors searching for hedges against both deflation and inflation will find their way to precious metals.

You don't need to worry about management fees, since the PMC Ounce is not a fund. There is a modest premium over the spot price, as with any bullion purchase. You can find the real-time PMC Ounce spot price easily through the PMC Index on Neptune Global's site.

You can also own the PMC ounce within or outside your IRA. For more information, visit **http://www.neptuneglobal.com/pmc-ounce/**, or call Neptune Global at (302) 256-5080. Be sure to mention that you're a *Jim Rickards' Strategic Intelligence* reader.

What I like best about this is that the index actually outperforms three of the four index components with less volatility. That means a much higher Sharpe ratio — a measure of risk-adjusted performance — than either gold or silver.

The reason is that when gold is getting smashed, silver is not, and vice versa. The blended product dodges these bullets and reduces volatility, for a higher total return.

Of course, this product has been beaten down lately, like the precious metals themselves, but that actually makes this an attractive entry point.

Gold Coins

I recommend you have a 10% allocation to physical gold if you don't already. Here I recommend American Gold Eagle or American Buffalo gold coins from the U.S. Mint.

The American Eagle is 22-karat gold, and the American Buffalo is 24-carat gold. The Eagle is more durable than the Buffalo because it has some alloy, but both have 1 ounce of gold.

You should not buy so-called "collectible" gold coins or older coins, because dealers charge a premium that is not worth it in terms of numismatic value. Stick with new or relatively uncirculated Eagles or Buffalos.

Prices are usually at the daily market price for 1 ounce of gold plus a premium, which can range from 4–8%, depending on the dealer. Storage should be with a reliable, insured, nonbank vault near your home or in a home safe. The best security is not to let anyone know you have the coins in the first place.

Monster Box

If you haven't already, I recommend buying a "Monster Box" issued by the U.S. Mint. You can buy them through reputable precious metals dealers. A Monster Box is a sealed container of 500 1-ounce pure silver American Silver Eagle coins. The box is colored "Treasury green."

You should not break the seal on the box unless you actually need the coins for transactions. The price varies with the market, but one box would be about $8,000 plus a small commission based on the current price of silver.

This is not only a good store of wealth, but the coins will prove useful for shopping and smaller transactions in the event the power grid and banking systems break down in a future financial crisis or natural disaster. You can store the Monster Box in a reputable nonbank vault or in a home safe — just don't let anyone know you have it.

Emerging Markets

Some investors wonder if they should put their money into emerging markets.

Go back to the spring of 2013 when Bernanke first mentioned the "T word" — tapering. He implied that the Federal Reserve would reduce their long-term asset purchases and perhaps get on a path to taking the program all the way to zero. What happened to emerging markets? They collapsed immediately.

Why is that? It's because of the "carry trade". That's when interest rates are at zero, and investors say "Okay, I'll borrow dollars at almost no cost, convert them into another currency, and buy local stocks and bonds in places like South Africa, India, Brazil, Indonesia, Thailand and other emerging markets that have much higher yields."

Investors do this on a leveraged basis. That means they have a low cost of funds, a high returning asset, probably an appreciating currency — all of which could lead to thirty percent returns on equity.

What's wrong with that trade? Well, the risk is that U.S. interest rates go up and the whole thing falls apart. The minute that Ben Bernanke started talking about tapering in 2013, people reversed the carry trade.

They dumped emerging market stocks and currencies… went back to dollars… paid off their debts… reduced their balance sheets and went to the sidelines. It's a good example of why emerging markets are not necessarily a safe haven. Think about the linkages we've discussed so far. If you're going to invest in emerging markets, put in the due diligence beforehand and don't go all in.

Istanbul

I recently returned from Istanbul, Turkey. I had the opportunity to meet with a director of the central bank, along with stock exchange officials, regulators, major investors and one of Turkey's wealthiest men, Ali Ağaoğlu, a flamboyant property developer known as "the Donald Trump of Turkey."

I also spent time with everyday citizens from storeowners to taxi drivers and more. Invariably, such a range of contacts produces information and insights beyond those available from conventional research channels and buy-side reports. It was a great chance to gather market intelligence on the world's eighth-largest emerging market.

If you visit Istanbul, you cannot help but be impressed with the indelible beauty of the city. It's easily on a par with Paris, Venice and other beautiful cities of the world. Istanbul also has more than its share of history, having witnessed the rise, fall and clash of empires from late-antiquity Romans, through Greek Byzantines, Ottoman conquerors and Persian rivals. The mix of East and West, Christian and Muslim and old and new is like no other city in the world.

Today, Istanbul is an emerging financial center not just for Turkey but also for a broad region including Eastern Europe, Central Asia and the Middle East. Although Turkey is classified as an emerging market (EM), it is closely aligned with major developed countries as a longstanding member of NATO. It also aspires to join the European Union.

Turkey is a test-tube study in how EM countries reach developed status. As such, it is subject to the interactions between developed and emerging markets, including hot money capital flows, currency wars and the struggles with interest rate policy and inflation.

I returned with good news and bad news. The good news is that the banking system is functioning well, inflation is contained and the currency is fairly stable against the dollar and euro.

This contrasts sharply with a disastrous period of hyperinflation from 1995–2005, at the end of which a short taxi ride cost 20 million Turkish lira. In 2005, the government engaged in currency reform that started by dropping six zeros so that the 20 million lira note became a 20 lira note. The currency has been fairly stable for the past 10 years, and inflation has been mild.

The bad news is that Turkish financial markets are now subject to many of the adverse trends affecting all EM economies around the world. The central bank is under pressure from politicians to cut interest rates and devalue the Turkish currency to promote exports and tourism.

This is a typical case of a country being pushed to join the currency wars. Of course, what results from the currency wars is not growth, but inflation, as recent experience in Brazil and Australia has demonstrated.

Turkey has a large, well-educated population, good infrastructure, strong exports and tourism and is strategically located to act as a conduit for energy flows from the Caspian and Central Asian regions to the Balkans and Central Europe. Based on these accomplishments and resources, Turkey seems poised for continued growth and should be a magnet for foreign direct investment from countries with capital surpluses, including China and Russia.

The Turkish individual savings rate is low, while consumers continue to spend freely using credit cards and other forms of consumer credit. The banks are happy to accommodate this credit expansion, because they are flush with deposits. Turkish consumers prefer to leave their money in the bank, where deposits rates are 8% or higher.

This impedes capital formation because most investment products such as stocks and bonds cannot compete with the high rates offered by the banks. The result is that Turkey is underinvesting, and over consuming, fueled by easy credit. The credit boom has the makings of a future credit collapse similar to the U.S. subprime fiasco in 2007.

The bubble dynamics are not confined to consumer credit. Real estate, both high-end residential and commercial, is in a bubble also, with rapidly rising prices and a skyline filled with construction cranes. This boom is also being fueled by cheap bank credit.

Much of the residential demand is coming from wealthy international buyers, many trying to get money out of unstable home countries such as China, Russia, Argentina, Venezuela,

Syria and Egypt.

Recep Tayyip Erdoğan has been president of Turkey since August and was prime minister from 2003 until his election as president. The decisive victory by Erdoğan in Turkey's first-ever direct presidential election last August has important implications for the politics and economy of Turkey, but the international implications are no less profound.

The large size of Erdoğan's margin of victory, 13 points ahead of the next closest candidate, and the fact that he avoided a runoff by obtaining an outright majority in the first round of voting are both sources of strength and leave him with a powerful mandate to pursue his pro-Sunni, pro-nationalist, conservative, religious agenda at home and abroad. Erdoğan will now be dealing from a position of strength, and that strength will likely grow for years to come.

Erdoğan also serves as a beacon for a specifically Muslim political identity, especially after the suppression of the Muslim Brotherhood throughout the Middle East. His brand of pro-Muslim politics may prove attractive when compared with the secular Egyptians, conservative kingdoms in Saudi Arabia or Jordan or the extreme radicalism of the Islamic State.

Erdoğan is now stronger at home and more influential in the region than ever. He will be able to leverage Turkey's economic and geopolitical power to tip the balance in various disputes among large powers such as the U.S., Russia and China. With the U.S. in retreat around the world, Turkey will emerge as the arbiter of regional disputes involving other powerful players such as Iran and Israel.

Erdoğan's personal star has risen, and he hopes that Turkey's national star will soon follow. Turkish power is on the rise. The danger is that Erdoğan's power rests on the polarization of Turkish society. Erdoğan's victory depended in part on his polarizing rhetoric and emphasis on ethnicity.

If this polarization goes too far, Erdoğan's prospective gains at home and abroad may be undermined in the long run by the divisions that helped him to victory. His AK Party now appears to be involved in the same kind of corruption for which AKP rightly criticized opposition parties in years past.

It hardly needs noting that Turkey is in a bad neighborhood, sharing long borders with Syria, Iraq, Iran and the Caucasus. Its southern border is in crisis, with Syrian refugees fleeing the Islamic State and civil war. The risk of an independent Kurdistan comprised of parts of Iraq, Turkey and Iran is another danger to Turkey's stability, and even the global financial system.

Longer term, Turkey is a highly attractive emerging market with excellent growth potential based on its people, industry, infrastructure and strategic locations. Yet for the next two years, higher inflation, currency devaluation and bursting credit bubbles are potential problems for investors, and geopolitical danger is a problem for the nation as a whole. Investors need to tread carefully in choosing stocks and be alert to the dangers of devaluation, inflation and a banking crisis once the multiple credit bubbles burst.

Turkey is a typical case of a large emerging market with good long-run potential but plenty of short-run political and economic problems. We'll be watching for a good entry point in the Turkish market in late 2015 or early 2016 if the U.S. dollar rally starts to weaken as we expect. For now, you should keep away despite the emerging-markets sales pitches from many retail brokers.

Third Time's a Charm: The UAE's Comeback Story

I recently returned from Dubai, where I was a speaker at an international monetary conference of bankers and investors from the Middle East, Iran, North Africa and Asia Minor.

Dubai is one of seven emirates that collectively make up

the United Arab Emirates, a strong ally of the United States with a potent military in a strategic location near the Strait of Hormuz in the Persian Gulf.

It is one of the two most important emirates, along with the capital of Abu Dhabi. Dubai is the best known emirate because of its efforts to make itself a resort, shopping and commercial center and transportation hub serving a vast region from South Asia to Africa, Europe and beyond.

This was my third visit to Dubai in recent years; I had been there in December 2008 and September 2011. Those two prior visits came just before and after the November 2009 collapse of Dubai World, a government-sponsored holding company, which had $60 billion in debt.

The Dubai World collapse marked the beginning of the global sovereign debt crisis that rolled through Greece, Ireland, Portugal, Spain and Italy over the course of 2010, 2011 and 2012. My 2008 visit came at the height of the bubble.

My 2011 visit came in the depressed aftermath. This latest visit was a chance to see how Dubai was doing five years after the crash of one of the biggest commercial real estate bubbles of all time.

The financial collapse of Dubai World and its affiliates in 2009 was handled in a fairly conventional way. Some debt was written off, some was restructured on new terms and still other debt was converted to equity.

Abu Dhabi provided working capital and new investment to keep projects afloat and to keep systems operating during the workout and restructuring process.

Eventually, the balance sheet was cleaned up and Dubai World was in a position to grow again, albeit with much tighter financial controls and more oversight of projects.

This newfound capacity to grow was evident in the new projects and improved sentiment I saw on the ground there. Rents are now rising and investors are again buying up multiple apartments in projects with waiting lists and flipping them for quick gains.

But alongside this revival of confidence, I found a great deal of skepticism and concern. Bankers and investors are now less worried about Dubai than the world around them.

Everything from U.S. political dysfunction to Russian adventurism in Ukraine, African Ebola and the rise of the Islamic State seems to cast a shadow on whatever upbeat news is emerging from Dubai. Above all, the sense that the world is nearing another global financial meltdown worse than 2008 is foremost in the minds of many I spoke with.

Notwithstanding this generalized global gloom, it was clear from my conversations and observations that Dubai has recovered financially and is once again in an upbeat mood. Despite the overbuilding that led to the crash in 2009, new construction can be seen everywhere.

There were five new skyscrapers being built in a row immediately adjacent to my hotel, the JW Marriott Marquis Dubai. The hotel itself is relatively new; it was completed in 2013, and is the world's tallest hotel, at 1,166 feet.

The most visible sign of Dubai's comeback is the Burj Khalifa, the world's tallest building, with 163 floors, at over 2,700 feet high. Everything in Dubai, it seems, is over the top.

The Burj Khalifa opened shortly before my 2011 visit, but this recent visit was my first chance to go to the top observatory.

What was most impressive, perhaps, was not the view, which one can see from an airplane, but the elevator ride. It took 40 seconds to rise 1,500 feet, and the elevator was silent (except for some piped-in disco music as we prepared to disembark) and produced no vibration or sense of motion.

It was a masterpiece of 21st-century engineering that combined precise manufacture with computerized performance. I recalled my first trip to the top of the World Trade Center in New York in 1975. That elevator trip involved heavy vibration, some banging and a need to change elevators halfway because the lift could not be completed in one ride.

The name Burj Khalifa is a constant a reminder of the out-of-control development and investment policies of Dubai before the 2009 crash. The building was originally called Burj Dubai. However, Dubai received its financial rescue in 2010 from the ruling family of nearby Abu Dhabi and the central bank of the UAE, which is based there.

As a sign of gratitude and respect, the ruler of Dubai, Sheikh Mohammed bin Rashid Al Maktoum, changed the name of the building to honor the ruler of Abu Dhabi, Sheikh Khalifa bin Zayed Al Nahyan.

Burj Khalifa reminds Dubai that despite its glitz and status as a destination in that part of the world, it is still financially subordinate to Abu Dhabi, which holds the real oil and financial power in the UAE.

Surrounding the Burj Khalifa is the Dubai Mall. This is the world's largest mall, with over 1,200 shops, and is the largest visitor destination in the world, with over 80 million visitors per year — more than Disney World or the Eiffel Tower.

I walked through Dubai Mall on my way to the observation deck elevator for Burj Khalifa at 10:00 p.m. It was jammed with shoppers and gawkers from Asia, Africa and Europe and felt like a true crossroads of the world.

One way to participate in the UAE comeback story is to buy the iShares MSCI UAE Capped ETF, (NASDAQ: UAE).

It consists of the largest property developers, banks and industrial companies in the UAE. Since oil prices are near recent lows and the dollar is near recent highs, this could be a good entry point for UAE.

Any reversal in these macro oil price and dollar trends will amplify the underlying returns from the companies in the UAE ETF. We won't be making UAE one of our portfolio holdings. But an investment of this type allows you to diversify away from U.S. equity and fixed-income investments.

It may be an easy way to participate in a good growth story abroad. I encourage you to take a closer look at it.

The Risks of Owning Bitcoin

In late 2014, I met with senior officers of the U.S. Special Operations Command (USSOCOM) in a secure location near their headquarters at MacDill Air Force Base.

USSOCOM includes the Navy SEALS, DELTA Force, Green Berets, and other highly trained and specialized units operating under joint military command to carry out the most difficult combat and intelligence missions. They conduct these missions both alone, and in conjunction with CIA paramilitary units depending on the theatre of operations.

The particular unit of USSOCOM that sponsored our meeting was "J36," the Transnational Threats Division. J36 is commanded by U.S. Army Lt. Col. Joshua J. Potter, and is assigned the task of detecting, disrupting and defeating threat networks that transcend geographic and regional boundaries. Such networks are both criminal and terrorist in nature, and may be involved in narco-terrorism and terrorist finance among other activities.

Our meeting was attended not only by USSOCOM operators but also by members of other combat commands including CENTCOM and AFRICOM, and other government agencies including the U.S. Treasury, CIA and the Federal Reserve. Our purpose was to consider ways to disrupt financial support for the Islamic State and other transnational actors.

In particular, the Islamic State and associated terrorist groups have the ability to use crypto-digital currencies such as Bitcoin to transfer funds from wealthy Saudi Wahhabi supporters to arms dealers and other suppliers of provisions and services. We had assembled financial and computer experts to work with the USSOCOM operators to disrupt the use of

Bitcoin by terrorists.

The particular counter-threat techniques we discussed cannot be disclosed because it would give an advantage to enemies of the U.S. But the session was an excellent opportunity to consider just how far the crypto-currency community has come in a relatively brief period.

So-called crypto-currencies such as Bitcoin have two main features in common. The first is that they are not issued or regulated by any central bank or single regulatory authority. They are created in accordance with certain computer algorithms and are issued and transferred through a distributed processing network using open source code.

Any particular computer server hosting a crypto-currency ledger or register could be destroyed, but the existence of the currency would continue to reside on other servers all over the world and could quickly be replicated. It is impossible to destroy a crypto-currency by attacking any single node or group of nodes.

The second feature in common is encryption, which gives rise to the "crypto" part of the name. It is possible to observe transactions taking place in the so-called block chain, which is a master register of all currency units and transactions. But, the identity of the transacting parties is hidden behind what is believed to be an unbreakable code. Only the transacting parties have the keys needed to decode the information in the block chain in such a way as to obtain use and possession of the currency.

This does not mean that crypto-currencies are fail-safe. Large amounts of crypto-currency units have been lost by those who entrusted them to certain unregulated Bitcoin "banks" and "exchanges." Others have been lost to old-fashioned fraud. Some units have been lost because personal hardware holding encryption keys or "digital wallets" has been destroyed. But on the whole, the system works reasonably well and is growing rapidly for both legitimate and illegitimate transactions.

It's worth pointing out that the U.S. dollar is also a digital crypto-currency for all intents and purposes. While we may keep a few paper dollars in our wallets from time to time, the vast majority of dollar denominated transactions, whether in currency or securities form, are conducted digitally. We pay bills online, pay for purchases via credit card, and receive direct deposits to our bank accounts all digitally.

These transactions are all encrypted using the same coding techniques as Bitcoin. The difference is that ownership of our digital dollars is known to certain trusted counterparties such as our banks, brokers and credit card companies, whereas ownership of Bitcoin is known only to the user and is hidden behind the block chain code. Another difference is that dollars are issued by a central bank, the Federal Reserve, while Bitcoin is issued privately.

The future of Bitcoin and other crypto-currencies is uncertain. One problem is that the value of a Bitcoin is not constant in terms of U.S. dollars. In fact, that value has been quite volatile, fluctuating between $100 and $1100 over the past two years.

This gives rise to tax problems. For example, if you acquire a Bitcoin for $200 and later exchange it for $1000 of good or serveries, you have an $800 gain on the purchase and sale of the Bitcoin itself. From the perspective of the IRS, this gain is no different than if you had purchased a share of stock for $200 and later sold it for $1000. You have to report the $800 as a capital gain.

It seems unlikely that most Bitcoin users are reporting these gains. Those who do not may be involved in tax evasion. The IRS has broad powers to investigate evasion, and may require counterparties to reveal information, including computer keys, which can lead to discovery of the transacting parties.

Given the fact that the IRS has engaged in selective enforcement against Tea Party activists and other political opponents in recent years, this is a serious potential problem for libertarian users of Bitcoin.

Another problem is that Bitcoin and the other crypto-currencies have not survived a complete business and credit cycle yet. Bitcoin, the first crypto-currency, was invented in 2009. The global economy has been in a weak expansion since then, but has not experienced a financial panic or technical recession.

Investors have some experience with how stocks, bonds, gold and other asset classes might perform in a downturn, but we have no experience with Bitcoin. Will liquidity dry up and prices plunge? Or will investors consider it a safe harbor, which will lead to price increases? We don't know the answer.

In the end, it may be the case that Bitcoin will fade as a currency, but survive as a technology. The encrypted block chain technology is useful for a variety of asset transfers beside currency. It can be used to transfer title to land, securities, and other assets in secure, inexpensive ways.

It is this technology potential, more than the currency itself that has attracted the interest of investors such as the Winklevoss twins and Marc Andreesen. While start-up companies in Bitcoin may be highly speculative for the time being, there may be attractive investment opportunities in this arena in the years ahead.

My day with the operators, as the Special Forces are called, was a fascinating blend of technologists, commandos, and economists working together to counter a threat to U.S. national security from the use by terrorists of crypto-currencies to finance terror. I have participated in such collaborations before and it's always heartening to encounter the brilliance of our military leaders and elite forces.

Many of the colonels and generals whom I meet have graduate degrees in demanding technical fields, speak multiple languages, and have deployed in diverse civilizations and cultures on every continent. The U.S. has the finest military in the world capable of defeating any threat including new threats arising from the blend of technology and finance.

In addition to being a threat, Bitcoin and its crypto cousins also represent an opportunity. It is still too early for investors to hold Bitcoin in their portfolios due to excessive volatility and unresolved tax issues.

But the time may come, sooner than later, when some Bitcoin technology companies might warrant investor interest based on their possible role in the future of payments and in other forms of wealth transfer. Companies such as Western Union and PayPal dominate the private payments systems space today. They may have company from crypto-currency start-ups soon.

Get Paid 2.6% For Having Hyperinflation Insurance By Dan Amoss, CFA

My top investment analyst, Dan Amoss, researched one play he believes will benefit during a hyperinflationary scenario. It pays a handsome dividend while providing you with "hyperinflation insurance"...

With a few clicks in your brokerage account, you can own hyperinflation insurance *while* getting paid 2.6%.

"Hyperinflation does not affect everyone in a society equally," wrote Jim. "There are distinct sets of winners and losers."

The best hedges to protect you from hyperinflation are gold, foreign currency, land and other hard assets. Jim defines "other" hard assets as: factories, natural resources and transportation equipment.

Fortunately, through my research, I've uncovered an exchange traded fund (ETF) that combines the very best hard asset businesses in the stock market.

It's called the **Schwab U.S. Dividend Equity ETF (SCHD:**

NYSE) and it will maintain or even build your wealth through the chaos of hyperinflation...

SCHD tracks the total return of the Dow Jones U.S. Dividend 100 Index. That's a list of U.S. companies with track records of paying reliable cash dividends.

All the stocks held in SCHD — which currently pays you a 2.6% dividend yield — must have sustained at least 10 consecutive years of dividend payments. The managers of this ETF review its holdings annually and rebalance them quarterly.

Two top reviewers of ETFs agree: the Schwab U.S. Dividend Equity ETF is among the best.

Morningstar, an independent investment research firm, says SCHD's mix of top-quality businesses is better than other dividend-focused ETFs. Their yardstick is what's called a "wide-moat" rating. It quantifies how likely a company is able beat its competitors over time.

Through a hyperinflation, you'll want to own companies that are most likely to be thriving for decades into the future. Sixty-three percent of SCHD's holdings receive a "wide-moat rating" from Morningstar — the highest among dividend ETFs. In other words, SCHD is primed to thrive through thick and thin.

Another independent review by New Constructs, gives SCHD the highest possible marks. New Constructs is an investment research firm specializing in quality-of-earnings and forensic accounting analysis of U.S. public companies.

While many of the stocks held in SCHD are expensive, its valuation won't matter much in a hyperinflationary episode. Since SCHD charges a management fee of just 7 basis points, or 0.07%, you're paying a tiny sum to own a portfolio of the market's very best companies.

If you decide to reinvest the dividends when you place your buy order, and hold SCHD over the long term, your hyperinflation hedge will strengthen. Here's why: dividends that build up as a cash stockpile in your account can be devalued in a hyperinflation. Reinvesting dividends would increase the number of SCHD shares you own over time, growing the strength of your hyperinflation insurance.

Your specific circumstances and risk tolerance will determine how much you allocate to this idea. As always, Jim recommends maintaining a diversified portfolio, including cash and Treasury bonds. Cash and Treasuries are hedges against deflation. Deflation may be more likely in the near term. But history shows that hyperinflation is a long-term risk for any paper money system.

Recommended Reading

In addition to actionable investment opportunities, there are several books I recommend to my readers. Each will help investors understand our complex financial system...

Money and Tough Love

The Washington, D.C., area is thick with secret agencies with "three-letter names" such as CIA, FBI, NSA and less well-known outfits such as the Defense Intelligence Agency (DIA) and the Director of National Intelligence (DNI).

One of the most powerful, and also most secretive, of these agencies is an institution that is not even part of the U.S. government. It's an autonomous part of an emerging scheme of global governance accountable only to a small elite of central bankers, finance ministers and heads of state. That institution is the International Monetary Fund, or the IMF.

Everything about the IMF is designed to deceive you — beginning with the name. The IMF is not really a "fund" in the sense of an endowment or mutual fund; it functions as the central bank of the world taking deposits, called "borrowings," from countries around the world and making loans to its members.

It prints money like most central banks, but this world money has the opaque name of special drawing right, or SDR. It has a convoluted governance structure in which the highest decision-making body, the Board of Governors, has little power, because the votes are weighted in favor of the largest economies, such as the U.S. Actual power rests with the blandly named International Monetary and Finance Committee, the IMFC.

Everything about the IMF is designed to make it difficult for outsiders like you to have any idea what is going on. The insiders like that arrangement just fine.

Given this culture and history, it was surprising to see the recent publication of a book by Liaquat Ahamed, *Money and Tough Love — On Tour With the IMF.* The book is the most detailed account yet from behind the scenes at IMF headquarters.

The author also reports on an IMF annual meeting in Tokyo and goes on the road with IMF "missions" as they monitor large and small governments around the world. These missions are the key to forcing governments to conform to the "rules of the game" as established by the global monetary elites.

Ahamed had difficulty getting the cooperation of the IMF and access to IMF meetings and missions he needed to write the book. In the opening section, he writes, I soon discovered that gaining access to the world behind its doors would not be easy. The fund is the repository of many secrets, which it guards ferociously. It does its work behind the scenes, out of the public eye, and has a history of being wary of the press… The Fund benefited from a certain mystique that could be lost by too much openness.

In the end, Ahamed was granted access by IMF Managing Director Christine Lagarde. What follows is a revealing account that is part history, part economics and part James Bond as Ahamed travels from Washington to Tokyo, Dublin and Maputo, Mozambique. He describes IMF interactions with other members of the global power elite as well as the IMF's member countries in both the developed world and among the poorest.

Importantly, the book is highly accessible. Ahamed avoids the arcane jargon that fills most accounts of the IMF as well as the IMF's official publications and reports. Anyone with the slightest interest in the workings of the international monetary system will find this book an excellent guide to how the IMF goes about its business on a day-to-day basis, and how the IMF has the power to make or break sovereign governments by deciding whether or not to make loans when those governments are in financial distress.

One of the book's main takeaways is the demonstration that the IMF is just as powerful as the military and CIA when it comes to forcing regime change in governments that do not follow U.S. orders. Of course, the IMF does this without firing a shot. They use money as a weapon just as effectively as the military uses special operations or the CIA uses drones.

Second, if Western nations lose votes in the IMF and those votes are given to communist China — as is currently planned — then the IMF money weapons may be aimed at the U.S. in the future.

In recent decades, the emerging markets and southern Europe have needed IMF bailouts. In the future, the U.S. may be the one that needs to be bailed out, and we may have to accept conditions imposed by China or the BRICS using the IMF as their monetary agent.

The book is also timely. While the IMF has always been opaque, its importance to global finance has waxed and waned over the decades. Now the IMF is about to enter its most powerful stage yet. Central banks bailed out the world in 2008. The next financial panic will be bigger than the ability of central banks to put out the fire. At that point, the only source of global liquidity will be the IMF itself.

The issuance of 5 trillion of SDRs, equal to $7.5 trillion, to paper over the next financial panic will be highly inflationary. The difference between this coming inflation and those in the past is that few investors will know where the inflation is coming from. Politically, it will not be easy to hold the U.S. Treasury or the Federal Reserve accountable, because they will just point a finger at the IMF.

This book will make you better acquainted than most with this hidden source of inflation. Ahamed's book is a good chance to meet the financial world's fire department before the next great fire.

The Downfall of Money

Despite the widespread identification of "Weimar" with hyperinflation, few investors know the detailed history and political dynamics that led to Germany's catastrophic outcome. The facts that Germany had recently been defeated in the first World War and bore a heavy debt burden in the form of reparations to France, the U.K. and other victorious powers are necessary background.

You may also know that communists and proto-Nazis fought street battles, led regional rebellions and engaged in assassinations of high-profile political figures. But even this backdrop does not tell the whole story.

To understand exactly what happened, and why a repetition in the U.S. is a real possibility today, I highly recommend *The Downfall of Money: Germany's Hyperinflation and the Destruction of the Middle Class,* by Frederick Taylor. This is the best and most thorough account of the Weimar hyperinflation yet and is likely to remain the definitive history.

Most accounts of the Weimar hyperinflation focus on Rudolf Havenstein, the director of the Reichsbank, the central bank of Germany. Havenstein had control of the printing presses and was directly responsible for the physical production of the banknotes, eventually denominated in the trillions of marks.

At one point, the Reichsbank printed such huge volumes of currency that they were physically constrained by paper shortages. They even resorted to printing on one side of the banknote in order to save ink, which was also in short supply. Havenstein is routinely portrayed as the villain in the story — the man whose money printing ruined the German currency and its economy.

Yet Taylor makes almost no mention of Havenstein, referring to him only a few times in this 400-page book. Instead, Taylor takes aim at the political leadership that refused to compromise on the structural reforms needed to restore growth to the German economy so it could begin to deal with its debt burden.

Politicians looked to the central bank to paper over their problems rather than fix the problem themselves. In this analysis, Havenstein is not an autonomous actor out to destroy the currency. He is simply the handmaiden of a weak, dysfunctional political class who refuse to make hard choices themselves.

This insight, which is well documented by Taylor and clearly described, is of the utmost importance as you try to assess the risks of hyperinflation in the U.S. today. Investors like to point fingers at Ben Bernanke and Janet Yellen for "printing" (actually digitally creating) trillions of U.S. dollars out of thin air.

But today's problems in the U.S. economy, too much debt and too little growth, are identical to the problems confronting Germany in 1921. Then, as now, the solutions were mainly structural. Then, as now, the politicians refused to compromise on solutions and looked to the central bank to paper over the problems. Then, as now, the central bank accommodated the politicians.

The name for this phenomenon is *fiscal dominance*, something described by former Federal Reserve Governor Frederic Mishkin in a classic academic paper in 2013. Mishkin says that central bank independence is largely a myth and only appears to be a reality during stable economic times.

But when the legislative and executive branches become dysfunctional, as they are today, and when debts and deficits spin out of control, as they appear to be, then central banks must bow to the politicians and monetize the debt by money printing. This is what happened in Germany in 1921–23. Something similar may be starting to happen in the U.S. today.

The U.S. is not yet at the point of no return that Germany reached in 1921. But it is moving in the same direction. It has a dysfunctional political class and accommodating central bankers. Taylor's book is must-read if you want to know about the warning signs of hyperinflation before its most virulent stage wipes out your savings and pensions.

Mark Twain once wrote, "No occurrence is sole and solitary, but is merely a repetition of a thing which has happened before." Taylor's insightful and lucid account offers an historic guide to something that has happened before and that may repeat in the U.S. under remarkably similar conditions.

When Money Dies

Taylor's book is the second account of the Weimar hyperinflation published in recent years. An earlier book, *When Money Dies*, by Adam Fergusson, was republished in 2010 and received excellent reviews. I recommend it too, but it does not have the depth of Taylor's account.

Fergusson extensively chronicles events and includes moving anecdotes about food riots, starvation and suicide, showing the social impact of hyperinflation. Taylor's book does too, but dives deeper into the political dynamics that allowed the hyperinflation to begin and continue. In short, Fergusson gives you the *what* and *when* of Weimar, while Taylor gives you the why.

The Forgotten Man — A New History of the Great Depression

The Great Depression in the United States is conventionally dated from 1929 to 1940. It began with the stock market crash in October 1929, and only ended when the U.S. massively restructured its economy to produce war material, first for our allies, particularly the U.K., in 1940, and later for our own forces after the U.S. entered the Second World War in December 1941.

Like any dating scheme, these dates are somewhat arbitrary. The U.S. depression was part of a larger global depression that was visible in the U.K. in 1926, and in Germany in 1927, and that was not fully resolved until the new international monetary arrangements agreed at Bretton Woods in 1944 and implemented in the post-war years. But the core period, 1929–1940, covering President Hoover's single term, and the first two terms of President Franklin Roosevelt, are the object of intensive interest by historians and scholars to this day.

The term "depression" is not well understood and is not in wide use today. Economists prefer terms like "recession," which means two or more consecutive quarters of declining GDP with rising unemployment, and "expansion" which covers periods of rising GDP between recessions. Economists like the fact that *recession* is mathematically defined and measurable, whereas *depression* is subjectively defined and somewhat in the eye of the beholder. Policymakers avoid using words like depression for fear that the public may become depressed and stop spending — the opposite of what is desired. As a result, the word depression has been more or less swept under the rug of economic discourse today.

This is unfortunate because the term depression is useful in economic analysis. Depression does not imply long periods of declining GDP. It is possible to have rising GDP, falling unemployment and rising stock prices in a depression. Indeed, this is exactly what happened from 1933 to 1936 in the middle of the Great Depression.

What characterizes a depression is that growth does not return to long-term potential, and total output, labor force participation and asset prices languish below prior peaks in some combination. This definition was first laid out by John Maynard Keynes in 1936 in his magnum opus, *The General Theory of Employment, Interest and Money*. It is not mathematically precise, but it is highly serviceable.

The importance of Keynes's definition is that depressions are not merely longer or more persistent versions of a recession. They are qualitatively different. A recession is a cyclical phenomena amenable to liquidity and interest rate solutions applied by central banks, whereas depressions are structural and do not respond to central bank remedies.

Depressions are only cured by structural changes in areas such as fiscal policy, regulation, and labor markets that are not controlled by central banks, but rather by legislatures and the executive. Indeed, the U.S. is in a depression today, and its persistence is due to the fact that positive structural changes have not been implemented. Federal Reserve policy is futile in a depression.

Because depression has been dropped from the economist's tool kit, few are familiar with depression dynamics. Because the last depression was 80 years ago, there is almost no one alive today with a living memory of a depression. This vacuum of analysis and experience lends urgency to the historic study of depressions, and there is no finer history of the Great Depression than Amity Shlaes' *The Forgotten Man*.

The conventional narrative of the Great Depression is known by rote. Herbert Hoover and the Federal Reserve are the typical villains who committed a series of policy blunders that first caused the depression, and then failed to alleviate it.

Franklin Roosevelt is portrayed as the hero who saved

the day and led the country back to growth through activism, government programs and massive spending. This narrative has been the blueprint and justification for liberal government intervention and spending programs ever since.

What Shlaes show is that this narrative is almost completely wrong. Her book is a kind of alternative history, but one much closer to the truth of what happened in the 1930s. She shows that there was a great deal of continuity between the Hoover and Roosevelt administrations. Both were activists and interventionists.

Both believed in public works and government spending. Major depression-era projects such as the Hoover Dam were begun in the Hoover administration; Roosevelt merely continued such hydroelectric and flood control projects on a larger scale with his Tennessee Valley Authority and other projects.

Importantly, Roosevelt did not end the depression in the 1930s; he merely managed it with mixed results until the exigencies of war production finally helped the U.S. escape it. Indeed, the U.S. had a severe relapse in 1937–38, the famous "recession within a depression," that reversed some of the gains from the period of Roosevelt's first term.

Shlaes also shines a light on the dark side of government policy in the Hoover-Roosevelt years. She exposes the admiration that many at the time had for dictators such as Mussolini and Stalin who seemed to be achieving economic growth through top-down central planning.

She also describes the collectivist farming communities and labor concentration camps launched by the U.S. government in those years. The extent of socialist and communist leanings among major Roosevelt administration figures is well known and Shlaes covers that ground thoroughly.

The book is balanced in its approach. Shlaes is meticulous in describing the growth that was achieved and the jobs that were created by FDR's programs. She is also glowing in her praise for the artistic, literary and architectural achievements in those days coming from various government sponsored programs for writers and artists, and in public works.

The mystery of the Great Depression is not why it began but why it lasted so long. The U.S. had been in a severe depression in 1921, but it lasted 18 months, not 12 years. The answer appears to be something economists call *regime uncertainty.*

The Hoover-Roosevelt programs seemed to come out of nowhere and disappear just as quickly confusing business leaders. Programs were launched with great fanfare then abandoned based either on Supreme Court decisions declaring them unconstitutional or because of their failure to produce results.

In response, private capital went to the sidelines and refused to invest. Instead of a labor strike, there was a capital strike. No amount of government intervention could make up for the lack of private capital investment caused by the policy uncertainty of those years.

Shlaes makes this clear both through quantitative research, and through individual portraits of Andrew Mellon, Wendell Willkie, and less known figures such as Bill Wilson, the founder of Alcoholics Anonymous. These individuals kept private initiative alive during a decade in which government pretended to have all the answers

Shlaes has done prodigious research and writes indelibly. Her book is worth reading for its literary and historical qualities alone. But the book carries important economic lessons for investors and policymakers today.

As the U.S. struggles through a new depression, regime uncertainty in policies such as Obamacare, environmental and internet regulation, and changes in labor laws have once again caused capital to go on strike. The implication is that the current period of low growth in the U.S. will continue indefinitely until positive structural changes and greater clarity in public policy are achieved. This new depression may be a long one.

Shlaes' excellent book is a great work of history, but an equally great guide to where we are today, and where we may be heading. I recommend it to you.

CHAPTER 13

Thirty-Five Frequently Asked Questions Answered

I often receive questions from my *Strategic Intelligence* subscribers. We try to get to as many of them as possible during our monthly intelligence briefings and in our monthly issues. I've noticed that many are the same. Here are thirty-five of the most frequently asked questions answered. I hope you find them useful as you invest...

1) What is one book that I can read on complexity theory?

There's a book called *Simply Complexity* by Neil Johnson. I recommend that as an introduction.

2) Do you think the Ebola virus will be the snowflake that causes the financial avalanche?

I think it's a very serious matter that will have very serious economic impacts. But I don't think it's the snowflake that will cause the financial avalanche. The reason I say that is because the snowflake will, almost by definition, be the thing you don't see coming. It will be something that none of us have thought about. We can see Ebola coming and know that it's going to have some economic impact. Maybe it adds to the slowdown in global growth but it's probably not the snowflake that starts the avalanche — only because we know so much about it.

3) Would you recommend buying silver in addition to gold?

Silver has a place in investors' portfolio. I don't believe in a fixed silver/gold ratio. A lot of people put stock in that concept but silver's harder to analyze because it's a precious metal and also an industrial input so it moves on different vectors. That said, if gold's going to $7,000 per ounce, which I expect, silver's going to go to $100 or more. So silver's along for the ride and I think silver has a place.

By the way, I do recommend the monster box. The monster box comes from the U.S. Mint. It's 500 1-ounce American silver eagles. That's good to have because if the time comes when they shut down the ATMs and you need precious metal for walking-around money to buy groceries for your family, you're not going to want to hand over a gold coin. A silver coin's probably enough. Having a monster box is a good insurance policy.

4) Do you think inflation or deflation is more likely?"

I think they're both likely and that's what makes it so challenging for investors. Again, I go back to our friend Warren Buffett. He owns hard assets as his inflation insurance. But he also has $55 billion in cash — the most cash that Berkshire Hathaway has ever had — that's his deflation insurance. Buffett understands that both are possible.

I think we'll end up with inflation but we could go through a deflationary episode first. That's why investors need a barbell approach so they're ready for both outcomes.

5) Is money safer in a small local bank or a big "megabank"?

Small local banks are good if they're highly rated. Some of them are solid and some of them are not. I don't want to get into the business of recommending banks because I don't know every investors particular circumstances. But there are rating services out there. If it's a highly rated bank that's small and local, it may be a better option. I would also recommend just having some cash. Just have $5,000–$10,000 in hundred dollar bills so when they shut down the ATMs you'll still have walking-around money.

6) Do you think that gold will be confiscated like it was in the 1930s?

I don't think it will be. The government might want to do that but I think there would be pushback. In the 1930's trust in government was much greater than it is today. People went along with it because they felt desperate. Today they may feel desperate but they don't trust the government. I think the government knows that.

7) Are credit unions safer than banks?

Generally yes. Again, I don't want to be in the business of recommending specific names because I don't know everyone's circumstances. But I am familiar with the credit union business and they're very solid. They have not been a source of any problems over the last 30 years.

8) What are the chances of gold and silver mining companies being nationalized during the crisis?

There's some possibility of that. But in countries like the United States and Canada, where there's the rule of law, they could only be nationalized on one of two bases. One is they'd have to change some laws which you would see coming because the legislative process is so clunky. The second what is through the president's emergency dictatorial powers. When I say that to people roll their eyes and respond, "What're you talking about, he's not a dictator." Well, in a way he is — he's a dictator in a legal sense.

Few people know that the United States is operating under a state of emergency today. President Obama extended the state of emergency. Every September it expires and this past month, the president extended the state of emergency.

Using his emergency powers, the President could nationalize the mining companies. The government might do that in the extreme, but we're not at the extreme yet. I don't want to be binary and say what will happen or won't happen. What I would say is it's always a process. It's a dynamic. Some things might happen but we'll see it coming. Again, that's the importance of being a *Strategic Intelligence* reader. You'll be the first to know.

9) Why do you recommend a 10% portfolio allocation to gold. Why not 20% or more?

I'm not giving personal portfolio advice. I want to be clear on that.

There's no smart way to give individual investors advice unless you know all their circumstances. I do have private investment clients. When you do something like that, you sit down with the individual and you say, "Look, give me your whole portfolio. Give me your net worth. Give me your family situation. How old are you? What goals do you have?"

There's a lot of work you have to do. I'm not going to tell anyone, "You should have 10 percent. Or, you should have 20 percent." 10 percent is just a general recommendation.

Gold is very volatile, so if you're liquid, have a reasonable size net worth and you want to lean into the trade a little bit, there's nothing wrong with 20 percent.

10) Do you really believe gold could go to $7,000?

I'm very candid about the fact that I think gold is going to $7,000. But it could go to $800 on the way. In other words, it could go from the current level, around $1,200, to $7,000.

There could be some big jumps in between as this dynamic takes off. I think it's going to end up at $7,000, but I'm not going to say to anyone it couldn't go to $800 because it certainly could.

I think people spend too much time watching the ticker tape. Dollar by dollar, they get all excited when gold goes up a little bit and they get depressed when it goes down a little bit. I don't do that. I watch it. I analyze it. I have a view on where it's going and I explain it in my books and in *Strategic Intelligence.*

11) What do you mean when you say store your precious metals in a "reputable non-bank vault?" Where can investors find one?

Most banks will give you a safe deposit box and bigger banks have vaults for large amounts of gold. Of course, the government tightly controls the banking system. At the time you want your gold, or, if you really need your gold, there's a strong possibility that the banks would be closed, at least temporarily, and you wouldn't be able to get it. That means you need to find a non-bank vault.

When I say reputable, I mean one that's been in business a long time, which can give you good references and has insurance. You can find them online. They're all over the country. Just find one that suits your needs and has been around a long time. Make sure they have insurance.

12) Do you see the U.S. using bank bail-ins to recapitalize the banking system during the next crisis?

It's more than talk and more than a possibility. It's actually in one of the G20's working documents. You can find the G20 Final Communiqué, which says as much. It's just about five pages long, but there was one page of annexes and additional working papers. There were dozens of those. If you click on each one, you'll find thousands and thousands of pages. It's a bit of a geek fest, but I did go through that, quite a bit of it, and the bail-in language is there.

In an extreme crisis everybody wants his or her money back. Last time, they printed the money to give you your money back. Next time, they're going to say you can't have it. Instead, they're going to close the banks and close the accounts, at least temporarily. I do see something like that happening.

13) Do platinum or palladium play a role in an investor's portfolio?

They can. I like just gold for portfolio purposes, but I think for some investors, there is a place. There's also an investment called the PMC Ounce offered by a firm called Neptune Global. That's physical metal. You actually have physical metal. It's not a derivative contract. You get all four of them.

It does better than having any one of the metals because it reduces your volatility. I do think that's an attractive play.

14) Are Middle Eastern oil countries trying with concerted effort to drive down oil prices?

They certainly are in the sense that oil price is very much a product of output, and they control the output. Saudi Arabia has reduced its output recently. The question is why? What's going on? Are they trying to put pressure on Iran? Are they trying to put pressure on Russia as part of the penalty for what they've done in Ukraine?

There are some geopolitical reasons going on behind the scenes. But I also think we have to recognize that this is part of a global slowdown. Geopolitics are always intriguing, so there could be some of that going on. It's also indicative of deflation and a global slowdown, which we're seeing around the world. I think that's going to catch up to the U.S. by early next year.

15) Do you recommend expatriation?

That's a personal decision. I'll just say, factually, expatriation is going up. There are more and more people dropping their U.S. passports. I'm a U.S. citizen. I'm proud to be a U.S. citizen. I still have my passport and I have no plans to expatriate, personally. But it is a fact that expatriation is increasing.

16) Is there another country where a person could open a savings account that would be safe to hold funds?

I do like the Swiss banking system. The problem is you're not going to be off the radar screen. I don't, obviously, counsel any kind of tax evasion. But if you're a U.S. citizen and you have a foreign bank account, you have to check a box on your U.S. tax return, and that would certainly attract the interest of the U.S. tax authorities.

From a safety and soundness point of view, however, I like Switzerland because I think they have a well run banking system and well run economy. But don't think that that's going to get you off the radar screen because it will not.

17) In the coming bad period is it good to be a lender, a borrower, or neither? Should investors pay off their mortgages now, for instance?

That's really asking whether inflation or deflation is going to prevail. If inflation is going to prevail, you really don't want to pay off your debts, at least not accelerate the payments, because those debts could be worth a lot less in an inflationary world.

But right now, I see deflationary forces prevailing. My advice would be, if you have a legitimate reason to borrow, such as to finance a house or something like that, and you can afford it and you're not overleveraged, that's fine. I wouldn't necessarily run out to prepay a mortgage, though.

I would not be going out and borrowing a lot of money right now to lever up. That's a strategy that does work in inflation — but the inflation might not come right away. We might be facing prolonged deflation. My approach is to have a balance of hard assets and cash. The hard assets protect you in inflation. The cash protects you in deflation and reduces volatility. It's hard to know which one we're in for, so I like to prepare for both.

18) When you say 'hold cash', do you mean banknotes? If so, what currency?"

When I say cash, I mean the highest quality instruments you can get. For a US investor, that would be US Treasury bills or maybe kind of one-year notes. There are foreign equivalents. Basically, find treasury debt in your own currency. That's the lowest risk, I think. But I don't consider money market funds or bank CDs to be cash in this sense.

19) You recommend physical metals as well as long Treasury bond funds. Can both of these deliver at the same time?

The answer is no, they can't both deliver at the same time. That's exactly the point. I think people who say they know exactly what's going to happen don't really know what they're talking about. We could have inflation for a whole bunch of reasons. We could have deflation for a whole bunch of reasons. The smart investor has a little bit of protection in case of either. And by the way, the best example of that is Warren Buffet. Buffett is buying railroads, transportation assets, oil and natural gas, which are all hard assets. He also has $55 billion in cash. That way if things do crash, you have the cash to scoop up the bargains.

20) Do you see the G20 moving to 100% electronic currency so they can charge negative interest rates on deposits?

Yes, it's out there. Ken Rogoff and Larry Summers have mentioned it. The G20 doesn't do anything quickly, but the move towards a cashless society, which basically means you're trapped in the banking system and they can impose negative rates, is just a way to steal your money.

That trend is pretty well underway. It's another reason to have physical gold — because it's non-digital.

21) The dialogue between Russia and the U.S. has broken down. Has the economy deteriorated so much that the U.S. will opt for war, as it has in past depressions?

That's a compound question. Putin is a non-economic player. He's a power player.

I met with some top national security experts in Washington recently. We had CIA officials, US ambassadors, think tankers, people from the Defense Department, people from the Treasury Department and from the financial world. There were about fifteen of us around the table behind closed doors and we talked this through.

Believe it or not, I laughed at them. I did it in a nice, respectful way but I said, "This is the worst case of mirror imaging I've ever seen." Mirror imaging is an intelligence analytical flaw where you make the mistake of thinking the other guy thinks the way you do.

The mistake the U.S. is making is thinking that Putin thinks like us. The U.S. thinks that if we inflict enough economic pain on Putin you'll change his behavior because if he inflicted economic pain on us it would change our behavior. But Putin is not like us, and we are not like him.

In other words, sanctions don't work on Putin. He has other goals, priorities and ways of thinking about it. So, the short answer is no. But that doesn't mean that the U.S. won't persist in escalating the conflict because we are thinking about it the wrong way.

22) Is now a good time to consider the ruble and Russia's oil sector?

With the understanding that it is more of a speculation than investment — and only as a small slice of an investor's portfolio — yes, I don't think it's too soon to look at Russia. The ruble has been down almost 60 percent. Their stock market is down and their economy is in recession. That's a good time to buy, quite often. Russia's not going away. It's the eighth largest economy in the world. It has a population of about 150 million people, is a nuclear state and it's heavily integrated with Europe. So Russia's not going to zero.

It might be a little early, but keep your eye on it. There will come a time soon to invest a little bit there. As always, my suggestion would be don't go all in, have it be a slice and do other things with your portfolio.

23) Is it possible for the US government to raise interest rates? Wouldn't the cost of interest payments bankrupt the United States?

If you had normalized interest rates, meaning for this stage of recovery 3%–5%, yes, that would blow a hole in the budget the size of the one that sank the Titanic. That's not what we're talking today, however. Today, we're talking about 25 basis point increases.

Maybe the Fed funds goes to 50 basis points or 75 basis points. Maybe they try to get ten-year notes to 2.50%. I don't think any of that's going to happen by the way, but the question is, if it did happen, would it bankrupt the United States?

At higher, normalized levels, it could. But what the Fed's thinking about right now wouldn't — at least in the short run. I don't think they're going to do even those small rate increases because I think the economy's too weak.

24) Who are the power elites that really call the shots in this country?

When I say "power elites" I'm not referring to the boogieman or other conspiracy theories. I'm not talking about the Illuminati or anything like that, either. These are real people. We know who they are.

They are Treasury secretaries, CEOs of major banks, finance ministers, some other deputies, central bankers, Janet Yellen, Mario Draghi, etc. But also some academics and PhD professors, like Larry Summers, Marty Feldstein and some corporate CEOs of the largest corporations. It's not a huge group.

They all know each other and hang out — whether in Davos or on the sidelines of a G20 summit or at an IMF annual meeting. They all go to the Clinton Global Initiative and they like being in New York during the United Nations General Assembly.

I'm able to talk to a lot of them. What they tell me privately is not what they say publicly. And this is what I put in my books and in *Strategic Intelligence*. I don't always mention names because sometimes you're not at liberty to do so. But I do mention the conversations.

I've had conversations with central bankers, people who are on the FOMC and the Board of Governors. They tell me point blank: "We don't know what we're doing, we're making it up as we go along." Again, they will never say that publicly because it would freak people out.

Sometimes the power elite retire and new people come along. You have to watch for the newbies — guys like Michael Froman. He's not a household name, but he's one of Robert Reuben's protégés who's in very powerful positions.

The rules for the power elite club are never criticize another member and never say what you really think. The art of the exercise is to — even if you're not a full-fledged member — at least have enough access to them that you know what they are thinking.

25) What are SDRs?

They're essentially world money. Now when you say world money it sounds kind of spooky or scary but it actually has a funny name. It's called the Special Drawing Right or SDR. The global financial elites pick strange names for what they're doing so people don't understand what it is

The International Monetary Fund, the IMF, can print these SDRs. They have in the past — there's nothing new about it. They were invented in 1969 and they've issued hundreds of billions of SDRs over the years. But they only issue them when there's a financial panic. They don't issue them every day or when times are good.

26) Will we be able to spend Special Drawing Rights or SDRs?

You will not be able to use them, touch them, or feel them. You will not be able to spend them. You will not have them.

In Philadelphia, we have something called walking around money. SDRs are not going to be walking around money. You'll still have dollars, but the dollars will be a local currency, not a global reserve currency. So, for example, when I go to Turkey, I cash in some dollars and get some Turkish lira. I use the lira to pay for taxis in Turkey. Then when I leave, I cash them out again. That will be how the dollar is used.

You'll use the dollar when you come to the United States, but it'll be like Mexican pesos; something you use when you go there. The dollar won't be the important global reserve currency.

The SDR will be used for the settlement of the balance of payments between countries, the price of oil, and, perhaps, the financial statements of the 100 largest global corporations.

The impact on everyday investors will be inflationary. The difference, however, is that, right now, if we have inflation, everyone blames the Fed. In the future, however, you'll have inflation coming from SDRs. That means when people try to blame the Fed, the Fed will say "It's not us, it's those guys over there on G Street in Northwest Washington. Go blame them."

No one even knows where the IMF is. So the SDR is just a way to get inflation through the back door.

27) Can the U.S. ever recover from the economic situation it's in?

It is possible but it's not likely. There are a set of policies that would encourage growth. The key is growth. The problem is we can't do it by printing money. We can do it by structural changes. But since the White House and the congress aren't talking to each other, I don't see the structural changes coming.

28) If there is a "strong dollar" does that mean the dollar will not collapse?

The question confuses the cross rate with the systemic risk. If the dollar is strong, it's strong versus euro or versus yen. The people base that on what's called the DXY, which is a dollar index. The dollar index is heavily weighted to the euro.

A strong dollar, however, doesn't mean that the whole system isn't nearing a point of collapse. Looking at the cross rate is like you're on the Titanic while it's sinking and your chair is fine but the person's chair next to you is a little lower than yours. In other words, a strong dollar cross rate is actually adding to the instability because it's very deflationary from a US perspective.

Many people think I favor a strong dollar.

What I favor is a *stable* dollar. It could be stable at a strong level, but the point is when you go from 2011 where the dollar was collapsing, to 2015 where the dollar is king of the hill, there is enormous volatility, which is very destabilizing.

The death of the dollar or the collapse of the international monetary system means a loss of confidence in money as a store of value by markets, investors and people around the world.

You might get paid in dollars but you don't want them. You take them and you turn them into something else: land, hard assets, gold, silver, fine art or whatever.

If that's happening to the dollar, it'll be happening to everything else at the same time. There's no way that confidence in the dollar is going to collapse without confidence in other countries' currencies collapsing, also. You're not going to have a crisis of confidence in the dollar where everyone demands euros.

I would not judge the state of the dollar or international monetary system based on cross rates. I would judge it based on the instability of the system as a whole.

29) Should investors consider buying Treasury Inflation Protected Securities (TIPS)?

They have a place. They're a kind of cash equivalent with an inflation insurance policy inside. They are also very liquid. They give you liquidity and safety, which is good in deflation, but they have an inflation protection built in too. In the short-term, TIPS are actually one instrument that covers both sides of a barbell strategy.

In *Strategic Intelligence*, we've recommended ten-year notes, which are on the deflation side of the barbell, and some gold, which is the inflation side. But short-term TIPS are right there in the middle and might be worth considering.

30) What's the difference between Austrian Economics and Complexity Theory?

They have a lot in common. Complexity theory is a branch of science that only emerged in the 1960s. It's a relatively new science. It's come a long way in 50 years, but as the history of science goes, complexity theory is relatively new and a lot of that has to do with computers. When you want to actually solve complexity problems, you need massive computing power and that didn't exist prior to the 1960s.

The main Austrians, going back to Carl Menger, Ludwig Von Mises and Friedrich Hayek, were doing their work in the late 19th and 20th centuries. That's why there's little overlap with them.

What Hayek said, however, was exactly what complexity theory says. Essentially, central planning will always fail. This is what he said in *The Road to Serfdom*, and what he said in one of his very influential articles.

Hayek said that nobody is smart enough or has enough information to plan an economy, no matter how much power they have. At the time, he was thinking the Soviet Union.

That's exactly what a complexity theorist would say, too.

They would say that economic phenomena are what are called "emerging properties". They seem to come out of nowhere. They come out of the decisions of tens of thousands, or millions, or tens of millions or hundreds of millions of market participants all individually expressing a certain preference, but collectively producing results that no individual could possibly foresee.

I get into debates with hard shell Austrian economists all over the world. I am not anti-Austrian economics. I think Austrian economics has a lot to offer. The only thing I would say is that science moves on, and there are new tools that we can use to get an even better understanding of the world.

I like to use Austrian economics the same way Einstein used Newton. Einstein produced a special theory of relativity, which overthrew part of what Newton said about gravity. That doesn't mean Newton was a dope; it just means Newton took the science so far and Einstein built on it. Einstein would agree with that, and said as much.

Likewise, it doesn't mean Austrian economics is wrong, but that complexity theory can advance the state of the art. The way I shut down the debate is by saying that if von Mises were alive today, he would be a complexity theorist.

31) How is it that the "powers that be" still allow you access when you warn everyday investors about the things policymakers are doing to muck up the economy?

The short answer is that no one allows me to do anything. I do what I want.

This is a very loaded question. It suggests that I am a government puppet and that the government is a monolithic, unified force. All of that is wrong and untrue.

I do a lot of work for the US government. I have been a government contractor, I've worked on government projects, I talk to government officials all the time. If you knew how messed up they are, you'd be a lot more relaxed about conspiracy theories.

There is no "government". There are many, many, many agencies, individuals, bureaus, departments and branches all over the country and the world — and certainly all over Washington, DC and northern Virginia.

I like to joke that we have two governments: the downtown government and the Virginia government. Downtown are the Treasury and the Fed, and in Virginia are the Pentagon and the intelligence community.

The simple fact is that the government is not monolithic. You can go around the different agencies of the government, as I do, and hear different views. People reach out to me, saying, "Jim, you won't believe what my boss is doing," or "I can't even believe what my agency is doing."

There are individuals who are dealing in good faith, working hard and are patriotic who don't like what they see inside the bigger nexus. My advice is not to assume the government's monolithic or uniform.

One thing I've heard my whole career, which is now tiptoeing up to the 40 year mark, is that, "Jim, you never do what anybody tells you." There's some truth in that, and I think that's good because it enables me to have some originality, which is what I try to bring to my *Strategic Intelligence* newsletter. People who know me well will understand this, too.

The notion that the insiders have like wound me up a clock or a little robot and turned me loose to warn the world, it's not true. I take it upon myself to do what I do. I always tell people my 84-year-old mother motivates me. She lives on a retirement check. Thank goodness she's fine, but there's nobody who's more vulnerable to inflation than my mother because she relies on that check to make her ends meet.

She's a good anchor for me. She's helps me think of the tens or maybe scores of millions of Americans who are in the same place. They are why I do what I do. Those are the people who are victimized, who are most likely to be victimized again and have always been victimized throughout history by inflation. Meanwhile, it's always the insiders, the hedge fund types and the government officials who see it coming and are in the position to protect themselves.

Candidly, there are probably people who I've spoken to who wouldn't be entirely happy if they knew what I wrote in *Strategic Intelligence*, but maybe they're not subscribers.

My point is that the picture's a lot more nuanced and complex. The government's a lot more diverse. There are people inside who don't like what they see, and any suggestion that I'm operating within a monolithic system isn't true.

32) What does your personal portfolio look like? What percentage of your money is in physical gold and/or silver, and do you own any stocks?

My personal portfolio is a blend of cash, fine art, gold, silver, land and private equity. I do not own any publicly traded stocks or bonds, partly due to restrictions under various regulatory requirements applicable to my role as a portfolio strategist and newsletter writer.

The mix in my portfolio changes from time to time based on valuations of the particular asset classes. My recommended mix is 10% precious metals, 10% fine art, 30% cash, 20% land and 30% alternatives such as hedge funds, private equity and venture capital.

Currently, my personal allocation is overweight land, fine art and private equity and underweight cash and precious metals. However, this will change, because the fine art fund is currently making profit distributions, which are being reallocated to gold, at what I consider to be a good entry point, and to cash.

All investors should be able to purchase precious metals and land and hold cash without difficulty. Alternatives such as hedge funds, private equity and venture capital are not open to all investors, because they are frequently traded as private funds limited to accredited investors with high minimum subscription amounts.

If you are unable to purchase such private investments, there are still publicly traded equities such as high-quality bond funds and companies holding hard assets in energy, transportation, natural resources and agriculture that offer good protection from the dual dangers of inflation and deflation.

33) Fracking technology has been around for decades. Was the shale revolution a bubble fueled by low interest rates? Some say it will save our country, but I fear it may do the opposite.

The American energy boom on the whole is a triumph of American technology and entrepreneurship and will be good for long-term growth. But as with many disruptive technologies in the past, there will be excesses and losses and unintended consequences in the early stages of this technological revolution.

America benefited greatly from the railroad boom of the late 19th century, but railroads were overbuilt or poorly managed in some cases and many investors suffered losses on railroad stocks and bonds. Something similar is now happening in the energy sector, despite the clear advantages of the technology.

The benefits of fracking are obvious, which include plentiful low-cost energy and lots of high-paying jobs in the oil and natural gas fields. The problems are less obvious. For one thing, this low-cost energy is deflationary at a time when the Federal Reserve desperately wants to increase inflation.

If the deflationary impact of fracking causes the Fed to push monetary ease to the point where confidence in the dollar is destroyed, then the costs of this revolution will be very high. Of course, this will not be the fault of the frackers, but rather the fault of the Fed. Yet the dangers are there, nonetheless.

The other problem is that much of the euphoria in the fracking fields was financed with low-grade corporate debt. This debt was issued on the assumption that oil prices would remain above $80 per barrel or higher. With oil in the $45 per barrel area and likely to remain below $60 per barrel, much of this investment will have to be written off.

The amount is in the trillions of dollars, larger than the subprime mortgage crisis, and much of the debt is stashed away in bond funds buried in retail 401(k)s. As I mentioned earlier, you should check your 401(k) to see if there are any corporate bond funds, and if so, call your broker or adviser to find out if there are any fracking-related junk bonds tucked inside.

34) I read in the introduction of your book, *Currency Wars*, about the possibility of an 80-90-98% "windfall profits tax" on gold (if and when it goes up to $7,000-plus per ounce). If that's true, wouldn't that mitigate the benefits of holding gold?

My reference to a future windfall profits tax on gold in the introduction to my book *Currency Wars* was intended to form a contrast to the confiscation of gold in 1933. The point simply is that the government sometimes works to suppress the price of gold, but when gold goes up anyway, the government finds a way to steal the profits from private investors. A windfall profits tax is one way to do this, but not the only way. I mentioned it as an illustration of what could happen, not as a hard-and-fast prediction.

The possibility of such a tax is not a reason to avoid holding gold today. The surge in the dollar price of gold that I expect has barely begun. If the price does move up sharply, there should be time to sell the gold at a high level and reinvest in another asset class, such as land or fine art, which is less likely to be targeted for confiscatory taxation by the government.

Of course, deciding when the profits on gold are large

enough to justify the pivot into other hard assets will not be an easy call, but that's one of the things I will be thinking about and pointing out to *Strategic Intelligence* readers in the months and years ahead.

35) Why do you think that there is a corporate debt problem? Aren't U.S. companies sitting on hoards of cash?

Debt comes in many forms, including high-quality U.S. Treasury debt, high-grade corporate debt and junk bonds. Debt is also issued by both U.S. companies and foreign companies. Some of the foreign corporate debt is issued in local currencies and some in dollars. In discussing debt defaults, it's necessary to keep all of these distinctions in mind.

The U.S. companies sitting on hoards of cash, such as Apple, IBM and Google, are not the ones I'm concerned about; they will be fine. The defaults will be coming from three other sources.

The first wave of defaults will be from junk bonds issued by energy exploration and drilling companies, especially frackers. These bonds were issued with expectations of continued high energy prices. With oil prices at $60 per barrel or below, many of these bonds will default.

The second wave will be from structured products and special purpose vehicles used to finance auto loans. We are already seeing an increase in subprime auto loan defaults. That will get worse.

The third wave will come from foreign companies that issued U.S. dollar debt but cannot get easy access to U.S. dollars from their central banks or cannot afford the interest costs now that the U.S. dollar is much stronger than when the debt was issued.

The combined total of all three waves — energy junk bonds, auto loans and foreign corporations — is in excess of $10 trillion, more than 10 times larger than the subprime mortgages outstanding before the last crisis, in 2007.

Not all of these loans will default, but even a 10% default rate would result in over $1 trillion of losses for investors, not counting any derivative side bets on the same debt. This debt will not default right away and not all at once, but look for a tsunami of bad debts beginning in late 2015 and into early 2016.

Conclusion

Money is transitory and wealth is permanent. A lot of people confuse money and think "Well, I have a lot of money so I'm wealthy."

In the short run, that may be true but in the longer run, the money can go away. Wealth, on the other hand, is something that prevails. The value of money may collapse, but there are things you can do and strategies you can pursue to create and preserve wealth that will survive a monetary collapse.

When everyone else is getting wiped out, just surviving is coming out ahead. That said, I think it's possible for you to outperform most other asset classes and actually increase your net worth in real terms in the process.

You always have to think about things in real terms. It's not enough to talk about things in nominal terms. The stock market could go to 40,000. If the dollar loses 95 percent of its purchasing power, what good is Dow 40,000 if the dollar is only worth a nickel?

That's why it's imperative you prepare now. You can't wait until the crisis strikes. A lot of things could cause the next crisis. It could be a failure to deliver physical gold because gold's getting scarce. It could be a Lehman type of collapse of a financial firm or another MF Global. It could be a prominent suicide. It could be a natural disaster. It could be defaults in the junk bond market. It could be a lot of things, but my point is, it doesn't matter. It will be something.

What matters today is that the system is so unstable. The blunders have already been made. The risk is already there, embedded in the system. We're just waiting for that catalyst to trigger the collapse. It will happen sooner rather than later. This is not necessarily something that's going to happen tomorrow — although it could — but it's not a ten-year forecast either, because we're not going make it that far.

The dynamics — what are called the scaling metrics or the size of the system — are an exponential function. What that means is that when you triple the size of the system, you don't triple the risk. You increase risk by ten or a *hundred times*. That's what we've done today.

So, I would say two things. First, the crisis could happen very suddenly and likely you won't see it coming. Investors always say to me, "Jim, call me up at 3:30 the day before it happens and I'll sell my stocks and buy some gold."

But it doesn't work that way for the reasons I just explained. And even if it did, you might not be able to get the gold. That's very important to understand.

When a buying panic breaks out and the price of gold starts gapping up not by $10 or $20 per ounce per day but by $100 and then $200 per ounce and then, all of sudden, it's up $1,000 per ounce, people say "I have to get some gold." At that point, you won't be able to get it.

The big players will get it — the sovereign wealth funds, the central banks, the billionaires and the multibillion-dollar hedge funds — they'll be able to get it. But everyday investors won't be able to get it.

You'll find that the mint stops shipping it and your local dealer has run out of supply. You'll be able to watch the price on television, but you won't actually be able to get the gold. It'll be too late. That's why the time for action is now.

I like to say that every individual has a Ph.D. when it comes to managing his or her own money. You may not know a lot about economics, but you can and should focus on your own net worth.

You are not helpless. You don't have to feel like a cork on the ocean or like a victim of whatever policy the central bankers are putting out there.

You can take your net worth and take your retirement and take your portfolio into your own hands.

There are families in the United States, like the Rockefellers, that have had money for, say, one hundred years. That's the old money.

When you go to Europe, however, you find families that have had wealth for three hundred, four hundred and even five hundred years. That's the *really* old money.

Not long ago, I was at the magnificent Palazzo Colonna in the heart of Rome. The Colonna family's had their wealth since the 13th Century. For 800 years they've been wealthy and never lost it.

They not only survived 2008, but they survived the Thirty Years' War, Napoleon, Louis XIV, World War I, World War II, the Holocaust and more.

If you ask them how they did it they'll look at you and say, "a third, a third and a third" — one third land, one-third gold, one-third fine art.

Let's say you're living in Bavaria and it's 1620. The enemy is five miles away and they're burning down everything in sight. What do you do? You put your gold coins in a sack, you cut your painting off the wall, roll it up, put it in your backpack, get on your horse, and ride away.

Then a few years later when the dust settles, you come back and you should be able to reestablish title to the land, put your gold back on the table, put your art back on the wall. You're wealthy and your neighbors have all been wiped out.

My point is there are survival strategies you can use. You are not helpless. You can protect yourself. You can definitely see the crisis coming using the warning signs present today.

The idea is to take the story forward, see the collapse, see what comes next and then go back to square one and do what you can today to survive the collapse and survive into the new system and preserve wealth?

It can be done and as a *Strategic Intelligence* reader, you're in a better position than most Americans to make it happen.

Index

C

D

H

J

K

L

M

N

O

P

S

U

V

W

Y

Z